T0340233

By following traces, practices and 'devicification', the chapters of this edited collection take us through the profound transformations that characterise contemporary digital consumption. Digital consumers are now not more or less than their devices. Consumers, devices, data, infrastructures and algorithms form composites with consequence.

Professor Daniel Neyland, *Sociology, Goldsmiths, UK*

This is a terrific collection that takes the dynamic, material processes of digitalization, rather than 'the digital' as its departure point. As a result, the authors are able to expose the rhythms, traces and consequences of digitalization on consumption, and on social life more broadly. It should be required reading for anyone who wants to move beyond the hype to understand how digitalization is working through infrastructures that artfully combine the enterprises of consumers and professionals to monitor and frame consumption.

Liz McFall, *Senior Lecturer in Sociology at the Open University, UK*

The digitalization of consumption is an important field of research that, so far, has not been adequately explored. This book makes a much need contribution by combining in-depth empirical analysis with new theoretical insights. I think it is a must-read for anyone with an interest in this field.

Adam Arvidsson, *Associate Professor of Sociology, University of Milan, Italy*

Digitalizing Consumption

Contemporary consumer society is increasingly saturated by digital technology, and the devices that deliver this are increasingly transforming consumption patterns. Social media, smartphones, mobile apps and digital retailing merge with traditional consumption spheres, supported by digital devices which further encourage consumers to communicate and influence other consumers to consume.

Through a wide range of empirical studies which analyse the impact of digital devices, this volume explores the digitization of consumption and shows how consumer culture and consumption practices are fundamentally intertwined and mediated by digital devices. Exploring the development of new consumer cultures, leading international scholars from sociology, marketing and ethnology examine the effects on practices of consumption and marketing, through topics including big data, digital traces, streaming services, wearables, and social media's impact on ethical consumption.

Digitalizing Consumption makes an important contribution to practice-based approaches to consumption, particularly the use of market devices in consumers' everyday consumer life, and will be of interest to scholars of marketing, cultural studies, consumer research, organization and management.

Franck Cochoy is Professor of Sociology at the University of Toulouse Jean Jaurès, France, and a member of LISST-CNRS, France.

Johan Hagberg, PhD, is Associate Professor of Marketing at the School of Business, Economics and Law, University of Gothenburg, Sweden.

Magdalena Petersson McIntyre is PhD in European Ethnology and Associate Professor at the Centre for Consumer Science, University of Gothenburg, Sweden.

Niklas Sörum is PhD in European Ethnology and Senior Researcher at the Centre for Consumer Science, University of Gothenburg, Sweden and a Senior Lecturer in Marketing at University College of Borås, Sweden.

Routledge Interpretive Marketing Research

Recent years have witnessed an 'interpretative turn' in marketing and consumer research. Methodologists from the humanities are taking their place alongside those drawn from the traditional social sciences.

Qualitative and literary modes of marketing discourse are growing in popularity. Art and aesthetics are increasingly firing the marketing imagination.

This series brings together the most innovative work in the burgeoning interpretative marketing research tradition. It ranges across the methodological spectrum from grounded theory to personal introspection, covers all aspects of the postmodern marketing 'mix', from advertising to product development, and embraces marketing's principal sub-disciplines.

Consuming Books
The Marketing and Consumption of Literature
Edited by Stephen Brown

The Undermining of Beliefs in the Autonomy and Rationality of Consumers
By John O'Shaugnessy and Nicholas Jackson O'Shaugnessy

Marketing Discourse
A Critical Perspective
By Per Skålén, Markus Fellesson and Martin Fougère

Explorations in Consumer Culture Theory
Edited by John F. Sherry Jr. and Eileen Fisher

Consumer Culture, Branding and Identity in the New Russia
From Five-Year-Plan to 4x4
Graham H. Roberts

The Practice of the Meal
Food, Families and the Market Place
Edited by Benedetta Cappellini, David Marshall and Elizabeth Parsons

Digitalizing Consumption
How Devices Shape Consumer Culture
Edited by Franck Cochoy, Johan Hagberg, Magdalena Petersson McIntyre and Niklas Sörum

Digitalizing Consumption

How Devices Shape Consumer Culture

Edited by
Franck Cochoy, Johan Hagberg,
Magdalena Petersson McIntyre and
Niklas Sörum

Routledge
Taylor & Francis Group

LONDON AND NEW YORK

First published 2017
by Routledge

2 Park Square, Milton Park, Abingdon, Oxfordshire OX14 4RN
52 Vanderbilt Avenue, New York, NY 10017

Routledge is an imprint of the Taylor & Francis Group, an informa business

First issued in paperback 2019

British Library Cataloguing in Publication Data
A catalogue record for this book is available from the British Library

Library of Congress Cataloging in Publication Data
A catalog record for this book has been requested

ISBN: 978-1-138-12489-9 (hbk)
ISBN: 978-0-367-87549-7 (pbk)

Typeset in Times New Roman
by Taylor & Francis Books

Contents

Illustrations

Figures

Tables

Contributors

Ann-Sofie Axelsson is Associate Professor of Technology Management at Chalmers University of Technology, Gothenburg, Sweden, and Associate Professor of Library and Information Science at University of Borås, Sweden. Her research focus can be described as digitalization, with particular interest in how individuals, groups and organizations carry out their practices with the help of digital tools and services. Online gaming, digital advertising and sharing of research data are some of the practices she studies. Aspects of accessibility and sustainability are of particular interest.

Dominique Boullier is Professor of Sociology at the École Polytechnique Fédérale de Lausanne (EPFL), Switzerland, and Director of the Social Media Lab since 2015. He holds a PhD in Sociology (EHESS, Paris), a Habilitation degree in Information and Communication Sciences, and a degree in Linguistics. He worked as a research consultant in the fields of urban sociology and ICT uses (1981–89), was an invited scholar at University of California, Berkeley (1985–86), and served as CEO of a consulting firm (1989–96). He has held positions as Director of a social science team at the University of Technology at Compiègne (1998–2005), Director of Lutin User Lab, Cité des Sciences, Paris (2004–08), and Scientific Director of Sciences Po médialab, Paris (with Bruno Latour) (2008–13). He has published several books, chapters and journal articles on sociopolitical analysis of the digital sphere and social media analysis.

Oskar Broberg is a Senior Lecturer and Associate Professor at the School of Business, Economics and Law at University of Gothenburg, Sweden. His research is in the field of business history with a particular focus on the interaction between business and societal development at large over the last four decades. This has resulted in studies regarding organic milk, digital advertising and financial derivatives.

Franck Cochoy is Professor of Sociology at the University of Toulouse Jean Jaurès, France, and a researcher at the Laboratoire Interdisciplinaire Solidarités, Sociétés, Territoires at the Centre National de la Recherche Scientifique (LISST-CNRS). He works in the field of economic sociology, with a focus on the technical devices that frame or equip consumer behaviour, such as packaging, self-service, QR codes and other digital tools. Recent publications include articles in *Consumption Markets and Culture, Journal of Marketing Management, Marketing Theory* and *Urban Studies* and the books *On the Origins of Self-Service* (Routledge, 2015) and *On Curiosity: The Art of Market Seduction* (Mattering Press, 2016).

Barbara Czarniawska is Senior Professor in Management Studies at Gothenburg Research Institute, School of Business, Economics and Law at University of Gothenburg, Sweden. She takes a feminist and processual perspective on organizing, recently exploring connections between popular culture and the practice of management, and the organization of news production. She is interested in techniques of fieldwork and in the application of narratology to organization studies. Recent books in English include *Research Agenda for Management and Organization Studies* (editor, 2016), *Social Science Research: From Field to Desk* (2014) and *A Theory of Organizing* (second edition, 2014).

Janice Denegri-Knott is Associate Editor of *Marketing Theory* and Head of the Promotional Cultures & Communication Centre at Bournemouth University's Faculty of Media and Communication, UK. Prior to joining academia, she worked in both the corporate world and in marketing communications for not-for-profit organizations in South America. Her research deals with the intersections between technology and consumption. Her most recent work is on possession of digital objects and the mediating role of digital devices in consumption. She has also worked with major UK brands on projects dealing with the valuation and capitalization of digital content.

Aude Dufresne is Honorary Professor in the Department of Communication Sciences at the University of Montreal, Canada, and Director of the Laboratoire de Recherche en Communication Multimédia (LRCM). She is responsible for the Graduate Diploma in Art, Design and Technology. Her research focuses on the analysis and design of human--computer interaction systems. She is particularly interested in the development of personalization technologies in the areas of learning and e-commerce. She has written various articles and reviews of ergonomics and human–computer interaction in specialized journals in the areas of education and intelligent tutoring systems, and she has written many research reports for public and private organizations.

Christian Fuentes, PhD, is a Researcher at the Centre for Consumer Science at University of Gothenburg, Sweden, and a Senior Lecturer at the Department of Service Management and Service Studies at Lund University. He undertakes research in the fields of green marketing, sustainable consumption, mobile shopping, e-tailing, practice theory, and actor-network theory. He is currently involved in several research projects exploring how digitalization and digital devices enable and shape sustainable consumption and marketing practices.

Johan Hagberg, PhD, is Associate Professor of Marketing at the School of Business, Economics and Law, University of Gothenburg, Sweden. He received his doctorate in 2008 with a thesis on retail change. His current research investigates consumer logistics and the digitalization of retailing and consumption. His publications include articles in *Industrial Marketing Management, Journal of Marketing Management, Urban Studies, Marketing Theory, Journal of Historical Research in Marketing* and *Consumption Markets & Culture.*

Lena Hansson holds a PhD in Business Administration and is a Senior Lecturer and the Director of the Centre for Retailing at the School of Business, Economics and Law, University of Gothenburg, Sweden. Her previous research focuses on consumption and design related to social equality issues such as inclusion, accessibility, age and gender. Her current research deals with the analysis of the digitalization of consumption and specifically how digital market devices contribute to the shaping of ethical consumption and how gender is being performed.

Rebecca Jenkins is a Principal Academic in the Corporate and Marketing Communications Department, Faculty of Media and Communication at Bournemouth University, UK. Her PhD was a study of consumption in the everyday imagination and more recent research projects extend this area of interest while focusing on emerging areas of consumption. Recent and ongoing projects include the extended mind and distributed cognition, particularly in relation to digital devices and consumer practices. Her research received the 'Editor's Choice' award in the *Journal of Consumer Culture* as one of the 11 most noteworthy manuscripts in the journal since its launch.

Hans Kjellberg is a Professor of Marketing at the Stockholm School of Economics, Sweden. His research focuses on economic organizing, particularly the organizing of markets. Recent publications include articles in *Consumption Markets & Culture, Industrial Marketing Management, Journal of Marketing Management and Marketing Theory*, and the co-edited volume *Concerned Markets* (Edward Elgar). Currently, he is involved in an interdisciplinary research programme on the digitalization of consumption and a cross-country comparison of valuation and pricing of pharmaceutical cancer treatments.

Minna Lammi, PhD, is an expert in social construction of consumption and changes towards more sustainable practices in consumer society. She is currently researching business models in emerging circular economies as principal investigator at the University of Helsinki, Finland, located in the Centre for Industrial Sustainability, University of Cambridge, UK. She also participates actively in societal preparatory and policy-related processes. She holds the title of Docent in both Political Science (University of Helsinki) and Communication Studies (University of Vaasa) and has many years of experience not only in research but also in journalism, publishing and public relations.

Lucie Larnaudie graduated in social psychology of work and organizations. She specializes in the field of cognitive ergonomics of electronic documents. She is particularly interested in the role of motivation and self-efficacy in the uses of human–machine interfaces. She is the author of an article in a professional review specializing in psycho-social risks and an article in the academic journal *Human-Computer Interaction*.

Mika Pantzar is Research Director at the Consumer Society Research Centre at the University of Helsinki, Finland, and Adjunct Professor in the Department of Management at the Aalto University, School of Business in Helsinki, Finland. His research area ranges from technology studies and consumer research to practice theory.

Magdalena Petersson McIntyre is Associate Professor and PhD in Ethnology at the Centre for Consumer Science, University of Gothenburg, Sweden. Her research interests focus on gender studies, consumption, fashion and ethnography. Recent publications in English include articles in the *Journal of Cultural Economy* (2014), *International Journal of Small Business and Entrepreneurship* (2015) and *Fashion Practice* (2016). Her ongoing research involves fashion blogging and the marketization of gender equality.

Gustav Sjöblom has a PhD in History and is Assistant Professor in the History of Technology at Chalmers University of Technology in Gothenburg, Sweden. His primary research focus is on the use of information technology and the governance of transport systems.

Jan Smolinski is a PhD student in Sociology at the University of Toulouse, France, and a member of the CERTOP-CNRS. At the crossroads of economic sociology and science and technology studies, his dissertation studies the smartphone as a mediator that transforms market interactions in a context of digitalized mobility. His publications include book chapters and articles in *Communication*, *Netcom* and *Revue d'anthropologie des connaissances*.

Niklas Sörum holds a PhD in Ethnology and is a Researcher at the Centre for Consumer Science at the School of Business, Economics and Law, University of Gothenburg, Sweden, and a Senior Lecturer in Marketing at University College of Borås, Sweden. His research focuses on digitalization of consumption, second-hand markets, ethical and sustainable consumption, consumer logistics and marketization of cultural heritage. He works with an actor-network approach towards consumption and markets, and combines different ethnographic methods in his studies. His research has been published in *Consumption, Markets & Culture, Journal of Consumer Policy, Culture Unbound* and by Ashgate Publishing.

Jean-Sébastien Vayre holds a PhD in Sociology from the University of Toulouse Jean Jaurès, France, and works as an Attaché Temporaire d'Enseignement et de Recherche (ATER) at the CERTOP-CNRS. His research concerns the development of big data technologies in the commercial sphere. He is particularly interested in the design and uses of artificial intelligence applied to markets. He has written articles published in academic journals in the fields of sociology, innovation, human–computer interaction, information systems and digital technologies.

1 Digitalizing consumption

Introduction

Franck Cochoy, Johan Hagberg,
Magdalena Petersson McIntyre and Niklas Sörum

Contemporary consumer society is increasingly saturated by the digital. Despite this there has been, until recently, a relative paucity of studies concerning the intersection of digitalization and consumption (Lehdonvirta, 2012). Social media, mobile Internet, smartphones, QR codes, tablets, mobile apps, virtual fashion and digital shopping windows replace and merge with previous consumption spheres. Consumer activities such as purchasing, comparing and examining goods are increasingly handled through the Internet and mobile digital devices; consumers organize and disseminate service and product information on social media sites, blogs and forums; and money is spent increasingly on digital items. Furthermore, product searches, decision making and the relationships with physical stores are becoming more intimately dependent on smartphones, tablets and other digital devices. Growing numbers of available recommendation systems and online review platforms have also assumed a prominent role in consumption practices (Mellet et al., 2014). In their use and co-production of such recommendation systems for books, movies, restaurants, wines, music, electronics, musical instruments and clothes, consumers are relying increasingly on algorithms and artificial intelligence. Taken together, these examples are manifestations of the contemporary ongoing digitalization of consumption that results in the development of new cultures of consumption.

From the introduction of PCs in many homes several decades ago, through their subsequent connection to the Internet and the proliferation of laptops, tablets and smartphones, the digital has become increasingly intertwined in everyday life. "Digital" has become a prefix to so many aspects of consumption that the present time is commonly referred to as the digital age. Digitalization now impacts all parts of society, spanning large-scale calculations by mainframe computers to mobile digital devices in the hands of ordinary consumers. There is a budding delegation of everyday consumer practices to digital technology, and it is clear that consumption has been altered, enhanced and sometimes even lost by advances in digital technology; for instance, previous forms of expertise and advice recommendation systems are increasingly becoming replaced with a reliance on combinations of big data.

By using the term digitalization, rather than the digital, we aim to focus on the processes through which consumption becomes ever more digital. What interests us particularly is not so much the present state of the digital, but the processes in which the digital is performed, tried out, stabilized or destabilized, how users are enrolled and practices disrupted, and the ways in which digital technologies are integrated into markets and consumer practices. We approach digitalization as "integration of digital technologies into everyday life by the digitization of everything that can be digitized" (Businessdictionary. com, 22 October 2014; see also Hagberg et al., 2016, p. 707). We want to draw attention to the transformation of consumption that follows digitalization, as well as to how the relationship between consumption and production is challenged through such processes.

Thus, although a focus on the digitalization of consumption is what the different chapters in this volume have in common, only some have consumers as their topic of study. We see consumption as a phenomenon that involves many actors – such as marketers, producers, data scientists or even novelists – and encompasses a way to describe how various digital entities, together with consumers, pragmatically enact and format consumer actions, shape consumer culture and stage consumer dispositions. In that sense, the consumer and consumer culture are defined as "made up of human bodies but also prostheses, tools, equipment, technical devices, algorithms, etc." (Callon, 2005, p. 4). Digital devices help produce particular versions (or images) of consumer subjects; they may work to enable new ways of being a consumer in the 21st century; they may even challenge the gender constructions inscribed in more conventional shopping practices, and may work as disciplinary and governing devices that encourage certain forms of consumption and discourage other forms.

Several contributions in this book explore the mundane market(ing) and consumer uses of digital devices in marketing processes and communication systems, and offer different vantage points on the digitalization of consumer society. The transformative potential of such devices challenges our conceptions of consumer choice, consumer insight, consumer practices, consumer subjectivities and communities, as well as market ideologies, marketing practices and innovation. Thus, the aim of this book is to examine how digital technologies interact with consumer society in a broad range of processes that can be termed the *digitalization of consumption*. This volume is not the first collective attempt aimed at accounting for the digitalization of the consumption sphere; see, for example, the edited volumes of Molesworth and Denegri-Knott (2012) and Belk and Llamas (2013). However, the effort is to complement and contribute to this literature in several ways.

Previous research on digitalization and consumption has focused mainly on the consumption of digital tools with questions concerning Internet access, smartphone ownership, mobile phone frequency or mobile application users. As several researchers have noted, incorporation of digital tools in mundane consumer activities also affects the way we consume *other* services or goods.

Smartphones, laptops, tablets, smartwatches (see Moats and McFall, 2016) and other digital devices are increasingly intertwined in everyday activities in numerous settings (at work, at home, on the move, etc.), and in various aspects of consumption. Thus, digital market devices are not only consumed in their own right, but are also used increasingly by consumers as part of other consumption practices, such as payment tools, information providers and virtual shops. As such, these devices contribute to shaping new consumer identities and raise issues about gender, ethics and power. The development, marketing and adoption of digital tools interact with consumption and sometimes promote and trigger change within more or less ordered practices and institutions.

Another important aspect of the digitalization of consumption is the hybridization of the Internet and everyday life, as spectacularly illustrated by, for example, the recent craze for the "augmented reality" game *Pokémon Go*. After two decades of relative separation between the Internet (based on desktop home searches) and the marketplace (favouring physical behaviour), contemporary market settings rather favour the hybridization of the two and the associated dimensions of interactivity, mobility, portability and ubiquity connected to real, ordinary practices. We thus join Ruppert, Law and Savage (2013, p. 2), who argue that digital devices and digitalization are "simultaneously shaped by the social world, and can in turn become agents that shape that world". The chapters in this book provide support for such a view by engaging with the specificities of digital devices in order to understand the transformations revealed through the digital.

Focusing on the digitalization of consumption also means focusing on both demand and supply in an effort to get a more complete picture. Whereas consumption studies, including those that attend to digitalized forms of consumption, primarily have focused on the consumer side, this move means that we also pay attention to the role of producers in the digitalizing of consumption. We want to highlight the dynamic and transformative character of the implementation of digital devices in consumer markets, as this is a way to contribute to the current shift of market studies from "market agencements" (Callon, 2013) to "market agencing" (Callon, 2016; Cochoy et al., 2016) – for example, the process through which various materially heterogeneous agencies evolve and combine to colonize and shape consumer behaviour. In this respect, our book shares the view that consumption cannot be understood through studying consumers only, and thus calls, like other works, for studying how marketing knowledge, devices and practices shape consumer behaviour (Araujo and Kjellberg, 2010; Cochoy and Mallard, n.d., forthcoming; McFall, 2014).

We address the processes of digitalization in four main ways: 1 the implications of digitalization for society and markets; 2 how digital devices are "devising consumers"; 3 how digitalization reshapes consumer subjects and practices; 4 through astute marketing knowledge, tools and strategies. In the following, we present the chapters of this book under these different headings.

We start by discussing the more general implications for society and markets and the social sciences. This is followed by an introduction of the chapters that particularly attend to the devising of consumers, i.e. the processes of entanglement of devices and consumers in everyday life. A third section focuses on the construction of consumer subjects and practices through digitalization processes. Moving on from issues of subjectivity and practices, the last section introduces three chapters that explore various forms of marketing practices and their role in digitalizing consumption, and some concluding notes concerning the digitalization of consumption.

Implications for society and markets

The opening chapters by Boullier, and by Pantzar and Lammi address the larger implications of digitalization processes for society and markets, including the social sciences, companies, consumers and citizens. As Boullier implicitly suggests, chances are great that a main contribution of the digital world to contemporary society is the amazing proliferation of a new kind of entity: digital traces. These traces invade artificial memories, computer networks and social media, as well as business talks and market intelligence, both eager to learn how to extract knowledge and value out of so-called "big data".

Such evolutions are good reasons for the social sciences to pay attention to these new digital traces. On the one hand, social sciences are about making sense of social matters, and it is their duty to consider these new entities that colonize and transform the world. On the other hand, the growing attention of business actors for the same entities reinforces this need; not only is this attention part of the phenomenon that deserves to be studied, but responsible social scientists cannot allow business to exploit the new goldmine of digital traces alone, given the risk of a privatization and marketization of social knowledge that such monopoly would entail.

In his chapter "Big data challenge for social sciences and market research: from society and opinion to replications", Boullier interprets the recent development of digital methods (Rogers, 2013) as the emergence of a third generation of social sciences. According to Boullier, the first generation aimed at studying "society", based on secondary data such as official statistics produced by the state. The second generation of social sciences aimed at exploring public opinion, thanks to polling techniques. With the magic of great numbers and sampling procedures, polls helped to build the image of the social "whole" from a small set of data accessible at a reasonable cost. Now, Boullier says, big data and digital traces have made us enter a third generation of social sciences, no longer based on official records or survey samples, but on the huge flow of information collected automatically through Internet traffic and digital usage. These data are subject to instant analysis by various digital methods and algorithms. With third-generation social sciences, Boullier claims, the topic at stake is neither society nor public opinion, since most of the time traces neither reflect the big collective nor express the isolated individuals, but produce "replications". What matters is not studying these traces to gain knowledge about the social whole they belong to, or to portray the individuals who originate them, but studying the moves, trends, issues and rhythms created by the circulation of the traces themselves (see "likes" on Facebook, "tweets" on Twitter and so on).

This emerging issue of replications is systematically explored by Pantzar and Lammi, whose chapter "Towards a rhythm-sensitive data economy" studies how the spread of digital traces and their growing interconnection renew and transform the rhythms of social life: like never before, the use of the Internet, smartphones, self-trackers and other connected objects redistributes social practices by creating a time for collective "wired" social interactions. These networked flows challenge or overlap other, more traditional moments, such as working hours or family gatherings, further reshaping social rhythms and leading towards their synchronization. Moreover, the use of the same devices and the conduct of the same interactions generate a flow of traces that document the underlying behavioural patterns of market actors. As the authors convincingly argue, this knowledge is a source of business opportunities: the successful companies of today and tomorrow are not only the ones who prove capable of addressing the price and quality challenges raised by their immediate competitors, but rather the ones who show their ability to "synchronize" their activities with their clients' rhythms. In other words, the competitors are not only the other companies that produce the same kinds of goods and services, but also the ones that address the same moments. Economic value does not rest solely on the material characteristics of a given good, but on businesses' ability to propose timely offers, at the right place, and with the appropriate price (see the example of Netflix, whose distinct economic advantage lies in its capacity to adapt flexibly to consumers' changing rhythms and even social configurations, according to the number of simultaneous "screens" they need for the same subscription). As the authors note in their discussion, these evolutions call for our vigilance, given the rising control of social knowledge by companies through big data analytics, and the related capacity of businesses to "learn how to shape and manipulate rhythms" (cf. Epp et al., 2014, for a similar argument regarding brand competition).

If Boullier is interested in the life of traces per se, Pantzar and Lammi remind us that the same traces are attached to and produced by consumers, so that "big data analytics" is both an issue of social knowledge and a source of market control. However, Pantzar and Lammi join Boullier on one major point: they both argue that companies no longer necessarily need to come back to individuals. By identifying relevant rhythms, they may develop proactive and performative market segmentations that both meet and create the consumers they target. Trained in traditional social analysis and survey research, for too long marketing experts have been (and still largely are!) obsessed with the idea that they should know who the consumers are in order to answer their needs. This prejudice has ironically and, paradoxically, efficiently protected consumers from managerial control. Indeed, "real consumers" have remained elusive (Ekström and Brembeck, 2004), far from the distorted image of them produced through innumerable but often vain marketing surveys, focus groups, market ethnographies and so on. Now, digital-focused companies and new data analysts show that knowing consumers is misleading and becomes unnecessary (Cochoy and Mallard, n.d., forthcoming). What matters is knowing the traces produced through market transactions, Internet activity and Web searches, retrieving the hidden associations existing between these traces, and adjusting market offers accordingly, thus creating the consumers that meet and propagate them, along with the "replication" or "synchronization" logics well identified by the authors.

In this sense, both chapters more or less implicitly raise similar political and ethical issues. On the one hand, it is important to remember that the power of big data is greatly exaggerated, for the good reason that big data do not speak by themselves, and that most business actors either do not know what to do with them or do not make great use of them. On the other hand, it is equally important to observe that despite such difficulties, big data analytics are growing, especially in the media and marketing sectors, thanks to the development of third-party players who propose and sell "big data analytics" tools, solutions and services. This growth raises serious issues in terms of privacy ownership, data management and consumer protection (Milyaeva and Neyland, 2016).

Again, though, things are not as simple as one might think. Privacy is not only challenged, but also deeply transformed by the new practices. As Moats and McFall (2016) recently noted, it is unclear whether "our" data are still really ours anymore; these data also belong to our devices, to the technical networks and to the companies that make them exist. Latour and his colleagues go even further by observing that the modern subjects of the digital society are no longer isolated persons, but rather monads (see, for example, the "profiles" of individuals on social media). A profile published on a social media platform can be defined as a nexus that combines the subjective projection of a given spirit concealed in a particular body, as well as the information and links the profile gathers, connects and displays (Latour et al., 2012). Finally, and ironically, protecting data from business has become a business in itself, through the development of data protection companies (Milyaeva and Neyland, 2016; Neyland and Milyaeva, 2016). All in all, these issues raised by the two chapters call for a thorough study of digitalized consumption practices, and the following chapters of the present book contribute in their own way to such a programme.

Devising consumers

The processes of human and non-human entanglement in everyday consumer practices are examined critically and discussed in the chapters under the heading "Devising consumers", in tribute to McFall's (2014) book titled *Devising Consumption*, in which "devising" refers both to how consumption is practically enabled, and to how the design of particular market devices helps to do so. In this section, we examine three different empirical sites: recommendation agents, practices of digital virtual consumption, and ethical smartphone applications. Together, the chapters work as prisms for studying the digitalization of consumer culture and gaining a deeper understanding of many consequences of digitalization.

Vayre, Larnaudie and Dufresne's chapter, titled "Serendipitous effects in digitalized markets: the case of the DataCrawler recommendation agent", is a study of how commercial applications and systems inscribe functions designed to enact discovery and chance encounter as part of the shopping process in order to increase levels of purchase in an e-commerce website environment. They develop a case of technologically mediated and digitalized forms of serendipity. Serendipity refers to the accidental discovery of something that the consumer did not know that s/he could want. Paradoxically, in its commercial application form as an inscribed design feature, serendipity works as a funnel towards purchase that leads consumers to discover, explore and select available products or offers. The authors argue that recommendation systems or agents solve problems of the sales process. They develop a theoretically informed argument about the agency of such digital merchant devices and how they shape consumers' purchase process through the Web shop experience and through interaction with goods recommended by the agent. Results show how a successful journey – where staged serendipity leads to purchase – through a Web shop visit is aided by an active recommendation software that effectively manages consumer dispersion and even increases the consumer's interest in particular goods. To frame such explorative consumer behaviour, the authors provide the concept of staged serendipity to understand the agency of digital agents and their impact on consumer dispositions (curiosity, surprise and interest).

Devices not only assist and channel consumers, but also rework their dispositions, emotions and values, as recently noticed by McFall and her colleagues (McFall et al., n.d., forthcoming). In the chapters by Jenkins and Denegri-Knott, and by Hansson, we learn that consumers' cognitive capacities as well as their (ethical) decision-making skills and emotional abilities are extended by, entangled with and externalized to digital technologies with particular effects on everyday consumer cultures, including values, skills, practices and morals. In "Extending the mind: digital devices and the transformation of consumer practices", Jenkins and Denegri-Knott present a study of consumers in the south of England and their relationships to digital devices (smartphones, laptops, the Internet). In this chapter, the authors focus on how consumers' knowledge, imagination, desires and memory related to given consumer practices such as product search, choice and cooking become something different when "devised" through digital tools. Consumers can do new and different things when associated with digital tools than they can without such tools. Jenkins and Denegri-Knott note that a consumer "using digital devices to construct desire for an object, or seeking knowledge to carry out consumption-supported practices, like cooking or motoring, is a very different consumer, with a new repertoire of capabilities and skills". The authors' suggestion is rather radical for a humanistic concept of intention or agency but also for traditional views of responsibility and morals. Indeed, they propose "that digital devices and consumers form a hybrid cognitive system". Brains, the authors proclaim, are no longer limited to the human body but are extended through various prostheses that are not neutral but are often inscribed with commercial, ideological or normative intentions or programmes of action (a theme also developed in Hansson's chapter). This idea of consumers' minds being extended and modified through digital devices begs the analysis of how and why consumers engage with digital devices in different practices – like, for example, collecting and cooking. According to the analysis, digital devices are good for remembering things and extending important consumer skills. In this sense, they aid consumers in their activities as collectors and cooks beyond their initial capabilities. An important finding stressed by the authors is that as digital devices enter the elemental set-up of consumer practices, consumers tend to shift focus and commitment from the consumer practice towards becoming a competent and committed user of the technology itself. For example, a committed cook could shift interest and become more engaged in mastering the technology. The authors also find an accompanying shift in the teleo-affective or emotional investment in the practice among consumers following such alterations.

In "Promoting ethical consumption: the construction of smartphone apps as 'ethical' choice prescribers", Hansson pursues the exploration of the cognitive and normative effects of digital consumer assistants by developing a cross-case analysis of three ethical smartphone apps. Hansson applies an actor-network-theory perspective to disclose how ethics is coded into software applications and the potential effects that such digital devices can have on practices of ethical consumption. In detailing both the various functions and the versions of ethics inscribed in these devices, the author shows how marketers and developers of digital tools work to change the meaning of what it is to be an ethical consumer. This is mainly accomplished through mobilizing a particular image of the consumer: "the choosing consumer" as the main figure at work in the apps. This configuring of ethical consumer representations is critically examined and discussed in the chapter in a detailed cross-case analysis of ethical smartphone application "scripts", a concept borrowed from Akrich (1992) that details the lines of action designed into technology through functions and user representations. Hansson argues that not only are ethical smartphone apps designed with a particular consumer representation in mind, but they are also scripted in order to alter the consumer practices of ethical shopping by equipping concerned consumers with new capabilities for ethical action through the extended functionalities provided by the apps. Issues like interactive databases, algorithmic decision making, barcode readers and extended memory capacities assemble a new form of ethical consumption culture based on the identity of a hybrid form of ethical consumer action. Accordingly, Hansson argues that ethical smartphone apps carry the potential to counteract the conventional market devices in stores that prescribe purchases (how to move; face arrangement and shelves, products and packaging; and salespersons) (cf. Cochoy, 2007). In that sense, marketing of ethical apps might be interpreted as something along the lines of a counter-programme for ethical action where some traditional market devices are being challenged through digitalization and the equipping of consumers with new forms of choice guides, preferences and qualification of goods in ethical registers (traceability, social justice claims, environmental performance, etc.).

All in all, these three chapters turn our attention to wider considerations regarding transformations of consumer cultures. New possibilities for consumers equipped with, for example, barcode scanners and access to previously hidden databases of product information – a sort of new "empowered consumer" – are emerging. Or, as Thaler argues, with "smarter information" come "smarter consumers" (Thaler, 2013). In the footsteps of applications and digitalization based on algorithmic power and the potential of digital information access, a wider transformation of consumer culture can be attested and imagined as more and more consumers make use of digital tools and become enrolled in technologically mediated practices. That ethics and morals or dispositions such as serendipity are becoming codified, designed and inscribed in digital devices, or "choice engines" (Thaler, 2013), and marketed to consumer mass markets points towards the importance of considering how cultural elements like meanings, norms and values are distributed through the medium of digital technology. As Hansson writes, "choice is framed differently in the apps and thus prescribes particular ways of behaving in an ethical way. The GreenGuide app prescribes free or 'open choice' as long as consumers act and consume in an environmentally friendly way". This is similar to how labels can work as a "vehicle for providing consumers with information that turns credence attributes into search ones" (Valor, 2008, p. 320). In her concluding discussion, Hansson joins Vayre et al., and Jenkins and Denegri-Knott in arguing for a better understanding of the impact of digitalization on consumer preferences, consumer culture and consumer choice.

These chapters about the devising of consumers suggest that digital artefacts can be seen as market devices. In such a framing, devices play a crucial role in the shaping of both markets and consumers, including their roles, capacities, desires and dispositions (Callon et al., 2007). Digital devices programmed with algorithms exemplify that devices contribute to give shape to smaller- and larger-scale alterations of cultural practices (Amoore and Piotukh, 2015). Algorithms have become deeply integrated in our society (see Facebook, Google, Netflix, Spotify, etc.), and they express sometimes dominant and sometimes alternative or subordinate values and beliefs in our culture, and thus codify beliefs and values. For example, the moral that limits images of naked breasts led Facebook to censor images of breastfeeding and led to the use of male breasts in a video that instructed how to self-examine for breast cancer. Digitalization results in changes throughout the world via the values that are coded or inscribed into the design of the Facebook algorithm that searches for and hides nudity. Other actors, such as Amazon, Uber and Airbnb, make good use of ordering and organizing digital information by putting algorithms to work. Recommendation systems fuel algorithms and alter purchase behaviour on the mundane and micro levels of consumption that seem to be more and more entangled with invisible digital technologies (Mellet et al., 2014). This might hold great consequences for how scholars can study and understand "the socially extended mind" in terms of other consumers being part of a digitally extended cognitive system. As Belk argues, digitalization "potentially changes the nature of humans, non-human things and the relations between them" (Belk, 2014, p. 1107), and consumption research therefore must consider "the full entanglements of humans and things" (ibid., p. 1113). As a result, one may wonder if it is still appropriate to think in terms of consumer culture, or if we should not rather talk in terms of consumer "cultivation" (Cochoy and Mallard, n.d., forthcoming).

In sum, this digital devising of consumers and consumer practices has effects on different levels and in various ways. Such processes make explicit how, for example, cultural values and ethical relations can be inscribed in digital devices. Seemingly human capacities, such as imagination, and dispositions, such as curiosity and surprise, become codified into the design of computer programs and technologies to trigger consumer interest and commitment, and alter their line of acting and thinking. In fact, given how digital devices form deep connections with human brains (and bodies), it can be argued that not even imagination, desire or ethics can be thought of as particularly human categories, but rather as the outcome of hybrid systems consisting of consumers and their devices. This might have an even greater impact in the future, following technological innovation and software development where consumers form even deeper *relationships* with devices (cf. Belk, 2014). The digital "devicification" of consumer culture, where more and more forms of action are digitally mediated, places emphasis on the dynamic and non-determinist influence of digital technologies on consumption and consumer behaviour.

Consumer subjects and practices

The chapters by Petersson McIntyre, by Sörum and Fuentes, and by Hagberg and Kjellberg discuss the consumer subjects and practices that are enabled by digitalization. The authors approach questions of subjectivities and power in varying ways. Three different types of setting are examined: music consumption on Spotify; trade fairs for e-commerce; and a Facebook group for ethical consumption. These settings are analysed as sites that bring consumers, everyday life, devices and markets together in specific ways. The authors use the examples to discuss the roles that new digital devices and technologies have for practices and meaning-making of consumption. Through what is inscribed in the technologies and how consumer subjects respond to the data produced, the algorithms produced by Spotify, the socio-technical construction and mediation of consumption on Facebook, and the mythologies of big data mediated at e-commerce trade fairs all convey particular versions of consumption and of what it means to be a consumer. Thus, these chapters contextualize the constitution and design of devices and services, and analyse the formation of the resulting consumer subjects. The changing cultural and social patterns of consuming groceries and music found in these chapters are related to sense-making processes regarding ethics, privacy, gender and subjectivities.

The transformations introduced by digitalization processes are not only material, but also discursive. The chapters by Petersson McIntyre, and by Sörum and Fuentes particularly address the material-discursive construction of consumer subjects and their relation to questions of power, more specifically regarding gender (gendered images of consumers), and ethics (the ethical consumer).

In the chapter "Tracing the sex of big data (or configuring digital consumers)", Petersson McIntyre examines how the digitalization of consumption is presented to visitors at trade fairs for e-commerce. Here, big data appear not primarily in terms of sets of data and traces, but as entangled in market actors' sense-making of the future of e-commerce. The mythologies of big data were not only mobilized to explain and market business opportunities (boyd and Crawford, 2012); big data also represented a shift in configuring the consumer, as elusive as it may be. The idea of the choosing consumer, as described by Hansson (this volume), now also contains a choice of gender. On the one hand, the consumers of the future are presented as individuals who stand above traditional segmentations. Marketing will now become completely individual, as new data make gender segments a superfluous category. On the other hand, speakers and presenters seem unable to imagine such a genderless world, and presentations of the functions of new devices are still firmly anchored in statistics on gender, leaving the future of gender categories ambivalent at best. Building on a methodology of tracing the gendered and cultural meanings that are mobilized in explanations of new market devices, Petersson McIntyre outlines the implications of the mythologies behind big data for making sense of gender categories. Speakers and presenters at the trade fairs were nearly always white, middle-aged men dressed in grey suits. Consumers were nearly always configured as young women. Thus, to understand the cultural and social meanings of digital devices, these devices need to be related to the bodies, subjects and categories of identity by and with which they are presented. Masculine symbolism with heavy metal, motorcycles and digital technologies framed many events, and is significant for the establishment of e-commerce as a new field that contrasts to mail order. The chapter attempts to understand digital consumption – not by studying what consumers actually do with devices, or by understanding consumers and devices as assemblages, but by understanding the mechanisms through which particular ideas of consumers come into existence, and how they matter for how gender is understood.

In the chapter "'Write something': the shaping of ethical consumption on Facebook", Sörum and Fuentes analyse the Facebook group "Conscious Consumption" and specifically focus on how ethical consumption is shaped by the technical affordances of the Facebook platform. The authors argue that social media sites actively co-shape what ethical content or information looks like, and images of the ethical consumer. In the digital environment, ethical rules are no longer pre-constructed, but rather emerge as results of online connections and continuous negotiations among connected members, as members share, comment and "like" various contents in public. Thus, Sörum and Fuentes understand the cultural meanings appropriated to ethical consumption as socially and technically constituted. The Facebook platform is approached as an important context for these collective meaning-making processes, as it allows members to coalesce around issues of ethics regarding their shopping and consumption habits as well as social change associated with detrimental effects of contemporary consumption. Due to technical properties of the medium – the multiple processes of connecting with other profiles and users, the ability to share content and the feature of publicness or visibility – certain forms and images of ethical consumption prevail (campaigns, homemade projects or "to-do lists"). The forms and images promoted seem to encourage social change through quite easy transitions, for example a simple exchange of products (certified instead of regular food for a period), or through campaigns aimed at reducing consumption levels with small threats of forcing consumers to adopt larger lifestyle changes. The chapter includes a perspective of power to analyse how a system of Foucauldian self-governance can become inscribed in digital tools. The Facebook group and disclosed member practices are interpreted as a form of "technology of the self" through which consumers learn to control their purchases and consume "consciously" with the help of collective norms mediated through these platforms.

In "Digitalized music: entangling consumption practices", Hagberg and Kjellberg continue to elaborate on how technological changes affect patterns of consumption. Different digital technologies (CDs, MP3s, streaming) have given rise to new ways of accessing, listening to and talking about music. Due to technological changes, not least the mobility of listening devices, music has become ubiquitous in contemporary society (Oakes et al., 2014). Based on interviews with Swedish music consumers, the chapter discusses the effects of digitalization on music consumption practices such as buying, listening to and socially interacting with music.

Sweden is the country of origin for several music innovations, such as Pirate Bay and Spotify, making it a particularly interesting setting to study how changing technological conditions affect consumption practices. The authors stress that music consumption has become increasingly integrated with other everyday activities, such as exercising, walking, biking, commuting, working, hanging out, being at home and driving. While such integration is not unique to digital music, digitalization has influenced the occurrence and intensity of these crossover practices. Hagberg and Kjellberg develop a typology of how listening to music intersects with everyday life, which includes four types of intersections. The increasingly prevalent intersections of music listening with other everyday activities transform the practice of music listening as such, they argue. Although digitalization, even if specific in its different forms, has made it easier to transport and consume music in all kinds of settings, music listening has simultaneously become a less social activity than before. In spite of the new functions for sharing and interacting that are enabled by these devices, music listening also works as a way to shut out the outside world. Yet, in spite of the ability to shut out competing sounds, Hagberg and Kjellberg find that the quality of listening has become impaired. This last point, which may at first be considered a "side observation", is highly important: it stresses that it would be wrong systematically to associate the digital with progress, or to study it in isolation. Rather, digitalization should be seen as a reconfiguration process, introducing novel social and market "agencements" (Callon, 2016). The study of such transformation is key to understanding the dynamic of contemporary markets.

The chapters in this section highlight how digital devices, services and technologies attract consumers and how consumers make use of them. Taken together, these three contributions shed light on the cultural meanings and practices of digital technologies. New devices and technologies present certain ways of being a consumer, and they shape and alter how consumption is understood and shaped by market processes. Ideas about what consumers like and find important are "inscribed" in digital devices, and specific technologies "prescribe" certain consumer actions: in the search possibilities of Spotify's algorithms, in the discussions on Facebook groups that encourage some behaviours and discourage others, and in the attempts to capture consumers with automated product offerings. Thus, devices form the ways consumers act by affording, and sometimes explicitly encouraging, certain types of behaviour – to share, to buy more or less, etc. – and discouraging others, such as buying unethically produced products. Devices act as prostheses, offering to enhance consumers' competence to perform certain actions, such as calculation and choice. Moreover, the devices can be used a little, for a short while, or simply not at all, points that also need to be taken into account, and aspects that are explored further in the following three chapters more particularly attending to the practices of marketing.

Marketing practices

All in all, the journey in the digitalized consumer world evidences the ambiguities of the digitalization of consumption as a movement that helps to enlarge and exert our choices but also gives more control over our consumption behaviour to market professionals. An exploration of how market devices contribute to shape consumption motivates paying closer attention to the professional discipline that is perhaps mostly associated with this kind of endeavour: marketing. Three chapters explicitly explore marketing practices in relation to consumers, although in distinctively different ways. These chapters explore the relationship between marketing and popular culture, digital marketing campaigns, and the tracing of the traces of such campaigns.

In her chapter "Marketing and cyberspace: William Gibson's view", Czarniawska explores the relationship between digital consumption and marketing by turning to popular culture and, particularly, to the work of science-fiction writer William Gibson. Through an analysis of three of his novels, she shows how these works relate to contemporary marketing and consumption fads and trends. Using characters and events from *Pattern Recognition, Spook Country* and *Zero History*, Czarniawska discusses examples ranging from "buzzadors" to neuromarketing as subtle marketing techniques to attract contemporary consumers. She proposes that this could be understood as a circular relationship that is aided by the digital. This circularity blurs distinctions between the digital and material, selling and buying, inscribed (e.g. texts, objects) and lived cultures, theory and practice, science and fiction. This theme relates to Petersson McIntyre's chapter (this volume), in which "fictions" about associations between new devices and consumers are represented at fairs and thus blur similar distinctions. Further, in her analysis of Gibson's novel *Zero History* and the secret brand "Gabriel Hounds", Czarniawska draws attention to secrecy and exclusivity, which may become an even more important part of marketing in a digital world increasingly characterized by instant availability. In a discussion that disrupts boundaries between bodies, technologies, senses and data, Czarniawska's chapter questions principles of linearity, temporality, the real and the (science) fictional that are attached to ideas of consumption and digitalization.

Sjöblom, Broberg and Axelsson's chapter, "Digital advertising campaigns and the branded economy", moves into digital marketing campaigns and how they have developed with the Internet. Similar to the mutual relationship between popular culture and marketing in Czarniawska's contribution, the relationship between such campaigns and the Internet is characterized by a co-development. Digital marketing campaigns have contributed to this development through attempts to attract consumers into various forms of Internet activity. Such campaigns have often been confronted with the paradoxical situation that some digital aspects of the campaign must be innovative and novel in order to attract consumers, while at the same time there is a danger of being ahead of their time and facing the risk of passing unnoticed. Here, marketing campaigns are often bold moves that may push the limits of what until then has been possible, thinkable or doable.

Sjöblom, Broberg and Axelsson analyse five award-winning digital marketing campaigns, which in combination provide insights into how digital marketing has developed over time in the relatively short history of Internet marketing that began in the mid-1990s. Through these campaigns, it becomes obvious that the development of digital marketing has always been a form of integration between online and offline. Today, this integration is further fuelled by the use of mobile devices such as smartphones and tablets, and perhaps even to the point where talking about off- and online is becoming superfluous. Throughout the cases presented, we may see how interactivity becomes an increasingly important part of the campaigns, involving more people and making more possibilities available, but also being more difficult to control. Borrowing a metaphor from the field they study, they refer to this as a "pinball effect", i.e. that the effects of different moves cannot be carefully controlled in advance but rather depend on change as they occur. This can also be compared with the way that Vayre, Larnaudie and Dufresne discuss the commercial application of "serendipity" in their chapter of this volume. All in all, the digital campaigns exemplify the co-development of marketing and the Internet, from introduction of the digital, to increased interactivity and, subsequently, mobility. The analysis of advertising agencies by Sjöblom, Broberg and Axelsson reminds us that despite the early prophecies about the removal of different types of intermediaries due to the Internet, they remain important, though their roles have shifted in some cases (cf. Doherty and Ellis-Chadwick, 2010; Hagberg et al., 2016).

While Sjöblom, Broberg and Axelsson focus on the campaigns, they refrain from making claims about possible impacts on behaviours, attitudes and actions, which moves us to the chapter "From the logs of QR code readers: a socio-log-y of digital consumption", by Cochoy and Smolinski. They take these effects as a serious challenge in their endeavour to trace the traces of digital campaigns. More specifically, they explore the "traces of marketing" campaigns that include QR codes. While Sjöblom, Broberg and Axelsson describe innovative digital campaigns as a "pinball effect", Cochoy and Smolinski expand the set of metaphors by comparing such campaigns with "reversed thunder". Whereas traditional advertising campaigns worked like thunder (lightning coming from the sky and hitting a few at the cost of its noise), digital campaigns turn it all around. With QR codes, data come from the ground and go up to the clouds (in the IT sense of the word) with greater silence, although supposedly creating noise with a rapid and extensive increase of data for the providers to handle, interpret and try to transform into action. QR codes are, at least in principle, a form of mediator able to bridge the physical and digital as well as increase interactivity, what Sjöblom, Broberg and Axelsson describe as a more important part of marketing campaigns over time. Cochoy and Smolinski discuss how data that result from QR code campaigns often are poor and require much work in order to make sense for the user. This is also important in relation to the praise and fears in relation to the emergence of big data in various forms of businesses. Thus, access to an increasing amount of data is a reality for many companies, but analysing and using these data is quite a different story. The proliferation of big data among businesses is also a key issue for researchers in the study of markets who pay attention to such data (see also Boullier, this volume). The authors propose not staying with this type of data, but rather enriching, extending and connecting it to other types of data by tracing these traces to their origin and use. Facing data that are poor and messy thus requires creative approaches to make sense of them.

Tracing data brings us back to where we started. The initial proposal by Boullier – to pay more attention to the circulating entities of data – has been further emphasized by the subsequent chapters in a call for what Cochoy and Smolinski refer to as "tracing the traces" into such practices. This issue becomes even more important, as we see throughout the chapters, because the digital and the physical are intertwined in different ways and are increasingly difficult to separate due to the increasing digitalization of more and more spheres of society, including consumption.

Taken together, the final three chapters in this volume complete what the previous sections of the book point towards: that an interest in the digitalization of consumption requires that sufficient attention also be paid to the professions that attempt to digitalize consumption in different ways. With the addition that this last section provides to the collective effort represented in the book, it seems fair to conclude that the volume offers a number of distinct contributions.

First, it contributes to the emerging tradition of practice-based approaches to markets (e.g. Araujo et al., 2010), and specifically to the study of market devices and their use in everyday markets (Callon et al., 2007; Cochoy et al., 2016), by highlighting how consumption and market processes are deeply intertwined with and mediated by different digital market devices.

Second, this volume contributes to practice-based approaches to consumption, particularly the use of market devices in consumers' everyday lives (Epp et al., 2014; Hansson, 2014).

Third, it explores the digitalization of consumer culture and thus extends previous contributions along these lines (Miller and Horst, 2012; Molesworth and Denegri-Knott, 2012; Lehdonvirta, 2012), by specifically attending to the meaning of digital devices and digitalization in consumers' everyday lives, the inscriptions of meanings of consumption in devices, and the role of devices for the making of subjectivities.

Finally, this book contributes with insights regarding the contemporary ongoing digitalization of consumer markets and consumer culture. Studying digitalizing processes renews the analysis of market-framing and market-shaping dynamics (Araujo and Kjellberg, 2010). By accounting for digitalizing processes, the different chapters aid in understanding how digital solutions are part of a "market for market devices", where the suppliers of varied solutions work hard to sell their tools (to retailers) along the argument that the latter will sell (to consumers) (Cochoy, 2016). It explores how marketers and market tools heavily equip, channel and impact consumer cognition and action. Such impact deserves all the more attention in that digital devices (such as smartphones, smartwatches and other quantified-self appliances) are used and perceived as empowering, tiny, friendly, "wearable" and "private" extensions of the self (cf. Belk, 1988, 2014), rather than as part of a larger infrastructure aimed at framing and monitoring consumption. In fact, and paradoxically, these artefacts share both characteristics: with digital devices, we are controlled through the expression of our very freedom, as if the "wired ball" of today were replacing or supplementing Weber's old iron cage – an evolution which, of course, deserves our best scrutiny and vigilance.

Acknowledgements

This book was published as part of the Digcon project (Digitalizing Consumer Culture) funded by the Swedish Research Council (grant number: 2012-5736), and the Omniscan project funded by the Région Midi-Pyrénées (France, Agile-IT program).

We would like to thank the authors who have contributed with chapters to this volume. We would also like to thank the reviewers for their constructive comments on these chapters: Magnus Bergquist, Julien Brailly, Helene Brembeck, Janice Denegri-Knott, Christian Fuentes, Bente Halkier, Lena Hansson, Hans Kjellberg, Alexandre Mallard, Mika Pantzar and Stefan Schwarzkopf. We also express our gratitude to Hans Kjellberg for his valuable comments on an early draft of this chapter.

References

Akrich, M. (1992) "The De-Scription of Technical Objects", in Bijker, W.E. & Law, J., *Shaping Technology/Building Society: Studies in Sociotechnical Change*, Cambridge, MA: MIT Press, pp. 205–224.

Amoore, L. & Piotukh, V. (2015) *Algorithmic Life: Calculative Devices in the Age of Big Data*, Abingdon: Routledge.

Araujo, L., Finch, J. & Kjellberg, H. (2010) *Reconnecting Marketing to Markets: Practice Based Approaches*, Oxford: Oxford University Press.

Araujo, L. & Kjellberg, H. (2010) "Shaping Exchanges, Performing Markets: The Study of Marketing Practices", in MacLaran, P., Saren, M., Stern, B. & Tadajewski, M. (eds) *The Sage Handbook of Marketing Theory*, London: Sage, pp. 195–218.

Belk, R.W. (1988) "Propriétés and the Extended Self", *Journal of Consumer Research*, 15(2): 139–168.

Belk, R. (2014) "Digital Consumption and the Extended Self", *Journal of Marketing Management*, 30(11–12): 1101–1118.

Belk, R. W. & Llamas, R. (2013) *The Routledge Companion to Digital Consumption*, London: Routledge.

boyd, d. & Crawford, K. (2012) "Critical Questions for Big Data", *Information, Communication & Society*, 15(5), 662–679.

Callon, M. (2005) "Why Virtualism Paves the Way to Political Impotence", *Economic Sociology*, 6(2): 3–20.

Callon, M. (2013) "Qu'est-ce qu'un agencement marchand?" in Callon, M. et al., *Sociologie des agencements marchands*, Paris: Presses des Mines, pp. 325–440.

Callon, M. (2016) "Revisiting Marketization: From Interface-Markets to Market-Agencements", *Consumption Markets & Culture*, 19(1): 17–37.

Callon, M., Millo, Y. & Muniesa, F. (eds) (2007) *Market Devices*, Sociological Review Monographs, Oxford: Blackwell.

Cochoy, F. (2007) "A Sociology of Market-Things. On Tending the Garden of Choices in Mass Retailing", in Callon, M., Muniesa, F. & Millo, Y. (eds) *Market Devices*, Sociological Review Monographs, Vol. 55, No. 777, London: Blackwell, pp. 109–129.

Cochoy, F. & Mallard, A. (n.d., forthcoming). "Another Consumer Culture Theory. An ANT Look at Consumption, or How 'Market-Things' Help 'Cultivating' Consumers", in Kravets, O., MacLaran, P., Miles, S. & Venkatesh, A. (eds) *Handbook of Consumer Culture*, London: Sage.

Cochoy, F., Smolinski, J. & Vayre, J.-S. (2016) "From Marketing to 'Market-Things' and 'Market-ITing': Accounting for Technicized and Digitalized Consumption", in Czarniawska, B. (ed.) *A Research Agenda for Management and Organization Studies*, Cheltenham: Edward Elgar, pp. 26–37.

Cochoy, F., Trompette, P. & Araujo, L. (2016) "From Market Agencements to Market Agencing: An Introduction", *Consumption, Markets and Culture*, 19(1): 3–16.

Coll, S. (2013) "Consumption as Biopower: Governing Bodies with Loyalty Cards", *Journal of Consumer Culture*, 13(3): 201–220.

Doherty, N.F. & Ellis-Chadwick, F. (2010) "Internet Retailing: The Past, the Present and the Future", *International Journal of Retail & Distribution Management*, 38(11–12): 943–965.

Ekström, K. & Brembeck, H. (eds) (2004) *Elusive Consumption*, Oxford and New York: Berg Publisher.

Epp, A., Schau, H. & Price, L. (2014) "The Role of Brands and Mediating Technologies in Assembling Long-Distance Family Practices", *Journal of Marketing*, 78(3): 81–101.

Hagberg, J., Sundström, M. & Egels-Zanden, N. (2016) "The Digitalization of Retailing: An Exploratory Framework", *International Journal of Retail & Distribution Management*, 44(7): 694–712.

Hansson, N. (2014) "'Mobility-Things' and Consumption: Conceptualizing Differently Mobile Families on the Move with Recent Purchases in Urban Space", *Consumption, Markets and Culture*, 18(1): 72–91.

Latour B., Jensen B., Venturini T., Grauwin S. & Boullier D. (2012) "The Whole is Always Smaller than its Parts. A Digital Test of Gabriel Tarde's Monads", *British Journal of Sociology*, 63(4): 590–615.

Lehdonvirta, V. (2012) "A History of the Digitalization of Consumer Culture", in Molesworth, M. & Denegri-Knott, J. (eds) *Digital Virtual Consumption*, New York: Routledge, pp. 11–28.

McFall, L. (2014) *Devising Consumption: Cultural Economies of Insurance, Credit and Spending*, Abingdon: Routledge.

McFall, L., Deville, J. & Cochoy, F. (n.d., forthcoming). "Introduction. Markets and the Arts of Attachment", in Cochoy, F., Deville, J. & McFall, L., *Markets and the Art of Attachment*, London: Routledge.

Mellet, K., Beauvisage, T., Beuscart, J. & Trespeuch, M. (2014) "A 'Democratization' of Markets? Online Consumer Reviews in the Restaurant Industry", *Valuation Studies*, 2: 5–41.

Miller, D. & Horst, H.A. (2012) *Digital Anthropology*, Oxford: Berg.

Milyaeva, S. & Neyland, D. (2016) "Market Innovation as Framing, Productive Friction and Bricolage: An Exploration of the Personal Data Market", *Journal of Cultural Economy*, 9(3): 229–244.

Moats, D. & McFall, L. (2016) "Devising Wellbeing Markets: How Wearables Track, Marketise and Financialise Movements", 4S/EASST Conference, Mundane Market Matters: On the ordinary stuff (and actions and sometimes people) that make markets, Barcelona (Daniel Neyland, ed.), 31 August–3 September.

Molesworth, M. & Denegri-Knott, J. (2012) *Virtual Digital Consumption*, London: Routledge.

Neyland, D. & Milyaeva, S. (2016) "The Entangling of Problems, Solutions and Markets: On Building a Market for Privacy", working paper, Sociology, Goldsmiths, University of London.

Oakes, S., Brownlie, D. & Dennis, N. (2014) "Ubiquitous Music: A Summary and Future Research Agenda", *Marketing Theory*, 14(2): 141–145.

Rogers, R. (2013) *Digital Methods*, Cambridge, MA: MIT Press.

Ruppert, E., Law, J. & Savage, M. (2013) "Reassembling Social Science Methods: The Challenge of Digital Devices", *Theory, Culture & Society*, 30(4): 22–46.

Shove, E., Pantzar, M. & Watson, M. (2012) *The Dynamic of Social Practice: Everyday Life and How it Changes*, London: Sage Publications.

Thaler, R. H. (2013) "THE BIG IDEA – Smarter Information, Smarter Consumers – How a Potent Mix of Modern Technology and New Government Policy is About to Transform Disclosure – and with it the Workings of Many Parts of the Economy", *Harvard Business Review: HBR*.

Valor, C. (2008) "Can Consumers Buy Responsibly? Analysis and Solutions for Market Failures", *Journal of Consumer Policy*, 31: 315–326.

2 Big data challenge for social sciences and market research

From society and opinion to replications

Dominique Boullier

Translated by Jim O'Hagan

A new generation of social sciences is knocking at the door. To put it simply, marketing and computer sciences take the lead and generate tools for monitoring brands, reputations, communities, social networks, etc. They can do without the interpretations and models of the social sciences because they compensate with computing power and the unprecedented traceability of "big data". Their main concern remains the action and reaction, not the analysis or understanding, as the traditions of sociology and other social sciences have defined. Traces rather than data, reactivity rather than reflexivity, the digital world finds itself shaped by principles that leave less and less room for social sciences.

First, we will discuss the peculiar status of these traces to understand the justifications and limitations of such hype. Then we will compare our times of tremendous technical change to those of the 1930s, when sampling was invented and opinions made visible in the same socio-technical and marketing moves. Finally, another time frame will serve for comparison, when "society" began to be thought of as an entity of its own and computed with novel devices at the same time. Finally, we will discuss how social sciences and market research can repurpose these digital sources for their own goals, while brands use them for their reactivity requirements. The three ages of social sciences are not mere questions for quantification sociologists: they frame our collective reflexivity. The table of their features gives striking evidence of the correspondence between these three ages.

The digital age

Neither people nor identities, traces are the raw material

For many years, computer science (in a way extended with social networks) has calculated and modelled society as if the traces collected allowed access to the "truth" about individuals in a more effective way than polls, surveys and censuses. Consider two examples, one academic and the other commercial:

- "The Web does not just connect machines, it connects people" (Knight Foundation, 14 September 2008). This was declared by Sir Tim Berners-Lee, founder of the World Wide Web (WWW) in 1991 with René Caillau, emphasizing the transition to a dimension of networks that are neither technological (Internet) nor documentary (WWW), but rather social (GGG, for Global Giant Graph).

- Facebook, for its part, has managed the tour de force of "normalizing" in terms of the actors themselves and the declaration of their true identity. That is to say, those provided by the civil state, their name and surname, in opposition to the tradition of anonymity on the Web. The platform thus claims to become the world of reference or even a civil-status alternative, competing with Google in this regard.

However, there is no guarantee whatsoever of any connection between identities on Facebook or Berners-Lee's "people" and persons identified by their civil registry. What are connected are merely the retrieved accounts and data, and these are only the traces of activity from an entity that could possibly take on the form of civil status. This uncertainty should lead to a careful examination of results in order to differentiate registered accounts and active or engaging accounts, and prevent anyone from allegations about "society" or "people" when using social networks analytics. For the scores that classify sites on a search engine such as Google, the resulting topology of sites and blogs never discusses their contents as such, but the inbound and outbound links that produce a rank of authority or hub, as defined in the network topology (Kleinberg et al., 1998) and not a civil status.

What we mean by "traces" should be noted here, in order to distinguish them from data. Traces can range from signals ("raw" generated by objects) to unstructured verbatim. Traces can be exploited in databases (links, clicks, likes, cookies)[1] and by operators or platforms, but they can also be captured independently of this through the application programming interface (API). Traces are not necessarily pre-formatted for a specific calculation, nor are they dependent upon aggregation that can then be applied. It is easy to argue that, despite everything, "behind" these sites or "behind" these clicks there are most certainly people, but that does not alter the fact that the algorithms do not take this into consideration and that, furthermore, no guarantees can be given in this regard. Traces understood in the restricted sense are produced by platforms and digital-technological systems, but are not "signs" or evidence of anything other than themselves as long as relationships with other attributes are not created and validated. This differs radically from the data that can be recovered en masse from client files or administrative acts. Certainly, the big data methods for calculating can be applied here in both cases, but the traces are *a priori*, independent of other attributes, in particular socio-demographic factors that are rarely mobilized in correlations sought between traces. Relationships with more conventional parameters in data sciences are limited to time (a timestamp) and location (geolocation tags), which allow for the production of timelines and maps that become simplified modes of representation for traces.

Traces are produced by platforms

Amazon and Apple do not focus on the same features as Facebook or Google (since the Web is no longer distributed but rather monopolized by these four GAFA platforms that centralize the majority of traffic, with Twitter extending the traces industry). It is not people who are put into relation with each other, but, above all, tastes (books or music originally), expressed by traces of purchases and choices, which can be treated en masse to produce patterns and profiles, independent of personal information. It should certainly not be forgotten that all these platforms, without exception, are also very fond of civil status-type data, phone numbers and other highly attractive resources to advertisers to whom they are resold. The ensuing marketing methods are largely based on the addressing of mass advertising or email to IP addresses or email accounts that have clicked on an article (retargeting), but much more rarely via sophisticated links with other attributes of the supposed people attached to these addresses or those clicks (profiling).

Traces of digital behaviour are thus a particularly profitable "raw material", without the need to appeal to the social sciences. How should the social sciences deal with this situation? Two options are open to them: either they are confined to their world of administrative data, surveys and polls, relativizing the interest of such traces and focusing on data; or they decide to take the bull by the horns and take these traces as raw material provided for "repurposing", as proposed by Richard Rogers (2013). Thus, they must accept being dependent on the platforms that produce these traces, without being able to influence, or even being totally dependent on the conditions of production for such data, which may vary over time and across platforms. The powerful viral phenomenon specific to the Facebook platform and its "likes" mechanism nevertheless does not leave researchers indifferent, since they are so spectacular, such as when pages generate substantial likes in a few days. This arouses all types of analyses from the most constructivist and critical ("all the likes are bought", i.e. artefacts), to the most realistic ("it is solid proof that opinion, and even 'the people' think that way"). The limited quality of the traces is observable on all platforms, but these limits may be intrinsic when they do not meet the criteria for traceability that we consider crucial in order to exploit them, or extrinsic when we criticize their lack of reliable relation to the "real" world. The latter stance is found in boyd and Crawford in relation to Twitter:

> Some users have multiple accounts. Some accounts are used by multiple people. Some people never establish an account, and simply access Twitter via the web. Some accounts are "bots" that produce automated content without involving a person. Furthermore, the notion of an "active"

account is problematic. While some users post content frequently through Twitter, others participate as "listeners". Twitter Inc. has revealed that 40 percent of active users sign in just to listen.

(boyd and Crawford, 2011)

Other studies (Driscoll and Walker, 2014) tested the data produced from various access methods offered by, for example, Twitter, and showed that the Search API, the Streaming API, and the Gnip PowerTrack (paid service) provide very different results, the latter method collecting a much larger number of tweets, but not uniformly according to the requests! This means that the traces collected are entirely dependent on the mechanisms of collection. This is not surprising, although we do tend to forget this for other, older methods that have become conventional.

The brands' grip on traces

Where does this fascination with traces – despite their limitations – come from, compared with data from registries and surveys? The traces are actually a key resource for brands to monitor the effects of their actions on the public. Reputation and notoriety no longer translate audience measurement, which would be a simplistic import of measures, largely built for the mass media. On networks, one must measure both a form of audience (the reach), the most basic activities of its uncertain public (likes, stars), and also more sophisticated activities such as comments, which constitute what is called "the engagement rate". Brands are fond of these traces and they fuel the turnover of all these platforms, and thus, of the entire Web. The opinion-mining and sentiment-analysis tools (Boullier and Lohard, 2012) are thus the answer to the marketer's anxiety after the product launch. However, the extension of this brand domain reaches all activities, whether commercial, cultural, political, institutional or even interpersonal, when each must measure excellence with rankings, as researchers are requested to do (Bruno and Didier, 2013). Thus, it is the brands' methods that take precedence everywhere and impose their law and their pace, even on public services.

However, what primarily concerns these brands is not structured and constructed data to test, for example causality, but many traces that function as indicators and alerts, even approximate, not at the individual level but at the level of trends. Similarly, it is not reflexivity that is sought but primarily reactivity, the ability to determine which lever to act upon in relation to the dimensions (features) of the brand that are affected. The closer the relationship with the devices that monitor the activity and the offers made to the customer, such as in customer relationship management (CRM) systems, the more efficient the reactivity. Algorithms that decide the prices of advertisement placement no longer depend on negotiations or decisions made by experts in pricing and market segmentation, but instead on the previous amount of traces collected by the systems (clicks, for instance) and assembled in correlations that generate automated decisions. These methods and the calculation devices that have been built for market purposes were imported from the financial market, where reactivity is the key factor, to the point of high-frequency trading, where expectations and moves on the markets can be manipulated automatically at a millisecond pace. The political world is now caught up in the spiral of reactivity and its addiction to tweets leads us to consider that we have entered the era of *high-frequency politics* (Boullier, 2013).

We have drawn up a table that merits systemization. Digital networking generates:

- Traces
- Assembled and formatted by platforms
- For brands
- With a view to reactivity
- In order to produce rankings or patterns.

This situation is not new. Two other key moments in the existence of the social sciences, especially sociology, market studies and political science, must be paralleled on the same basis to understand the scope of the changes underway. These two main periods of quantification for societies (Desrosières, 1998) must teach us how new methods and principles can be arranged in such a way that they transform themselves "into socio-technical conventions". The emergence of big data can be as challenging for social sciences as were sampling methods in the 1930s, for instance. Big data's ability to become a shared method to quantify social phenomena may produce the same lasting effects.

The construction of "opinion"[2]

The contemporary situation is undoubtedly not that far from a key moment in the history of the social sciences, especially when dealing with consumption behaviour issues that would help us understand what is happening: this is why we will review some features of the period to guess the equivalent in our times. If we gave the current era of digital traces the label "3G" for "third generation", we would then have to give the emergence of public opinion in the late 1930s the label "2G". Indeed, in 1936, George Gallup was able to predict the election of Franklin D. Roosevelt over Alf Landon with a study of 50,000 people. Thus, this dramatic gesture founded the reliability of the survey and of investigative sampling methods,[3] which certainly sacrificed the exhaustiveness of inquiries on entire populations but managed to produce correct results provided that the terms of *representativeness* were respected. The issues of sampling were addressed previously by the social survey of Rowntree (1901) studying urban poverty in York and using Booth's "poverty line" as a statistical marker. However, as Converse (1987) told the story, it is certainly in the context of the mass media that their importance was recognized and their method systematized. With Ogilvy, Gallup studied film audiences and then with Crossley at Young & Rubicam, he studied radio audiences using telephone interviews before even making a proposal to conduct the election polls (Converse, 1987). Considerable media transformation, and the mass media (radio at the time), has established the conditions for the emergence and validation of a survey technique, which thus opens up a whole new era for marketing and political science. Moreover, it is "public opinion" that takes on a measurable existence with these sampling methods.

Communication agencies such as polling organizations indeed cannot live solely from their campaign activities, even if these do bring them high visibility and notoriety. From the outset, their target is constituted by the mass media for one essential reason: audience measurement becomes key to the distribution of advertising space. This has been true since the dawn of radio and then later with television (in 1941 the first ads were aired on American television for Bulova watches, during a baseball game). However, these measures also allow us to monitor the effects of these campaigns on the minds of consumers, giving an unprecedented boost to marketing that drives increasingly sophisticated communication strategies (Cochoy, 1999). Agencies that provide the main reliable feedback on audiences are used to design the programmes and the ads as well, targeted at the same populations and generating revenue from companies. Brands are thus present from the beginning in methods of inquiry into opinion via sampling from the moment when such investigations were aimed primarily at mass-media audiences.

Public opinion exists. I measured it!

The work done by Gallup for the operational side, and Lazarsfeld for the scientific side, is therefore not a simple marketing operation or a facelift for the social sciences: it provides whole societies with methods with which to auto-analyse and to represent themselves as opinions. Tarde (1989 [1901]) certainly highlighted the importance of these views; it is only when the metrics are established and produced in a conventional way that opinion finally exists. Only the media's control and their ability to produce a unified public in a national territory enabled this methodological assembly to hold on. The "whole" referred to by the polls is in fact originally the *public* formed by the media, which allows the audience to emerge as *public opinion*, and to make it permanently visible and measurable with the aim of being exploitable for brands to measure the influence of their campaigns. The parts (Latour et al., 2012) that are individual expressions are pre-formatted to be recordable and calculable, but the link between the parts and everything else is made only by the pollsters' black boxes. The rigorous, scientific precautions are upheld through "confidence intervals" (defined by Neyman in 1934), which keep a reference on the comprehensiveness of the studied population. Such successful convention work focuses on the same assemblages of mediations already mentioned for traces:

- The "surveys" and "polls" (from individual expressions framed by questions and thus made calculable)
- Assembled and formatted by pollsters
- Guarantee the representativeness of samples (sampling)
- Made for the media
- Made for the purpose of monitoring
- Generate public opinion (and audiences).

The fabrication of "society"

This historical reference to opinion might seem too close to the digitally networked world because of the involvement of the media and brands. Therefore, the world of traces produced on the Web may ultimately be restricted to a permanent extension of the domain of brands and other metrics. Yet, to us it seems that another historic moment for the social sciences would allow us to complicate the panorama and perceive it in the long term. Let us effectively pretend here that Durkheim succeeded in an operation identical to when Gallup and Lazarsfeld invented "public opinion" because he managed to make "society" exist. If the conventional nature of the concept of opinion may still be admitted, it stands that evidence about society does not bear discussion, not only for academia but also for the layman and the experts of markets. This is especially true since the term did not begin with Durkheim, although its history is not so long. Durkheim's early work on the "division of labour in society" (1893) was not based on statistical methods, but instead laid the foundation for a model of social types, aggregated in mechanical and organic solidarity. With *Suicide* (Durkheim, 1897), the method was set up to extend the discussion of the types that would reveal anomia to be a problematic situation. However, reliance on data records produced by states, from their various components (ministries, prefectures, governments), becomes key to the demonstration. It is these aggregates that are explained or explanatory, using a method of comparison between countries, regions, counties or districts where possible and necessary. The method depends entirely on the available data and cannot afford to criticize or question the procedures for the production of these data, despite the countless limitations identified upon publication. By organizing all his systems of proof around these national administrative statistics, Durkheim finds a quantitative analogue for his conceptual choice that puts "society" in a separate status from all manifestations and individual behaviours. Durkheim's *whole* becomes an entity of the second degree, "society" (Latour, 2005), while the censuses and other state-data registers simply conduct the task of recovering individual, administrative events (marital status, judicial procedures, etc.), formatted in identical categories and aggregated to reveal the behaviour of populations. All Durkheim's force of conviction would have been to make these statistics exist as equivalent to his "society".

The statistical apparatus makes society visible in the same way that the survey makes opinion visible; regardless of the statistical validity, the framing that operates here gains power. It is indeed necessary to notice that a form of "objective alliance" was formed between data producers from the state administrations and the emerging social sciences. Together they produced the entity "society" as the object to be tracked by the state for the government and to be explained for scientific reasons. The result is the widely shared and obvious fact that "society" exists and the methods that allow it to do so have no grounds to be questioned because they demonstrate both their scientific and operational value; they are "tools of proof" and "tools of government", as Desrosières (2014) put it. These processes and alliances look absolutely identical to those we encounter between the media and the polling organizations which get on well with one another in order to fabricate opinion and make it seem natural, *taken for granted*, after a long work of implementing conventions.

Technical devices should be considered as parts of the assemblage for these conventions. In 1890, Hollerith used his machine to conduct the American census because the Census Bureau had failed to finish processing the previous 1880 census before starting the next. Hollerith's company would later be transformed into IBM by Watson in 1926 and would spread among all countries' administrations. This specific feature of new devices enrolled in this new quantification era is exactly what is at stake in the digital revolution, as it was at the times of phone lines and mass media for opinion. This socio-technical setting is well known in science and technology studies, and becomes very useful in times of ongoing innovations that generate so much disorientation. The ability of socio-technical designs to assemble a specific set of features, to make them last long after the innovation breakthrough, and to become a "taken-for-granted" part of the "social environment" are what make technologies powerful in maintaining "a sense of the social structure", as Schütz (1962) used to say.

Durkheim's performance would have been to hold an assemblage of very powerful mediations:

- Censuses
- Assembled and formatted by public administrations
- Under guarantee of exhaustiveness
- For states
- With a government in mind
- To produce "society" (based on population)
- Using tabulating calculation machines.

What the social sciences can do with the digital, and what the digital does to the social sciences

Replacing digital transformations in the long history of the social sciences allows us to better understand contemporary movements in the use of traces. Three positions are possible:

- One that aims to take up the course of the social sciences of previous generations and applies their methods and concepts of "society" and "opinion" to trace the Web.
- One that accepts this new world of traces, immersing itself in its demands and principles by abandoning traditions and scientific requirements.
- One that confronts the radical novelty of this socio-technical configuration and attempts to understand what the social sciences' place might be in the production of new conventions to exploit these traces.

The digitalization of opinion and society traditions

The first direction consists of taking up well-known methods and concepts and applying them to traces collected on the Web, or, even more sensibly, exploiting the potential of digital networks to implement exactly the same methods. Thus, surveys via questionnaire and polls are not only computer-aided on platforms equipped for this, but can be conducted entirely on the Internet and sometimes permit the recovery of enough of the respondents' socio-demographic attributes to ensure the sample's representativeness. These online surveys are ideal for making opinion more responsive and tracked on a more frequent basis. Thus, the digital amplifies (Eisenstein, 1983) "the reality of public opinion". Sampling is used in online surveys for market research that makes the rationale of consumers tastes, opinions and judgements appear through their formatted individual expressions. Likewise, input modes for censuses could be equipped with computer terminals to speed up and standardize the collection of data, which makes the now visible "society" even more reliable. However, Web studies, a by-product of the social sciences, implement the same framework on these new media formats: economic studies, preferably from Google queries, studies of sociability, longitudinal monitoring of "communities" around themes or specific sites, "opinion mining" and "sentiment analysis" methods (Boullier and Lohard, 2012) are implemented to increase the monitoring of public opinion or the identification of trends in consumer behaviours. In this approach, digital traces on social networks or blogs are just one more way to get access to these opinions that are not questioned and not dependent on the platforms where they appear.

The end of social theory?

Another orientation is available, a rather radical one when phrased by Chris Anderson. The editor of *Wired* magazine raised concerns with his 2008 short paper entitled "The End of Theory". Extending his provocative statement to social networks analysis, for instance, one can say that Facebook likes do not need theory. The platform picks up traces of the actions and the clicks of Internet users or machines, in a standardized format. It then aggregates them and produces a score that is displayed and can be used by the platform to show trends that guide the placements of advertisers who also seek to achieve certain effects and optimize their investment or communication choices. In a simplified format, this is the string of events that is produced. Social theory has virtually no use in such an operational system, where the performative mechanism works in almost the same way as audience measurement. Some have tried to develop a critique showing that the likes aggregate very different sorts of behaviour, including even purchased likes, but this hardly concerns operators, platforms or advertisers. Their action/reaction works in the performative mode, where the likes unearth a reality that will initiate strategies to influence the likes, in a self-referential cycle to which one could also assign audience ratings. However, in the case of audience ratings, all advertisers and programmers have agreed on stable criteria, producing a shared agreement. Evidence of this has come to forcefully impose itself every morning in the direction of programmes in the mass media. The platforms of social networks and advertisers have not yet reached a stable compromise, which explains the proliferation of services that claim to be standard (such as Klout) and want to become the Nielsen of these measures. However, no theory is necessary for all these institutes if there is high statistical quality (which is seldom the case!), as any theoretical advance in audiences and their processes would require a renegotiation of the agreements, which remains the only validity criterion of any theory. It is easy to see the difference between these principles and the traditions of the social sciences, as G. Bowker does to show their extreme reductionism:

> If I am defined by my clicks and purchases and so forth, I get represented largely as a person with no qualities other than "consumer with tastes". However, creating a system that locks me into my tastes reduces me significantly. Individuals are not stable categories – things and people are not identical with themselves over time [...] The unexamined term the "individual" is what structures the database and significantly excludes temporality.
>
> (Bowker, 2014, p. 1797)

Bowker has cause for concern from the point of view of "society", but the third generation of the social sciences is not so much interested in "society" as in other processes created by other devices, but which, nonetheless, cause us to act. Brands, reputations and recommendations, as exploited by Amazon, can certainly be forcefully re-injected into a "society" matrix to make them say what they are not made for saying, but they also say something of themselves, from another world: that of the power of recommendations and contagions that the social sciences are reluctant to understand. Censuses are no longer the vital statistics that are the reference base for the third generation of the social sciences, but are instead totally agnostic traces about the entities that are "behind" because all act almost equivalently and cause the others to act.

The properties of the third generation of the social sciences

What the third generation of the social sciences could be remains to be observed or even imagined if they:

- assume the radically new character of these heterogeneous traces without falling back on the status of traces as symptoms of something "truly" social ("society" or "opinion"; "market" being a hybrid of both);
- do not get caught up in the self-referential production system/monitoring of traces that dispenses with theory because of other aims.

We adopt a radical empiricism approach (James, 1890) in following the digital traces at their face value, looking for what they are (traces produced by platforms), and how they transform and are transformed by the very milieu they live within, refusing to reduce them to an equivalent of any other phenomenon in society or in opinion. This constraint strongly limits the power of "explanation" of these traces, but complies with other approaches that consider "platforms bias" as a component of the analysis. These high-frequency propagation phenomena cannot separate traces (elements) and platforms (milieux), and must account for the distribution of agency, which is never settled as an *a priori*. Following them allows us to compute these imitation processes, which, as Tarde said, include opposition and invention (Tarde, 2001 [1895]). This approach does not contest the legitimacy of other analyses of the social as long-term social structures, or as opinion movements of mid-range frequency (fashion and elections have almost the same wavelength), and should help more traditional social sciences seriously consider the extension of the social to new entities, these *replications* that could not be captured before the digital era. We would like to avoid two traps at the same time: using digital traces for the documentation of the "social-as-usual" (society or opinion); or reducing them to a set of clever tricks of methods. Our responsibility for the social sciences to be able to play their full role in the digital world dominated by platforms and brands is to build the conventions for a new layer of social sciences maintaining the requirements of scientific reflexivity.

The affinity of big data's quality criteria with the requirements of the social sciences is quite striking. They are often summarized with the 3Vs: volume, variety and velocity.

Volume and exhaustiveness

The volume, in some way, mimics the need for exhaustiveness famous in social sciences. However, this results in a somewhat limited mode, because nobody and nothing can define the boundaries of the universe of data collected. We clearly need to mourn the death of exhaustiveness when using Web traces, but that does not mean dispensing with the laying down of all conventional frameworks for social science's approach when dealing with digital traces.

Variety and representativeness

The second criterion, variety, is also a form of transcription for the representativeness requirements that allow all social sciences to proceed with inquiries and surveys based on sampling. Again, the test is a loose version of representativeness, which assumes that we accept a *sufficient* level of variety. The establishment of a set of sources (sourcing) in studies of the Web should then adhere to some criteria, specific to digital methods and to the field of study. Our work on opinion mining has led us to consider that no description of social society, social opinion or social traces can be produced "in general" on digital networks. The social sciences must agree to deal solely with "issues" (Marres and Weltevrede, 2013), on the focal points of attention, or on "oriented and situated engagements" (Hannerz, 1983), for which traces that are specific to each outcome or each engagement can be kept digitally.

Velocity and traceability

The last criterion, velocity, hardly finds a parallel in the first and second generations of the social sciences. Indeed, these dynamic processes were neither their *forte* nor their concern. It was essential to seek primarily to represent the positions at a given moment *t*, to show the strength of "society" on the diversity of individual behaviour, or to show how public opinion and consumer appraisal are structured beyond singular expressions obtained in surveys. Certainly, through a longitudinal follow-up of the same populations or by reusing the same questionnaire, it is possible to deliver the equivalent of dynamism, but without ever being able to track the mediations that would produce these changes. Velocity seems outside the scope of conventional approaches.

However, a branch of Web science has also seized upon the issue of velocity in its own way by exploiting the *meme* traces that spread on the Web. It is very significant that Kleinberg, the very man who exported scientometric methods to the study of Web topology – methods that were taken up by Google – has been interested in the technical development of a "meme tracker" with Leskovec since 2002 (Leskovec et al., 2009). Their most famous study looked at the propagation of citations throughout Barack Obama's presidential campaign, which allowed them to achieve a spectacular visualization of the focus of attention in rapid mounting and descending curves (*streams and cascades*) around certain incidents during the campaign. Their method aggregated all types of traces that these citations leave, and treated them as strings of characters that can be found throughout the entire Web. This produced a metric anchored in time, day to day and even minute to minute with Twitter. (The unit of measurement has become the tweet-per-second.) Taking memes into consideration seems promising to us, provided that we also track the transformations-translations of these memes (derived from memetics, Dawkins, 1976; Blackmore, 1999) in different environments.

Therefore, it becomes possible to find an equivalent for the velocity of big data: *traceability*. This becomes the essential quality criterion for entities that can be studied.

The third generation of the social sciences will hardly be able to do anything but associate with digital platforms and brands to produce a science of traces which are then treated as *"replications"*, as we propose below. The traces produced are platform-dependent; we can hardly expect to modify them at the source. Nevertheless, it is possible to exploit the traces produced by the platforms by diverting them from the purpose for which they were designed. The rule here is that we do not take any explanation at another level or another world into account, but that we might compare propagation speeds, rhythms and possible transformations (e.g. contamination of other areas, etc.). The difference should be the ability to see the processes that have not yet been identified, either because of the limits of pre-digital technology or because of the targets adopted by previous generations of social sciences. As R. Rogers has pointed to in his pioneering work, this "repurposing" of traces (Rogers, 2013) will suppose a fine-tuning of the "query design", on Google or on any API. For Rogers, this should rely on a well-defined hypothesis and not only follow the opportunity of inference offered by big data and machine-learning technologies. N. Marres seems more concerned by the critics about the overwhelming dependency of scholars on the platforms that deliver the data. The way she handles socio-political controversies as "issues" has proven very inspiring by designing limits of validity for empirical research. (For instance, no general tracing of tweets or weibos[4] or any other traces without delineating the arenas made by "issues".)

From traces to replications[5]

As we have highlighted, the production of traces is directly dependent on platforms that generate their own analyses. While cooperation with these platforms is required in order to reach conventional methods, it is still critical to produce the theoretical framework that would account for this phenomenon of traces. Let us then talk about *"replications"*. It may help social sciences to accept the shift achieved vis-à-vis the notions of actors, strategies and representations. All of these notions have their legitimacy in the context of other social sciences but do not allow for these circulating entities' *power to act* (the *replications'* agency) to be taken into account. We cannot say *a priori* what the size or status of these entities is, because it is only the mass corpus investigations that allow us to identify them when their vibration emerges from the sensors we exploit, certainly from platforms but also according to *our* objectives.

The principle of a sociology of *replications* relies on the need to follow the elements in order to detect waves, without knowing how they will join together to make a "whole" of variable geometry. The vibration approach allows us to build an infinite combinatory, following extensions, propagations and repetitions, provided we remain focused on "issues" that carry *replications*. It is then necessary to focus on the moments of emergence and not on the peaks that function as aggregates. The object of this science of *replications* is surely the agency of *replications* that spread and end up enveloping us. This is because people are actually traversed by ideas, and ideas do not make us act in the inverse, as Tarde (2001 [1895]) clearly indicated. "The imitation rays first and then the beings, whose existence we infer from the transformation they undergo with the flow of imitation" (Latour, 2011). It is then possible to study the properties of these *replications*, to potentially compare their chances of survival or contamination. This is made possible by differences in their properties, which are always directly related to the "issues" that they carry with them.

We started this work in 1987 with the monitoring of TV conversations and their transposition onto workplaces to make "local public opinion". In two different research projects, we proceeded to monitor the attributes of a photo from the Flickr database in the same way and to track the propagation of cultural signs (songs, flags, landscapes, etc.) in a corpus of websites linked to a region. In the first case, the attributes of the photo (e.g. crossed arms) became tag attractors and thus connected accounts or photos that would have no chance to get connected according to the traditional criteria of social explanatory variables. Tags or icons are *replications* that can be followed, even if they have neither the explicit character verbatim or expressions as in the meme tracker, nor their massiveness.

Potentially, all the traces that we have identified (such as likes, tweets, recommendations, etc.) may be the object of monitoring; however, they require specific tracking tools that exist largely for Twitter only. A detailed review of these tools should be done to ensure that they meet the specifications of a traceability of replications (not just traces for the sake of it or for the reactivity of brands).

Certain approaches from these digitized corpora (not native to the digital) can give an idea of the potential of such methods. Work done on the *n*-grams studied from Google Books (Michel et al., 2011) showed the evolution of the English language (the preterite of irregular verbs). Lev Manovich (2012) created a base of over 1 million examples of manga to compare their most basic attributes, such as the contrast, and produced a unique insight into influences between trends. He used similar tools to conduct cultural comparisons between countries from millions of photos on Instagram or from the Maidan Square in Kiev. The story of "JeSuisCharlie" as a hashtag and logo all over the social networks and media should be considered as a demonstration of the agency of an entity that is not related to a strategy, an intention, and not accounted for by simple society causations. By focusing on the entities that propagate, we change the distribution of agency and pretend to account for the specific role played by the very features of these messages in the waving of the network.

Some propagation patterns can be detected along with the social features of the nodes (e.g. popular Twitter accounts do not retweet but are retweeted), but the program to detect the agency of semiotic features of the messages (e.g. the tweet or the hashtag) still has to be built. This would give the opportunity of extending the agency apart from structures (the "society") and individuals ("opinion" extracted from the mind of individuals) to actants, such as messages that frame some issues. This is why a theory of *replications* (or vibrations) follows some principles of actor-network theory (ANT) (Callon and Latour, 1981). This is done by exploring this distribution of agency, thanks to the traceability of these elementary parts that produce the network and perform it, and not just follow social paths already well known by social scientists. The roles played by the founding fathers of ANT (Callon, Latour and Law) can be considered as twofold. The first is quasi-technical through scientometrics, because by describing how scientific facts are produced in this web of citations they paved the way for the topological principles of the Web, as previously mentioned, and also for the whole set of methods of traceability. The second role is of a more philosophical kind, because by "following the actants", they give the opportunity to repopulate the description of how social worlds are produced and maintained (including non-humans and messages, as well as clicks, likes and so on), and how to escape from the strategist view of the network. When computer scientists and market researchers enter the field of social networks, they immediately look for the "influential" (Rogers, 1983 [1963]) and treat these nodes as strategist actors. This is an extended version of decision-making theories (including rational choice theories and game theory), but it misses the point when trying to account for virality and propagation patterns. The network is always "enacted" and reconfigured along with each issue and with opportunities. This is why ANT always remains on the side of emergence theories, in order to account for what is not a mere effect of structure or of rational choices. Tracing the network is only possible by following the actants, be they artefacts or messages, provided that the observer adopts the right techniques to account for their specific agency.

The consequences of the way market research handles these traces can be listed as follows:

- The process under scrutiny or the central issues are not the same: from segmentation of the market (MR1G, marketing research first generation) or from trends (MR2G), we move to reputation, that is the way brands use digital traces, or to replications (MR3G) from the market research point of view.

- The entities that are populating this world and being computed are no longer socio-demographical categories nor market segments (MR1G), nor socio-styles, word of mouth, opinion leaders, the influential, consumer journeys, as in the MR2G approach. MR3G focuses on brands and communities when framed by companies and brands, or on viral content features when framed by social sciences. This is an important move, because the agency is not distributed to the same kind of entities. It means that segments or the influential no longer make sense from this point of view. Another set of entities emerge as candidates that had fallen into oblivion before the digital networks shed light on them. This is something content designers are eager to buy, even though they will get back to the omnipotent view of this viral approach, something Jenkins et al. (2013) criticized in favour of their "spreadability", with some reason.
- The data collection devices are transformed from the CRM, where all targets can be assembled and traced (MR1G), and from polls and focus groups (MR2G), to social listening platforms and community management processes for the brands, and to some kind of meme tracker for the social sciences (MR3G).
- The methods are intrinsically different from "targeting", borrowing on ballistics (MR1G) and from the influence processes (MR2G), because we focus on propagation patterns for brands as well as for social sciences (MR3G).
- The wavelengths that are investigated are different and do not compete with each other: the long waves of structural social features (MR1G), the mid-length cycles of market trends (MR2G), and the high-frequency waves of memes propagation (MR3G), typical of an emergence approach.

Any market research strategy should be aware of the strategy it adopts among these three generations and should not believe that one choice accounts for all the richness of social life, nor that strategies should be easily combined. We still need to build the conventions to make replications analysis as reliable as censuses and opinion polls. Table 2.1 summarizes these features more clearly.

Conclusion

A table summarizing the three ages of the social sciences allows the consistency of this approach to be made visible, and yet at the same time demands simplification and the elimination of the specificities of each age (see Table 2.2). Remember, however, that we are not dealing with the so-called "qualitative" aspects of the methods of social sciences.

Table 2.1 Market research generations

	First generation	Second generation	Third generation (from brands)	Third generation (from social sciences)
Issues	Segmentation	Trends	Reputation	Replications
Entities	Socio-demographic categories + market segments (e.g. dual income, no kids – DINK)	Socio-styles + word of mouth + opinion leaders + the influential + consumer journey	Brands + communities	Memes + viral content features
Collection devices	CRM	Polls + focus groups	Social listening + community management	Meme tracker
Methods	Targeting (ballistics)	Influence	Propagation	Propagation
Wavelengths	Long waves (structure)	Cycles (market)	High-frequency waves (emergence)	High-frequency waves (emergence)

Table 2.2 The three generations of the social sciences

	First generation	Second generation	Third generation
Concept of the social	Society/ies	Opinion(s)	Replication(s)
Collection devices	Censuses	Surveys, polls	Platforms, big data
Validation principle	Exhaustiveness	Representativeness	Traceability
Co-construction institutions/research	Registers, inquiries	Audience, polls	Traces, repurposed digital methods
Major players of reference (and financiers)	States	Mass media	Brands
Operational actors	National institutes	Polling organizations	Web platforms (GAFA)
Founding authors	Durkheim	Gallup, Lazarsfeld	Callon, Latour, Law
Key problems of scientific approaches	Division of labour and the welfare state (population metrics)	Propaganda and media influence (audience metrics)	Science and technology (scientometrics)
Technical conditions	Hollerith's machine (tabulating calculation)	Radio, telephone	Internet, the Web, big data
Semiotic formats	Crosstabs, topographic maps	Curve and bar graphs, pie charts	Graphs, timelines, dashboards
Metrics	Statistics (classic)	Sampling	Machine learning
Technical criteria for data quality	Relevance, accuracy, timeliness, accessibility, comparability, coherence	Confidence intervals, probabilities	Volume, variety, and velocity (big data)
The social sciences' dominant modalities	Explanations	Descriptive and predictive correlations	Predictive correlations

Brands may benefit from learning to react to using these metrics based on traces. Social sciences of "society" and "opinion" may also benefit in further developing their approaches by using these sources. In this sense, we plead to make these approaches coexist, to learn to change points of view, and to admit the conditions of possibility for each generation, relying on the states, media and brands. Each specific study of an issue arising from everyday experience or raised by prescribers, such as brands, must lead to a combination of the three generations. This is provided that research has a specific framework for these traces that invade our world. There is a new "raw" material that deserves a review of its own, and produces a third layer to the social measurable according to other principles, and not reducible to "society" or to "opinion". "Society" ended up existing, "opinion" ended up existing, and *"replications"* must eventually end up existing in the same way. The time may have come for the "buzz" to be translated in scientific terms and to gain some recognition of its own agency.

Notes

1 Cardon (2013) has proposed a typology consisting of links, clicks, likes and traces.
2 The works of Loïc Blondiaux (1998) and Jean Converse (1987) develop this story extensively.
3 Even though Kaier tested them in 1891 and Bowley established the principles of the probable error in 1912.
4 The Chinese equivalent of Twitter.
5 The original term used was "répliques", which could also be translated as "aftershocks" or "tremors".

References

Blackmore, S. (1999) *The Meme Machine*. Oxford: Oxford University Press.
Blondiaux, L. (1998) *La fabrique de l'opinion. Une histoire sociale des sondages*. Paris: Le Seuil.
Boullier, D. (2013) "Plates-formes de réseaux sociaux et répertoires d'action collective", in Najar, S. (ed.) *Les réseaux sociaux sur internet à l'heure des transitions démocratiques*. Paris: Editions Karthala.
Boullier, D. (2016) *Sociologie du numérique*. Paris: Armand Colin.
Boullier, D. and Lohard, A. (2012) *Opinion mining et sentiment analysis. Méthodes et outils*. Paris: Open Editions Press.
Bowker, G. (2014) "The Theory/Data Thing. Commentary", *International Journal of Communication*, 8: 1795–1799.
boyd, d. and Crawford, K. (2011) "Six Provocations for Big Data", paper presented at the Oxford Internet Institute's A Decade in Internet Time: Symposium On the Dynamics of the Internet and Society. Oxford: University of Oxford.
Bruno, I. and Didier, E. (2013) *Benchmarking. L'État sous pression statistique*. Paris: La Découverte, Coll. Zones.
Callon, M. and Latour, B. (1981) "Unscrewing the Big Leviathan: How Actors Macrostructure Reality and How Sociologists Help them to Do So", in Knorr, K. and

Cicourel, A.V. (eds) *Advances in Social Theory and Methodology: Toward an Integration of Micro and Macro Sociologies.* London: Routledge and Kegan Paul.

Cardon, D. (2013) "Du lien au like sur internet. Deux mesures de la reputation", *Communications*, 93, La réputation, 173–186.

Cochoy, F. (1999) *Une histoire du marketing. Discipliner l'économie de marché.* Paris: La Découverte.

Callon, M., Law, J. and Rip, A. (1986) "Qualitative Scientometrics", in Callon, M., Law, J. and Rip, A. (eds) *Mapping the Dynamics of Science and Technology.* London: Macmillan, pp. 103–123.

Converse, J. (1987) *Survey Research in the United States. Roots and Emergence 1890–1960.* Berkeley: University of California Press.

Dawkins, R. (1976) *The Selfish Gene.* Oxford: Oxford University Press.

Desrosières, A. (1998) *The Politics of Large Numbers: A History of Statistical Reasoning.* Cambridge, MA: Harvard University Press.

Desrosières, A. (2014) *Prouver et gouverner: une analyse politique des statistiques publiques*, ed. E. Didier. Paris: La Découverte.

Driscoll, K. and Walker, S. (2014) "Working within a Black Box: Transparency in the Collection and Production of Big Twitter Data", *International Journal of Communication*, 8: 1745–1764.

Durkheim, E. (1897) *Le suicide.* Paris: Alcan.

Eisenstein, E. (1983) *The Printing Revolution in Early Modern Europe.* Cambridge: Cambridge University Press.

Hannerz, U. (1983) *Exploring the City.* New York: Columbia University Press.

James, W. (1890) *The Principles of Psychology*, two vols. New York: Dover Publications.

Jenkins, H., Ford, S. and Green, J. (2013) *Spreadable Media. Creating Value and Meaning in a Networked Culture.* New York and London: New York University Press.

Kleinberg, J. (2002) "Bursty and Hierarchical Structure in Streams", Proc. 8th ACM SIGKDD Intl. Conf. on Knowledge Discovery and Data Mining.

Kleinberg, J., Gibson, D. and Raghavan, P. (1998) "Inferring Web Communities from Link Topology", in Proc. of the 9th ACM Conference on Hypertext and Hypermedia (HYPER-98), pp. 225–234, New York, June 20–24.

Latour, B. (2005) *Reassembling the Social – An Introduction to Actor-Network-Theory.* Oxford: Oxford University Press.

Latour, B. (2011) "Gabriel Tarde. La société comme possession. La preuve par l'orchestre", in Debaise, D., *Philosophie des possessions.* Paris: Les Presses du Réel.

Latour, B., Jensen, B., Venturini, T., Grauwin, S. and Boullier, D. (2012) "'The Whole is Always Smaller than its Parts': A Digital Test of Gabriel Tarde's Monads", *British Journal of Sociology*, 63(4): 590–615.

Leskovec, J., Backstrom, L. and Kleinberg, J. (2009) "Meme-Tracking and the Dynamics of the News Cycle", ACM SIGKDD International Conference on Knowledge Discovery and Data Mining (KDD).

Manovich, L. (2012) "How to Compare One Million Images?" in Berry, D. (ed.) *Understanding Digital Humanities.* New York: Palgrave Macmillan.

Marres, N. and Weltevrede, E. (2013) "Scraping the Social? Issues in Live Social Research", *Journal of Cultural Economy*, 6(3): 313–335.

Michel, J.B. et al. (2011) "Quantitative Analysis of Culture Using Millions of Digitized Books", *Science*, 331(6014): 176–182.

Rogers, E.M. (1983 [1963]). *Diffusion of Innovations.* New York: Free Press.

Rogers, R. (2013) *Digital Methods.* Cambridge, MA: MIT Press.

Schütz, A. (1962) *The Phenomenology of the Social World.* Evanston, IL: Northwestern University Press.

Tarde, G. (1989 [1901]). *L'opinion et la foule.* Paris: Puf.

Tarde, G. (2001 [1895]). *Les lois de l'imitation.* Paris: Les Empêcheurs de Penser en Rond.

3 Towards a rhythm-sensitive data economy

Mika Pantzar and Minna Lammi [1]

The novel digital tools, smart algorithms, and technical platforms of our contemporary era are introducing innovative ways of integrating various aspects of everyday life as, thanks to the Internet and billions of digital sensors, seemingly different activities are being brought together through and with data flows (e.g. Swan, 2015). With new data sources and algorithms, service operators are developing fresh, vital assemblies and descriptions of daily consumption practices, generating new "practice complexes" (Shove et al., 2012) in business contexts – better known as "platform economies" (Kenney and Zysman, 2015) – wherein data provide the driving force. Uber, Airbnb and AmazonFresh all provide highly successful examples of outcomes of this process. Yet, at the same time and as a result of the same factors, old and established businesses operating according to the conventions of even the quite recent past are experiencing disruption and loss of relevance.

This chapter examines the pulses generated by the emerging network-like entities that are the products of this nexus of developments, focusing in particular on commercially produced everyday products whose digitalization is changing the relative negotiating positions of consumer and producer. From this point of view, the perspective of rhythm analysis, the retail trade, banking and insurance services, and the entire entertainment and information industry provide the most interesting cases for examination. The data consist of original figures used in the company context in Finland, and therefore many of the figures in the article are in Finnish and some of the scales are manipulated for the sake of business secrecy.[2] More precise analysis of the broader questions raised by current technological change – how activities either erode or strengthen each other to form entire autocatalytic "circuits of reproduction," for example (Pantzar and Shove, 2010a) – requires new types of research tools (see Boullier, this volume) and perhaps, in the future, the birth of a whole "organization theory of time use." We shall take on a more modest task: to analyze and specify research questions by drawing parallels between the rich digital data and rhythm-theoretical approaches briefly described below.

The first bars of rhythm analysis were played more than 100 years ago, when researchers became interested in the quickening pace of life entailed by the new urban culture and the rational organization of factories (Taylorism), supported by the development of collective transportation systems and modernist architecture (Le Corbusier, 1929/1987; Meyer, 2008). More or less concurrently, the futuristic movement in the arts reflected an optimistic image of emotionally charged, intense rhythmic interaction between machines and humans, although Charlie Chaplin's film, *Modern Times* (1936), presented the critical side of this discussion. At about the same time as the latter, Lewis Mumford (1934), scholar of urban studies and philosopher of technology, Pitirim Sorokin (1937), sociologist of long cycles, and Robert Merton (Sorokin and Merton, 1937), sociologist of science, made their own contributions to the field by researching the tension between time measured on a human biological scale and clock time.

In the digital world, understanding changing periodicities and new rhythmic patterns becomes a crucial challenge for both academic and business-oriented research. Rhythm analysis questions the perception, typical of time use research, of linear, successive, separate periods of consumption (e.g. grocery shopping, cooking and eating). On the one hand, it emphasizes that human actions and practices are part of historically shaped network structures (e.g. snacking while watching TV or speaking on the phone while driving) or "practice complexes" (Pantzar and Shove, 2010a), while on the other, it brings into focus even tiny sequences that orient our daily practices, the so-called "performative fragments" (picking up, swallowing, digesting food, etc.) (Thrift, 2008). The repetition and periodicity of physiological states signal the life of complex, organic networks (Foster and Kreitzman, 2004; Koukkari and Sothern, 2006). In a similar vein, the rhythms of daily life could be seen as products of the combined effect of sequences of daily practices and localized synchronies. The order, orderliness, regularity, and repetitiveness of daily life are usually created as we spontaneously react to each other's behavior.

Some of our daily practices are connected with the annual or daily cycle of nature, some with biological needs, and some with economic cycles. Permanent deviations in biological rhythms usually signify a pathological condition (Kreitzman, 1999; Foster and Kreitzman, 2004; Koukkari and Sothern, 2006); when subjected to a continued state of stress, for example, the human heart no longer reacts positively to rest, which, in the long run, may lead to health failure or death. This insight offers an analogy that could perhaps also be applied to entire societies and their networks of practices. Both global natural resource crises and lifestyle diseases may indicate the kind of imbalanced development in which cycles of reproduction do not function properly.

Changing or coordinating biological, cultural, and social rhythms is often a violent yet slow process. Business analysts use the concept of "entrainment" to describe the problem of coordinating the internal rhythms of organizations (e.g. Ancona and Chong, 1996), and discovering or creating a common rhythm between the operative units or employers of a business is a challenging task. Nonetheless, what is today experienced as noise and disturbance may tomorrow be part of our normal experience, as Jacques Attali proposes in his book *Noise: The Political Economy of Music* (1985). Similar commentaries in the context of rhythm analysis have been made more recently by a number of researchers from very different backgrounds including history Professor William McNeill in his book *Keeping Together in Time* (1995), media artist Paul Miller (DJ Spooky) in his book *Rhythm Science* (2004), and Henri Lefebvre, posthumously, in his book *Rhythm Analysis* (1992/2004). For all four analysts, music was a source of inspiration, and they all concretize their somewhat obscure and abstract ideas by describing daily life as a music-like performance.[3]

Small practices in daily life, such as coming home, removing your coat, and opening the fridge, can be seen as an integrated whole, like a symphony orchestra. Each of us has many instruments in simultaneous use. Here the rhythm describes both the routine repetition of the daily practices and the unique tempos of their progression; these seek their own form, sometimes beating faster and more repetitively. Apart from rhythm, melody and harmony are also useful concepts from the perspective of rhythm analysis (cf. Southerton, 2006). The melody of daily life involves a series of successive consumption practices and can be identified both at the level of individuals and groups, where harmony (or lack of it) invokes the compatibility (or incompatibility) of simultaneous practices. Harmony is also a successive process: previous harmonious solutions determine (or socially construct) how the listener hears and feels about the solutions that follow.[4] This line of thinking emphasizes microscopic synchronies between the rhythms. It is the macroscopic viewpoint, however, which is emphasized in most existing rhythm analysis, and in the empirical examples discussed below.

Regularities in daily life, such as the flows of people in cities, are a consequence of millions of individual and collective time fragments, moments and episodes. At the same time, they are also expressions of collectively intertwined individual routines that relate to our attempts to coordinate the way in which we behave towards each other. As Henri Lefebvre (1992/2004, p. 75) remarks, "[i]n one day in the modern world, everybody does more or less the same things at more or less the same times, but each person is really alone in doing it."

It is obvious that shared sleeping rhythms make it easier to live in society, but would moving around be easier if people did not hit the streets en masse between eight and nine o'clock in the morning? Some of our daily practices are characterized by the very fact that they compete with each other. Meeting friends is one example of a co-production, while driving to work in private cars is an example of competing consumption. A rhythm analyst asks about the way that individual decisions and practices add to aggregate behavior such as national rhythms.

One could say that while daily routines serve as the raw material for collective practices, they also provide fuel for the service economy. As will be seen, Saturday evenings in Finland have become a kind of joint production event of spending "time together," which does not coordinate well with, for example, private chatting online or Internet bank visits. Along the same lines

Helene Brembeck (2012) has shown that in Sweden Friday is the evening when family members get together, thereby serving as an example of how in a certain space and at a certain time different practices support each other. Some activities can in turn be seen as eating away at other activities: bringing wage work home, for example, erodes the resources available for other daily activities.

Today's notion of differentiating between work time and free time, widely adopted in the Western world, is anything but a law of nature, or an evident or inevitable result of development (Thompson, 1967). Likewise, the temporal conventions of service businesses have been developed and passed down over a long period of time and should also not be regarded as foreordained. One might well ask why, for example, banks' valuation day practice follows principles dating from a time when money was transported from one region to another in sacks and on horseback. The digitalization of businesses and the changing power positions of consumers and producers may break this order of time conventions in which regulation, such as taxation and working-hour laws, has played a decisive role. As digital footprints increase and new kinds of market rhythms-based diagnostics gain ground, will we return to the time-optimizing, planned romantic vision presented by Le Corbusier? Or will a better understanding of time use reveal that our present life rhythms have only barely managed to adjust to a market economy (Foster and Kreitzman, 2004; Koukkari and Sothern, 2006)?

The combined effects of physiological, cultural, and economic rhythms have only rarely been studied simultaneously; rather, the practice has been to approach natural and cultural phenomena from the perspective of isolated sciences and isolated phenomena.[5] What is essential, however, is to emphasize that rhythms originate in, and are emergent properties of, networks. The entire pulse of a society develops as a result of interactions between the biological rhythms of individuals, and social and economic rhythms. Rhythms are embodied in our muscles and embedded in social and technical systems and are enacted more or less purposefully by various interdependent agents.

Academic consumer research has thus far reacted slowly to the data explosion of recent decades, meaning that media businesses, for example, have been compelled to recruit researchers from fields such as computational physics. Neither a business education nor knowledge of traditional market research provides sufficient preparation for studying the multidimensional and unstructured big data collected by large enterprises. Compared to data-mining expertise in various scientific fields – geo-informatics, bio-informatics and neuro-informatics, among others – consumer informatics based on large data sets consisting of both qualitative and quantitative data is in its embryonic form (see Cochoy and Smolinski, this volume). Today global consumer diagnostics based on versatile and unstructured data are being developed most actively in the offices of the giant data operators such as Amazon, Google, and Facebook. Combining numerical, textual, and visual data, for instance, requires totally novel methods and greater collective division of labor. Instead of focusing on research methods, however, this chapter aims to refresh rhythm-analytical views that were already being developed at the beginning of the 20th century, when Gabriel Tarde foresaw that mathematical sociology would one day move towards registering the pulsation of values in society via the so-called "Valuemeter" (see Latour and Lepinay, 2009).

A data economy, the move from the collection of big data to its use (World Economic Forum, 2014), seems to be among the hottest promiseware[6] being offered by international bodies such as the Organisation for Economic Co-operation and Development (OECD) and the United Nations (unglobalpulse.org), together with giant consulting agencies (e.g. Cap Gemini, Boston Consulting Group, O'Reilly Media), as a critical step towards digital wealth creation, a movement that the academic audience has recognized only recently (e.g. Swan, 2013; Andrejevic, 2014; Nafus, 2014). In the future it will become possible to contrast business data with physiological data, though it remains to be seen what will happen when, for instance, stress measurement or face recognition data are synchronized with time use and consumption data.

When rhythms and time use are chosen as the business perspective, three different forms of business content can be discerned: the first, "business based on consumers' time filling," is largely made up of leisure time services; the second contextual dimension can be found in "business based on consumers' time saving," which covers such utilities as home delivery, home services, and services performed by household appliances; the third, least recognized form of time-based (rhythm-sensitive) business, which is growing strongly due to digitalization, is "rhythm-based business." In the first two cases, business directed at time filling and time saving, firms largely base their operations on one-off services that are often defined by a strongly production-led view (see the discussion of insurance below). The point of departure for rhythm-based business is different, comprising as it does the repeated and possibly regular routines of consumers, and the openings between them where commercial services can find a specific niche.

In the past consumers have had to learn the rhythms of production. According to one optimistic view, however, in the future business companies will learn the rhythms of everyday life and adapt better to customers' daily routines. Inevitably, this will lead to traditional industrial patterns and offers being disrupted (e.g. World Economic Forum, 2014).

Rhythm-based and rhythm-sensitive business: empirical observations from Finland

Daily, weekly, and annual rhythms pertain to a very broad range of economic phenomena. Of the social sciences thus far, economics has made the most headway in empirical research of rhythmic movements, although it has mostly concentrated on those of five-year business cycles and, to a lesser degree, 50-year cycles. Indirect measurements such as gross domestic product (GDP) or exchange rates are the most commonly used pulse meters with regards to the economy. Underlying the emerging rhythms are price mechanisms that regulate the balance between demand and supply: when the supply is rigid, the demand fluctuates cyclically; when prices go down, demand increases, which in turn raises prices and decreases demand until prices start to fall again.

What is characteristic of economic rhythms is that variation in one sector of commerce usually correlates with variation in another. For example, free newspapers are usually distributed on Wednesdays because the rhythms of Friday and Saturday shop discounts require it. Similarly, textile shops start to prepare for Christmas early in the autumn, when they negotiate their orders, although fashion colors have been decided over a year earlier based on votes by various international color trend panels (e.g. Intercolor). Coordinated global activity directed at standardizing colors began as early as the 1950s, when producers wanted to ensure a sufficient amount of raw color materials for each season, and probably offers the clearest example of globally coordinated rhythms. Coordinated finance policies between states could be another example of centralized influencing of rhythms. It is, however, more common that the rhythms of consumption are born and establish themselves in the dispersed and complex interaction of numerous microscopic decisions.

Retail trade operators, for instance, regard rhythms at the level of both days of the week and months. In Finland, the highest sales volume per hour is achieved in the retail trade every year on December Fridays at 5:00 pm. Monday mornings in January are the quietest. The weekly rhythm is different in summer and winter; Saturday sales are much higher in winter than in summer. So far, for reasons of convenience and (menu) costs, prices have not reacted to rush hours, but with digital price tags we will see more active pricing favoring customers in quieter times.

Television watching is another good example of a rhythm-sensitive practice. Paradoxically, watching television, the fastest growing and dominant form of time use, has also become the chief locus of flexibility in individuals' daily schedules. It is not so much a question of television having appropriated time from other activities, but rather that it has effectively and flexibly found its own moments in people's freely determined time use. Western time use research has singularly revealed that the most remarkable change in the past four decades has clearly been the time consumers spend watching television. Currently, television takes up about one-third of people's six hours of daily free time in all Western countries. However, the time people spend watching TV varies considerably at the individual level. People watch TV to fill vacant time, but it is something they are also ready to skimp on when necessary (Robinson and Godbey, 1997). Meanwhile, watching TV has become the most significant form of time use that allows other simultaneous activities (Rideout et al., 2010; Sayer et al., 2004). Could these aspects of flexibility explain the rapid onslaught of television and its seemingly dominant place in people's daily lives? What will happen as the increasing amount of TV watching moves to services like Netflix which adapt flexibly to individual needs and time-use patterns?

The perspective of rhythm-based business emphasizes that even the popularity of prime-time programs may have more to do with the ability of media products to find their place in the routine melody of daily life than with attractiveness of content. The same applies to tabloid newspapers, whose role of providing a well-deserved "cigarette break" may be more important than their qualitative content. Watching TV late at night can also be seen as a rite of passage from being awake to going to bed; the program itself does not make much difference. Similarly, reading the morning paper may have to do with the ritual of waking up. The popularity of sending text messages or using social media could also be associated with the same phenomenon. Their serving size, place, and time can be adjusted to the requirements of daily life.

The inertia of many of today's markets can be seen in how commercial services are often offered at the wrong times (leading to long waiting and queuing times), in the wrong places (with consumers handling distribution), or in inappropriate (either too large or too small) portions. Meanwhile, the scarcity of services that enable the saving or optimizing of time can be seen as one expression of the ineffectiveness of markets like the construction industry. Indeed, examples of undervaluing the time and effort of customers can be found in all fields of business and the challenges vary to a large degree. The public economy, exemplified by institutions as varied as hospitals and legal trials, is probably the sector least sensitive to customers' time-specific needs. The (Finnish) school system (or homes for the elderly) is still characterized by a producer-led approach in which the customers' life rhythms are forced to adjust to the rhythms of a system that assumed its form in the 19th century. Even though elsewhere in society both bed and waking times have become later, along with more flexible working hours, this trend has not influenced the inflexible "working hours" of children. One result of this is sleep deprivation among young adults.

Perhaps the most obvious reason for the new synchronicity of practices lies in digitalization and mobile technology. The uses to which smartphones are put, for example, offer interesting possibilities for studying the rhythms of everyday life, although even in this field daily rhythms are only slowly being affected. In the 2010s, 20 years after mobile phones entered into widespread use in Finland, the fewest phone calls are still made on Sundays, but they are longer compared to the other days of the week. The busiest day for phone activity is still Monday, and winter Sundays are notably more active than summer Sundays (Elisa Communication, personal communication). The locations for phone conversations have changed, however; cars, particularly during the journey home from work, have become important hubs of communication. According to Zokem Mobile Media Insights (personal communication, 2010), phone calls and text messages reach their peak around the end of working hours.

People are also listening to music much more often on the move while the evenings are the peak time for using the camera (sharing images), and the calendar (scheduling) is naturally used more frequently in daytime. Thus smartphones are clearly used differently on weekends than on weekdays, when the peak is reached at the end of the work day and, to a lesser extent, also on the way to work. At weekends peak use is concentrated around noon and the early evening. Some daily activities are clearly more bound to a fixed "time space" (the wake-up alarm at home in the morning), while others are more strongly bound to other activities (surfing the Internet before or after lunch).

Along with the growing popularity of smartphones and mobile reading devices, the extent to which the use of the Internet is bound to the workplace will decrease. The increase in the supply and popularity of online newspapers has changed the way people read about current affairs and at present a growing number access them at the workplace, either soon after they arrive or right after the lunch hour. According to web monitoring data from the Sanoma Media group (autumn 2010), however, people read the online version of the *Helsingin Sanomat* newspaper differently depending on whether it is read from a fixed terminal or with a mobile device. On mobile devices the news is read earlier in the day than on fixed terminals, presumably while on the way to work. There are three peaks in the day, 8:30 am, 4:00 pm and 9:00 pm, and the services are most used on Tuesdays. In the future, in addition to weather forecasts, social media platforms may forecast shifts in the nation's interests as they change as the work week proceeds. For instance, prime time for the weekly entertainment section of the online version of the *Iltasanomat* tabloid newspaper is around 3:00 pm on Mondays. Readers are the most interested in the weather late in the morning on Tuesdays (IS.weather). Access to the mobile version of the *Taloussanomat* financial newspaper also reaches its peak on Tuesdays (8:30 am and 5:00 pm), but interest in economic matters decreases towards the end of the week. On Thursdays, right before the work day ends, minds wander in turn towards planning the weekend menu (highest visitor counts on the IS.ruokala food pages).

In printed media news needs to be updated only once a day, while news watched from a fixed Internet terminal needs to be updated once an hour, and mobile reading devices are assumed to require even more frequent updating. One could say in summary that mobile reading devices produce numerous peaks in time use, while reading tends to be concentrated during working hours on stationary devices. With the rise in use of mobile devices, old reading rhythms may make a comeback, and the workplace be freed once again for work as reading is fragmented into smaller and smaller episodes. Along with new data and better diagnostics, rhythm analysis will in the future delve into such questions as, for example, how individual practices like reading, eating or watching television, and the interactions between them, are reflected both in individual life paths and in the pulse of entire nations. Time geography may become one of the most scientifically innovative fields through its examination of time use on the scale of entire nations and regions.[7]

Another interesting example of rhythm-sensitive business is banking, which has undergone a radical change with the Internet and digital devices: where in the past people used to go to the bank a few times a month, a large number of people now visit online banks daily, at least in order to check their balance. Most Finns take care of their personal banking business at home, in the evening: around 8:00 pm on weekdays is the slot established by online banking in families with young children, and around 6:00 pm among older people. On Saturdays people do their online banking in the late mornings, if at all, and Saturday evenings commence an almost "bank-free time" lasting through until people clearly become active again on Sunday evenings (see Figure 3.1).

It is worth noting that in the not-so-distant past Finnish employers issued national guidelines about accepting online personal banking during working hours (1990s), which may have furthered the rationalization of banking activities. One could ask whether this has also contributed to Facebook updating or online gambling becoming more commonplace on weekdays than on weekends, during free time. The high activity during working hours could perhaps be understood through the concept of simultaneous activity; that is, "bank visits" or Facebook sessions find a natural space in the rhythms of waged work.

In bank visits regular patterns characterizing different weekdays seem to be quite fixed. The radical change in the banking business over the past decade is an effective example of how technological change also implicates cultural change. The growth in the "market share" of the time space of consumers might be explained with the observation that, along with the Internet, the personal banking business has started to accommodate its rhythm to other daily activities better than, for example, insurance companies and grocery shops, which are only beginning to offer online services. The number of "visits to the bank" has grown radically, while the separate moments of transaction have become shorter; meanwhile, probably more and more people think about their own finances and bank accounts more frequently.

What at the outset may appear as an irregularity often signifies the beginning of a new regularity, something clearly illustrated by the swift and widespread incorporation of the Internet into everyday use, and the new kinds of time-space dependencies thus produced. As mentioned above, Saturday evenings in Finland, for example, tend to be reserved for socializing with friends or providing family time for those with children, and there is little space for Internet sessions in those scenarios. Indeed, the "special" character of Finnish Saturday evenings becomes obvious in many Internet-based activities: for instance, there are far fewer visits to online travel agencies (Fritidsresor, personal correspondence) and gambling sites (Veikkaus, personal correspondence) on Saturday evenings than there are on Sundays. It is interesting to note, in passing, that these insights suggest that despite the potential the Internet offers for anytime/anywhere use, engagements with it seem to be slotted into already established weekly and diurnal rhythms.

Thus, while one would expect that rhythms concerned with relatively new activities and practices such as Internet chatting or online auctions would be

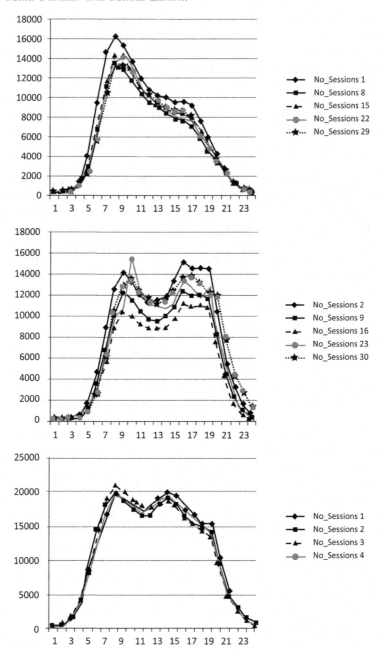

Figure 3.1 Daily profiles of Internet bank transactions in 2011 over a period of five
weeks on Saturdays (top), Sundays (middle) and Thursdays (bottom)
(Nordea)

fluid and unfixed, the evidence contradicts this assumption. Figure 3.2 depicts the weekly rhythm of participation in a major chat line in Finland. In this data set the quietest, the least "peaky" day, was Saturday 13 June 2009, with Saturday evening being exceptionally quiet. The activity is clearly lower during the day (and at night). Young people chatted online most actively around 7:00 pm and the most active day for them was Monday. A similar regularity in the lives of families with young children can be seen in online auctions, where people buy and sell a lot of products for children on Sunday evenings in particular (Figure 3.3).

Regular patterns seem to be the rule in Internet-based service businesses. Statistics on both firms and households speak of the repetition and regularity of consumption practices, at least at the level of the majority, and many firms, aside from media companies, are already engaged in rhythm-based business,

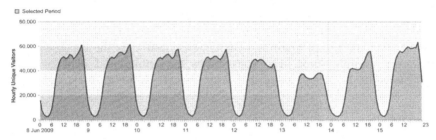

Figure 3.2 Hourly visitors on a major chat line in Finland from Monday 08.06.2009 to Sunday 15.06.2009
(Microsoft 2009, Helsinki, unpublished)

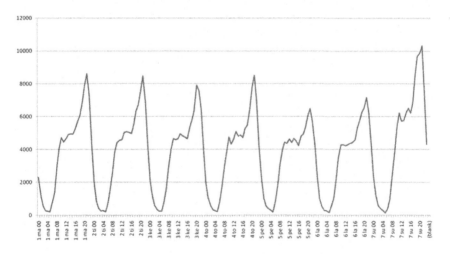

Figure 3.3 Weekly rhythm of an online auction: Friday, Saturday and Sunday peak (40% of sales connected with products for children)
(Huuto.net, scale distorted)

optimizing various sub-processes of customer relationships management. For example, tele-operators or electricity and energy companies develop their enterprise resource planning systems expressly to accommodate the rhythms of consumers. For tele-operators this means sizing and optimizing services (bandwidth, centers) while electricity and energy companies are adjusting to integrated energy markets with predictive and real-time pricing. Monitors constantly display real-time data on energy production, weather changes, and market prices, but also forecast data on changes in demand.

Service businesses manage customer flows in very different ways and are in very different situations with regards to developing online services; phones, however, still play a key role in the service network. An insurance company call center that is open on weekdays, for example, begins at 9:00 am and ends around 4:00 pm, and daily customer contacts are distributed fairly evenly over the day (Figure 3.4), with a small peak around 10:00 am.

The customer flow (or customer needs) of an insurance company may not be as even as one might conclude from Figure 3.4, however, since one should not forget the customers who are waiting in a queue to be serviced. This implies that the use of labor and capital is optimized at the expense of the customer's waiting time. The conventions of waiting and delivery times established in different fields of business are clearly resistant to change.

Discussion

The timing, duration, and amount of production, distribution and consumption activities (e.g. daily practices connected with eating), and their potential overlapping and mutual connections in time and space can today be diagnosed more and more effectively. Digitalization and new types of consumer diagnostics, for example, make it possible to effect changes in supply or prices on the basis of real-time customer information. Consequently, firms can increasingly learn, with the assistance of extensive customer databases, to

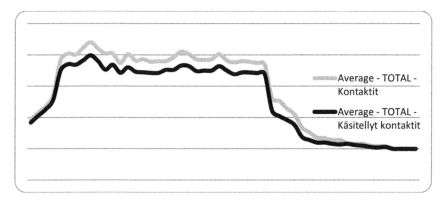

Figure 3.4 Daily customer contacts at an insurance company's call center

adapt better to the diverse daily rhythms of consumers (Prahalad and Ramaswamy, 2004). They can start to compete for a place in the daily lives of consumers by, for example, enriching their supply to serve the needs of ever smaller consumer segments and creating "portion sizes" for services that more effectively match consumers' time use. Taking a critical perspective, however, it should be noted that as businesses become increasingly able to control how consumers use their time and money through extensive data-bases, the power of consumers could be negatively affected (e.g. Zwick and Knott, 2009).[8] Businesses can also learn how to shape and manipulate rhythms.

When listening to the views of consumers it is crucial that one recognizes the logic of the melody and harmony of their daily lives and, most importantly, their reluctance to accede to radical changes (and learning) dictated from above in their own everyday environments. The fact that Internet-based grocery shopping has not yet established itself as a common practice – in Finland at least – has as much to do with resistance to change in the domestic sphere as it has with the difficulty of coordinating food maintenance (risk of spoiling) with customers' rhythms (receiving deliveries, readiness to be on call, home storage). Similar difficulties are probably faced in other fields of business that are trying to shift towards practices that are sensitive to customer rhythms.

Aided by various digital tools, the attention of market and consumer research concerned with rhythm-sensitive and data-driven business is increasingly shifting towards the time-space requirements of consumer activities. Competition over customers' time has long been a recognized form of combat among media businesses and, in the future, other fields of entrepreneurial activity will also learn to investigate the "prime times" of practices and to assess their own market share in the various key periods. At the same time they will learn to see that their worst rival may not be a similar, competing company but perhaps a chat service, the television, or even eating potato chips and drinking beer with friends. In order to discover these synchronies, service businesses will have to learn to understand how people, their customers, behave. Meanwhile, with the help of large data masses, it may also be possible to create pricing models that will have a stronger influence on consumers' time use. Digital price tags will increase the practice of active pricing, currently most prevalent and advanced in the pricing of air traffic where universal pricing is no longer recognized.

The architecture of time use is always also a question of well-being. Alvin Toffler understood this nearly 40 years ago when he spoke about "time shock," and his work has not lost its timeliness in the face of new research findings and methods (Pantzar, 2010). Undoubtedly, increased irregularity, fragmentation, and overlapping of activities in time use give rise to anxiety. The more we have learned to understand these changes, the more the problematic of hurriedness has shifted from the mere quantity of free time available to individuals, towards a structural problem in the temporal architecture of leisure. Indeed, some of our currently felt disruption of rhythms and experience of time-related stress can be attributed to the fact that the digitalization of services and distribution is still a work in progress.

Conclusions

The idea of a rhythm-sensitive digital service economy acknowledges the emergence of new diagnostic tools and policies such as active pricing. In the future, digitalization and population aging will change the rhythms of both service businesses and daily life, meaning, for example, that the practices of eating and interacting socially may move to new places and new times. On the other hand, even though the structure of commerce is changing, certain practices still remain strongly bound to specific moments and places. For example, cigarettes, mouth lozenges and breath fresheners will continue to feature prominently in the retail trade on Monday mornings in Finland. Early Saturday evening customers will remain predominantly young, while beer and potato chips will maintain their disproportionately high sales share. In the 2020s the weekly peak in alcohol consumption will still occur in Finland after the state lottery is drawn on Saturday night. However, changes are also to be expected. An increase has been noted in the United States in the practice of eating breakfast outside the home (often in the car), which may evidence development towards an even more work-centered society: "Nearly 10 percent of Americans reported no daily time spent eating – because they were eating only as a secondary activity" (Jackson, 2009, p. 121). It is likely that the daily pace of life will quicken rather than slow down (Gleick, 1999; Levine and Norenzayan, 1999).

The battle over market share in consumers' daily lives is a battle over their changing time space, and businesses have become more conscious of this competition setting thanks to new diagnostic tools. The success of Amazon-Fresh, for instance, offers evidence that in the future those companies most competent in the field of data analysis will also be the most competent in business because data-driven companies package their products flexibly into portions that match the daily time use of customers. Most likely weekends and holidays will continue to maintain their place as special days in the week with online shopping taking a day off on Saturdays and reactivating again on Sunday evenings as people begin to prepare for the work week.

The interactions between different fields and levels of business are hard to discern because there is no established research in the field due to, among other things, a lack of data. Not many of our predecessors could have guessed that the appearance of domestic refrigerators would mean a radical change in shopping practices, as well as in the structure of trade. When the task of storing meat and milk was transferred from shops to homes, daily visits to shops decreased and the dramatic disappearance of retail storefront trade from city centers began. In a similar vein, the Sunday opening of shops (in Finland) is affecting the weekly rhythm of activities such as childcare as first shop employees, then bakery workers, and eventually also those employed in other fields are increasingly shifting towards working on Sundays. This is despite the fact that, so far, the increase in Sunday opening has mostly been experienced as a decrease in Monday sales, followed by an increase in Tuesday sales and then a decrease in Wednesday sales (Nielsen PT-data, personal communication, 2010).

New digital customer-tracking tools and real-time data will change the game. The more companies recognize that they are competing not only against each other but also over consumers' time space, the more visible potential conflicts and cooperation between overlapping networks will become. In the producer-led world (e.g. in the marketing worldview illustrated by the insurance company call center mentioned above), still typical of many businesses, companies believe that they own the rights of possession and governance of the time and space of consumers. Philosophers (de Certeau, Schatzki, Lefebvre) have written extensively about time space, and our intention is not to delve into it any further than by stating that the time space of consumers should be seen as more than a container whose volume and extent can be somehow fixed, given, and open to manipulation.

However, one obvious reason why ownership of consumers' time space may be almost impossible in the future is related to the fact that consumption practices always live alongside other practices (in certain time periods and places): rush hours, hot spots, and prime time are temporal manifestations of the clustering of practices. Rhythm analysis, however, shifts our understanding and attention from time as a container to be rationally filled, towards the repetition of routines and practical sequences; in other words, in musicological terms, towards melody and the mutual synchrony of practices (Pantzar and Shove, 2010a, 2010b; Shove et al., 2012).

As digitalization proceeds, the battle for market share may well be won by those businesses that are best able to adapt to the melody, harmony, and rhythms of daily life. Services that are presented in suitable, sufficiently large or small portions, which are the most flexible in terms of time and place, and which allow for a consumer's personal rhythm, will win in this race. The fact that some services and fields of business (e.g. online auctions, banking, and chat services) have discovered their own regularities speaks of their adjustment to developments in daily social rhythms and perhaps also of their level of know-how in rhythm-based business practice.

Notes

1 This chapter was based on a research project that collected data from various fields of business on the kinds of consumer information collected by market research, especially in terms of the deployment of time (Pantzar, 2010, 2011).
2 What is essential is not the level of detail in company data, but rather the overall picture that is conveyed through a rich set of previously unpublished data.
3 In Lefebvre's perception rhythms are primarily associated with the customs of social coordination while McNeill places more emphasis on shared rhythms as a

precondition of emotional, collective commitment ("muscular bonding"). Miller (DJ Spooky), in turn, approaches rhythms from the perspective of a creator of artistic performances. At the same time he points out that firms are increasingly losing touch with artist-type consumers. Academic marketing researchers offer their own understandings of this phenomenon when speaking of the "co-creation of value" (see Prahalad and Ramaswamy, 2004; Zwick et al., 2008).

4 Schatzki (2007, p. 18) distinguishes harmonizations from coordination: the former achieve no overall result: "or rather the result they achieve is the absence of conflict, in other words, harmony."

5 The interface between various practices is an area largely obscured by current divisions of academic labor. As Canadian sociologist William Michelson points out: "Sociologists have tended to dissect human life into imaginable categories, each for study on its own right: work, leisure, family, crime, health, and so forth. Extremely little attention has been paid to the combination of activities constituting everyday life" (Michelson, 2005, p. 15). The same criticism can also be leveled at other sciences dealing with ordinary life.

6 So far the definition of "promiseware" as an "unfinished product delivered with defects and a promise of making it usable in an unspecified timeframe" (Wordreference.com) is an apt characterization of the data economy.

7 Media artists have also started to develop ways to record and map people's everyday movements using the various tracking tools of information technology such as "emotion mapping" and "biomapping" (Galloway, 2004).

8 One could, however, criticize business analytics for not acknowledging life in realistic terms. Managing consumers' time use purely on the basis of statistics or rationalized governance (e.g. "value co-creation" [Prahalad and Ramawamy, 2004], or "real-time economy") does not recognize the differences in the motive bases of consumers and different operating fields (Zwick et al., 2008). For example, the diagnostics of "digital footprints" which concentrate on separate transactions or situations of communication usually focus on the logic of isolated moments and situations (e.g. an anonymous bank transaction).

References

Ancona, D. and Chong, C. (1996) Entrainment: Pace, cycle, and rhythm in organizational behavior, *Research in Organizational Behavior*, 18: 251–284.

Andrejevic, M. (2014) The big data divide, *International Journal of Communication*, 8: 1673–1689.

Attali, J. (1985) *Noise: The Political Economy of Music*, Minnesota: University of Minnesota Press.

Brembeck, H. (2012) Cozy Friday: An analysis of family togetherness and ritual overconsumption. In Czarniawska, B. and Löfgren, O. (eds) *The Management of Overflow in Affluent Societies*, New York: Routledge.

de Certeau, M. (1980/1984) *The Practice of Everyday Life*, Berkeley: University of California Press.

Executive Office of the President (2014) *Big Data: Seizing Opportunities, Preserving Values*, Wahington, DC: The White House.

Foster, R. and Kreitzman, L. (2004) *Rhythms of Life: The Biological Clocks that Control the Daily Lives of Every Living Thing*, New Haven, CT: Yale University Press.

Galloway, A. (2004) Intimations of everyday life. Ubiquitous computing and the city, *Cultural Studies*, 18(2): 384–408.

Gleick, J. (1999) *Faster. The Acceleration of Just About Everything*, London: Abacus.

Jackson, M. (2009) *Distracted. The Erosion of Attention and the Coming Dark Age*, Amherst, MA: Prometheus Books.

Kenney, M. and Zysman, J. (2015) *Choosing a Future in the Platform Economy: The Implications and Consequences of Digital Platforms*, Kauffman Foundation New Entrepreneurial Growth Conference, Discussion Paper, Amelia Island Florida, June 18–19.

Koukkari, W. and Sothern, R. (2006) *Introducing Biological Rhythms*, New York: Springer.

Kreitzman, L. (1999) *The 24 Hour Society*, London: Profile Books.

Latour, B. and Lepinay, V. (2009) *The Science of Passionate Interests: An Introduction to Gabriel Tarde's Economic Anthropology*, Chicago, IL: Prickly Paradigm Press.

Le Corbusier (1929/1987) *The City of Tomorrow and its Planning*, New York: Dover Publications.

Lefebvre, H. (1947/1991) *Critique of Everyday Life*, London: Verso.

Lefebvre, H. (1992/2004) *Rhythm Analysis: Space, Time and Everyday Life*, London: Continuum.

Levine, R. and Norenzayan, A. (1999) The pace of life in 31 countries, *Journal of Cross-Cultural Psychology*, 30(2): 178–205.

McNeill, W. (1995) *Keeping Together in Time. Dance and Drill in Human History*, Cambridge, MA: Harvard University Press.

Meyer, K. (2008) Rhythms, streets, cities. In Goonewardena, K., Kipfer, S., Milgrom, R. and Schmidt, C. (eds) *Space, Difference, Everyday Life: Reading Henri Lefebvre*, New York: Routledge, pp. 147–160.

Michelson, W. (2005) *Time Use. Expanding the Explanatory Power of the Social Science*, London: Paradigm Books.

Miller, P. (2004) *Rhythm Science: A Mediawork Pamphlet*, Amsterdam and New York: MIT Press.

Mumford, L. (1934/1964) *Technics and Civilization*, New York: Harcourt, Brace & Company.

Nafus, D. (2014) Stuck data, dead data, and disloyal data: The stops and starts in making numbers into social practices, *Distinktion: Scandinavian Journal of Social Theory*, 15(2): 208–222.

Pantzar, M. (2010) Future shock – Discussing changing temporal architecture of daily life, *Journal of Future Studies*, 14(4): 1–22.

Pantzar, M. (2011) *Asiakkaan aika ja talouden rytmiliike, Tehokkaan tuotannon tutkimussäätiö 2*, Helsinki: Julkaisumonistamo Eteläranta ry.

Pantzar, M. and Shove, E. (2010a) Temporal rhythms as outcomes of social practices. A speculative discussion, *Ethnologia Europea*, 40(1): 19–29.

Pantzar, M. and Shove, E. (2010b) Understanding innovation in practice: A discussion of the production and re-production of Nordic Walking, *Technology Analysis and Strategic Management*, 22(4): 447–462.

Prahalad, C.K. and Ramaswamy, V. (2004) *The Future of Competition: Co-creating Unique Value with Customers*, Boston, MA: Harvard Business School Press.

Rideout, V., Foehr, U. and Roberts, D. (2010) *Generation M2: Media in the Lives of 8- to 18-Year-Olds*, A Kaiser Family Foundation Study, January.

Robinson, J. and Godbey, G. (1997) *Time for Life. The Surprising Ways Americans Use their Time*, University Park: Pennsylvania State University Press.

Sayer, L., Bianchi, S. and Robinson, J. (2004) Are parents investing less in children? Trends in mothers' and fathers' time with children, *American Journal of Sociology*, 110(1): 1–43.

Schatzki, T. (2007) *Timespace and the Organization of Social Life*, Workshop, The rhythms and routines of consumption, Florence, May.

Shove, E., Pantzar, M. and Watson, M. (2012) *Dynamics of Social Practices*, New York: Sage.

Sorokin, P. (1937/1941) *Social and Cultural Dynamics*, Cincinnati, OH: American Book Company, 4 vols.

Sorokin, P. and Merton, R. (1937) Social time: A methodological and functional analysis, *American Journal of Sociology*, XLII(5), March: 615–629.

Southerton, D. (2006) Analysing the temporal organization of daily life: Social constraints, practices and their allocation, *Sociology*, 40(3): 435–454.

Swan, M. (2013) The quantified self: Fundamental disruption in big data science and biological discovery, *Big Data*, 1(2): 85–99.

Swan, M. (2015) *Blockchain: Blueprint for a New Economy*, Sebastopol: O'Reilly.

Thompson, E.P. (1967) Time, work-discipline, and industrial capitalism, *Past and Present*, 38: 56–97.

Thrift, N. (2008) *Non-representational Theory: Space, Politics, Affect*, London: Routledge.

Toffler, A. (1970) *Future Shock*, New York: Bantam Books.

Toffler, A. (1981) *The Third Wave*, New York: Bantam Books.

World Economic Forum (2014) *Rethinking Personal Data: Trust and Context in User-Centered Data Ecosystems*.

Zwick, D., Bonsu, S. and Darmody, A. (2008) Putting consumers to work. "Co-creation" and new marketing govern-mentality, *Journal of Consumer Culture*, 8(2): 163–196.

Zwick, D. and Knott, J. (2009) Manufacturing customers: The database as new means of production, *Journal of Consumer Culture*, 9: 221–347.

4 Serendipitous effects in digitalized markets

The case of the DataCrawler recommendation agent

Jean-Sébastien Vayre, Lucie Larnaudie and Aude Dufresne

Introduction

The first recommendation systems, also called recommendation agents, were developed in the 1990s. Examples include:

- Those designed by the Xerox Research Center in Palo Alto (PARC; Parisier, 2011).
- The filter system and the sharing of information developed by Tapestry in 1992.
- The recommendation system available on Usenet GroupLens and the music recommendation system called Ringo, both developed in 1994.
- The Bellcore film and TV recommendation systems designed in 1995 (Nageswara and Talwar, 2008).

It was also during this period that Amazon employee Jeff Bezos developed a book recommendation tool based on customer purchase history (Baiocchi and Forest, 2014). The success of Amazon has played an important role in the dissemination of technical innovations such as recommendation agents (Martin et al., 2011). The spread of such technology has been significant and is evidenced in today's recommendation systems that are present in most e-commerce, culture and entertainment websites (Poirier et al., 2010).

In general, recommendation agents feed off various "signs of use" that consumers leave during their browsing activities, which market professionals now call "big data" (Vayre, 2014; Mille, 2013). These traces are often referred to as "attention deposits," which, once processed through more or less sophisticated algorithms, help reveal consumers' preferences and behaviors (Kessous, 2012). Recommendation systems are thus defined as customized filters which work by suggesting information that may be of interest to consumers (Park et al., 2012; Lynch, 2001).

Specifically, a recommendation agent's role is to customize e-commerce environments by ensuring the automatization of strategies to offer suggestions.

These strategies are relatively close to what Christian Licoppe (2006) calls "commercial rebound." According to Licoppe, for telemarketers, commercial rebound consists in offering, at the right time, one or multiple offers that may be of interest to consumers. This is somewhat close to the recommendation agent's role. Nevertheless, suggestions that come from recommendation agents cover different interactional forms from those at work in suggestions made by telemarketers (see Licoppe, 2006). Unlike the latter, commercial proposals from recommendation agents are not the result of verbal interactions between two human actors, but of nonverbal interactions between a human consumer and an artificial seller which is not always identified as such.

Thus, with reference to the work of Merton and Barber (2004), recommendation systems are technology that aims to produce serendipitous effects in markets – that is, they give rise to a certain disposition to the special human capacity that allows for discoveries by accidental shrewdness. Indeed, by means of the commercial rebound strategies deployed by recommendation agents, their designers want consumers to discover products they did not previously seek, but which attract their attention. In other words, recommendation agents are designed to elicit a certain disposition to serendipity in the sense that they must facilitate activities of discovery, comparison and selection of products while engaging consumers in the process of purchase. From the perspective of designers, recommendation agents thus have the function of solving a particularly crucial problem for retailers: getting consumers to discover deals from an online catalog without losing them along the way. The problem is significant because it involves managing the dispersion of the consumer's attention and being careful not to diminish his or her interest vis-à-vis the goods and services offered by the online seller.

From a consumer perspective, the serendipitous effects are therefore a double-edged sword, since they aim to facilitate the discovery of interesting products in such a way as to favor the financial interests of online vendors (Haübl and Murray, 2006). Thus, the serendipitous effects we are talking about here should not be confused with serendipity in the sense evoked by Merton and Barber (2004). In our case, chance is in fact the object of careful preparation: discovery is provoked (Muniesa, 2014) in such a way as to optimize the online vendor's sales. As the majority of promoters of big data commercial applications say, the purpose of recommendation agents is to allow stores to regain control of markets. In the context of the digitalization of commerce, they constitute technology that allows online vendors to better influence the behavior of consumers who are seen as ever more independent and informed.

Hence, in order to better understand the way in which recommendation systems can empirically produce serendipitous effects – as well as the associated sociocognitive implications – this chapter will set out to answer the following questions: What are recommendation agents able to do for consumers, and what are they able to make consumers do? Put another way, what is a recommendation agent's agentivity (Pickering, 1995)?

Before approaching these questions, we will first expose the theoretical and methodological frameworks used to carry out our investigation. We will see that the theory of performativity of economics is a particularly interesting approach to examine recommendation agents' agentivity. This approach allows us to account for the way in which retailers' devices offer particular representations of the world that, through their design, constitute performative actions that have some empirical effectiveness. We will then explain the methodology that we used to study the performativity of recommendation agents: in particular, the three intersecting methods used to study the design of – and the functions performed by – the recommendation agent developed by DataCrawler. We will report our results in two parts. In the first part we will show how, in terms of its physical placement and cognitive architecture, DataCrawler's recommendation agent contains a usage scenario aimed at producing serendipitous effects; that is, to make consumers discover products that must be sufficiently interesting to seduce them commercially. In the second part we will see the way in which the DataCrawler agent effectively performs these serendipitous effects, leading consumers to discover, explore and select available products more easily from an online store, while simultaneously enrolling them in the buying process. In conclusion, we will show how, on a purely interactional level, DataCrawler's recommendation agent constitutes a discovery aid device with true agentivity, tending to bring about in consumers the very behaviors intended by its designers. We will see the relevance of our work in leading to a better presentation of the way in which the DataCrawler agent, as a big data-type e-commerce system, may be used to economicize (Akrich, 1989) market exploration. Finally, we will point out the ways in which this economicization can be questioned.

Theoretical and methodological frameworks

As we have just explained, in this first section we aim to present the theoretical and methodological frameworks used to carry out our investigation. We will start by explaining how the theory of performativity of economics is a particularly interesting approach to studying the agentivity of retail technology such as recommendation agents.

Theory of performativity of economics

The performativity of economics is one of the most challenging research trends in contemporary economic sociology (MacKenzie and Millo, 2003). Generally, studies on the subject assume that the discipline of economics does not describe "economic" reality as it exists empirically, but actually as it happens through concrete economic activity. We can refer here to the work of Austin (1962), for whom the performative assertion, "I declare you husband and wife," while describing nothing real, makes the act of marriage happen by its enunciation. Similarly, economic science performs the real economy that it claims to observe. Hence Michel Callon, the originator of this performative turn (see Licoppe, 2010), offers a particularly interesting repossession of the notion of performativity. Performativity must indeed enable economic sociologists empirically to show how the commercial sphere "is not embedded in society but in economic science" (Callon, 1998, p. 30). This research program is one of the main alternatives to the new economic sociology which, for example in the works of Granovetter (1973), emphasizes the importance of intersubjective relationships (weak ties) in structuring the market (specifically the labor market).

Technical devices play an important role in the processes of performativity of economics (Callon, 1998). With reference to the works of Bruno Latour (2006) and Madeleine Akrich (1987), technical objects are carriers of action programs that reflect a number of representations. We can say that designers' views of the world are reflected in the objects they create. Specifically, technical devices are subjects of a "script" work that can be understood in three stages (Akrich, 1987). The first stage is the description, consisting of the way designers describe the object's role: that is, its functions are considered within the socio-technical network into which it must then be inserted. The second stage is that of registration and consists of introducing the action program (i.e. the usage scenario) that has been defined during the description phase. The third is that of prescription: the action program brought by the technical object constitutes a framework that must allow users to perform or not perform a number of actions.

For example, MacKenzie and Millo (2003) show how the Pricing of Options Theory, developed by Black, Scholes and Merton, has never described a state of the pre-existing world: "When first formulated, its assumptions were quite unrealistic, and empirical prices differed systematically from the model. Gradually, though, the financial markets changed in a way that fitted the model" (MacKenzie and Millo, 2003, p. 137). Thus, although MacKenzie and Millo nuance the performative power of the Black-Scholes-Merton model, emphasizing that players who use it never become morally fragmented, they nevertheless point out that these players typically assess options as the economic theory prescribes. In this sense, the theory performs (partially) according to the authors' economic rationality, since it is involved in empirically producing the figure of the homo economicus.

However, the financial sector is not the only form of trade that exists in our societies, and the homo economicus model is not the only representation that is performed in markets. For example, in the most trivial case of mass market retail, ordinary supermarket equipment (i.e. shelves, trolleys, packaging, labels, etc.) are all articles intended to bring about different calculation registers that can be about substantive rationality, axiological rationality, imitation or tradition (Cochoy, 2011b). In other words, in the sense of classical economics, rational calculation is not the only frame of mind found in the market. As argued by Cochoy (2011a), the functioning of markets implies being able to identify all the dispositions that occur during the process of consumer attachment to goods. Hence, curiosity constitutes a disposition that, like Callon's (1998) image of economic rationality, may be subject to a commercial performance (see Cochoy's (2011c) QR code).

Similar to MacKenzie and Millo's (2003) historical sociology aimed at identifying how the Black-Scholes-Merton theory eventually outperformed the world of finance, we propose an interactionist social and cognitive approach to highlight how recommendation agents are market devices that perform a certain disposition towards serendipity. We specify "a certain disposition towards serendipity" because, in the sense that we have mentioned in the introduction, the function of the DataCrawler recommendation agent is not to introduce serendipity in Merton and Barber's (2004) meaning of the word. We note that, for these authors, serendipity is indeed defined as a human ability to make discoveries by accidental sagacity. However, generally speaking, the purpose of recommendation agents has not so far been to foster those fortunate chance discoveries in the strict sense of the word. As we will see with the case of the DataCrawler agent, the main function of recommendation systems is to help consumers find products that are likely to be of interest to them so that they end up buying them. This does not truly correspond to serendipity, but rather to a kind of simulation of serendipity. It is for this reason that, to emphasize this distinction, we do not speak of serendipity but of serendipitous effects or even a leaning towards a certain serendipity.

It is important to emphasize, therefore, that in proposing to examine the performativity of the DataCrawler agent, we adopt a strong theoretical posture from the perspective of social science, since we do not see markets as subject to collective forms of overhanging structures which determine them from the outside. Instead, we see them as compositions of "inter-psychological" relationships woven into a variety of imitation and innovation processes (Tarde, 1973). However, we do not believe these inter-psychological relationships to be essentially human-to-human relationships. With reference to works on distributed cognition (see Hutchins, 1995), technical objects can be understood as psychological forms, in the sense that, as we have already said, technical objects carry out programmed actions that encapsulate their designers' representations of the world. Technical objects are cognitive entities as well as individuals (even if the two are different), and it is precisely in this that cognition is distributed (Hutchins, 1995; see also Jenkins and Denegri-Knott, and Sörum and Fuentes, this volume). In summary, we propose the adoption of a theoretical perspective similar to that of Bruno Latour (1994), for whom social interactions do not happen only between humans, but also between humans and objects. From the particular case of the recommendation system developed by DataCrawler, we wanted to examine how the forms of distribution of cognitive activities occurring between consumers and recommendation agents are made in practice.

Methodology of the DataCrawler recommendation agent case study

To do this, we used three types of method, from science and technology studies, information and communication science, and cognitive ergonomics.

First, as part of an 18-month partnership we collected a series of documents, observations and interviews to learn about how DataCrawler had developed its recommendation agent. Thus, with reference to work from science and technology studies, these materials have been the object of a systematic collection that allowed us to better know and understand:

- The social and material context in which DataCrawler's recommendation agent was designed.
- The socio-technical logic that guided its development as well as the algorithmic mechanisms at the heart of its functioning.

Referring to the theoretical frameworks that we have presented, the aim of this method is to account properly for the psychological forms – the action program – that are encapsulated by the DataCrawler recommendation agent. In other words, the materials obtained via this method should allow us to bring about the usage scenario (see Akrich, 1987) that is conveyed by this agent.

The second method used is based on the technique of recording eye movement, which is derived from cognitive ergonomics and is rarely used in human and social science (see Strahm et al., 2008). In our case study, this method is relevant because it offers the possibility to draw, with high precision, forms of interaction that take place between recommendation agent and consumer. Let us recall that these interactions are essentially non-verbal, visual-only. The study of eye movement thus provides a means to qualitatively perform an extremely precise pragmatic analysis of the uses of recommendation agents. Indeed, the method allows us to trace what consumers look at, thus making visible the way consumers read product information pages (see Figure 4.2). It also allows a concrete understanding of the attention consumers pay to recommendations the agent proposes, but also of the way this attention fits into very specific reading strategies. It is in this way that the technique of recording eye movement makes it possible to observe and measure interactions that would otherwise be only partially accessible through consumers' verbalizations or clicks made on recommendations. We will return to this point later.

To analyze uses of DataCrawler's recommendation agent from the study of eye movement, we asked 38 students from the University of Montreal to perform two searches for two different products from an online store using the agent. The first search was aimed at finding the best pair of binoculars for a maximum of €150. The second was to find the best pair of sunglasses for a maximum of €150. Each participant had 10 minutes to complete each search. None of the participants was paid. Of the 38 participants who completed the experiment, 17 were male (44.7%) and 21 female (55.3%); the average age was

24.26, with a standard deviation of 6.56 years; the median age was 21.50. With reference to what we have said above, the purpose of the materials collected from this first study was to give us a better understanding of the prescription power (see Akrich, 1987) of the usage scenario conveyed by the DataCrawler agent concerning participants' eye movements, namely the way they read product information pages.

The third method that we used comes from cognitive ergonomics and information and communication science. It is based on the recording of consumers' web browsing during research of information (see Amadieu et al., 2008). This method thus constitutes an excellent complement to recording eye movement, as it allows for an extremely powerful quantitative statistical analysis of the uses that consumers make of the recommendation agent. In contrast to the eye movement study, browsing history does not give information on how consumers read the recommendations suggested by the recommendation agent. Nonetheless, it constitutes a statistically powerful means of studying the way consumers use recommendation agents in non-experimental situations.

In order to carry out analysis of consumers' navigation history exposed to the DataCrawler recommendation system, we gathered data corresponding to visits made during the end of March 2014 to five online stores that use the DataCrawler system. We collected a total of 203,852 events. An "event" is a click made by a consumer in one of the five e-commerce websites considered. We analyzed these events after having grouped them by clickstream. A "clickstream" is defined as a sequence of one or more clicks made by the same customer on the same online store within a maximum space of 30 minutes. From the 203,852 collected events, we rebuilt a total of 35,701 clickstreams. The materials collected in this second study complement the material of the first. Indeed, its function was to allow us to better understand the prescription power (see Akrich, 1987) of the usage scenario conveyed by the DataCrawler agent, but this time concerning consumers' navigation history, that is, the way they use the site.

Design of DataCrawler's recommendation agent

To better understand how DataCrawler's recommendation agent is a market device intended to produce serendipitous effects on digitized markets, in this second section we will explain its usage scenario. In order to do this, we will rely on the various materials collected during the 18-month partnership we had with DataCrawler.

Physical positioning: encouraging exploration of the retail website

From the perspective of the sites in which it is implemented, DataCrawler's recommendation agent is an affordance (Gibson, 1966) that aims to promote the discovery, exploration and comparison of available products.

The five online stores that we considered in our study are systematically designed around four commercial spaces. The first is the homepage associated with the URL. The second is the product list that results from a consumer query through keywords or clicks on items included in a website menu. The third is that of the product information pages that present the various quantitative and qualitative properties of the consulted consumer goods. The fourth is the cart and contracting: this brings together all the pages that allow consumers to pay for and finalize their order.

On all of the commercial websites studied, DataCrawler's recommendation agent is located in the area of product information pages. This position is particularly important because it gives recommendations the status of information to discover. Indeed, from the perspective of developers, consumer information research activities necessarily involve the formulation of a need for information through one or more keywords, or through a click or multiple clicks on the items included on the website menu. Consequently, a product list is offered to consumers. They are thus driven to explore the list, assessing the relevance of the products and either reformulating the request or clicking on one of these goods. In the latter case, consumers are faced with information regarding the product's properties, but also a set of products that have not explicitly been subject to prior request, through the recommendations of the DataCrawler agent. These suggestions should thus lead consumers to discover a number of goods.

These recommendations are hyperlinked to their corresponding data information. In this way, they must help to encourage exploration of the website by allowing consumers not to return to the product lists space, for example through the formalization of a new research query by keywords. For its designers, DataCrawler's recommendation agent must foster a certain disposition to serendipity among consumers by leading them to discover new products that they had not previously sought, while simultaneously offering them the opportunity to explore these recommendations in greater detail via a single click.

Cognitive architecture: arousing consumer interest

Nevertheless, the physical positioning of the recommendation agent cannot, by itself, ensure serendipitous effects. Although its positioning covers a physical dimension that should not be ignored, it also refers to a cognitive dimension, which is central. The designers of the DataCrawler recommendation agent are fully aware of the importance of this dimension. They designed the agent not only to promote the discovery and exploration of products available in the catalog, but also to present every offer that may be of interest to the consumer: with reference to the works of Cardon (2015a), the DataCrawler agent must personalize the consumer's digital environment to maximize the usefulness of his or her discoveries and explorations.

To do this, the agent's designers have imbued it with special cognitive architecture to enable it to select the offers that should attract each consumer.

This cognitive architecture is based on five recommendation algorithms, which are supervised by a learning algorithm. As we will see, each recommendation algorithm systematically refers to particular assumptions that designers have vis-à-vis the appetites and navigational behaviors of consumers.

The first is the filter algorithm based on *content*. This algorithm uses the well-known principle of item-to-item correlation. The logic of this algorithm relies on suggesting products to the consumer that are similar to those that they have explicitly or implicitly declared as interesting (Bobadilla et al., 2013; Ochi et al., 2010; Olmo and Gaudioso, 2008). It can be made from the following inference rule: If consumer X likes product A, and A is similar to product B, then X likes B. The second recommendation algorithm is a *collaborative filtering* system based on the well-known principle of the user-to-user correlation. The logic of this algorithm relies on offering consumers products that have been explicitly or implicitly stated as interesting by other consumers with similar profiles (Bobadilla et al., 2013; Ochi et al., 2010; Olmo and Gaudioso, 2008). It can be made from the following inference rule: If consumers U, V, W, Y and Z are similar to X, and if U, V, W, Y and Z like product A, then X likes A. The third recommendation algorithm is one of *similarity*, and is based on scarcity. This algorithm qualifies as semantic because it analyzes the contents of the descriptions and images of products sold on the online store. The originality of this algorithm lies in its identification of informational units that are both the most relevant and the most specific to a given product. In other words, this algorithm's role is to:

- In each product description, look for the terms that are marked as relevant (i.e. those that are underlined, capitalized, in bold, italic, etc.) and which are equipped with a low recurrence rate compared with other product descriptions (e.g. in the case of a road bike website, the term "back-pedaling").
- In each product photograph, look for rare elements that allow the differentiation of the product from others (e.g. in the case of a road bike website, a dark brown leather saddle with chrome rivets).

Furthermore, this algorithm is based on real-time analysis of consumer navigation behaviors. Its logic can thus be exposed by using the following inference rule: If consumer X repeatedly clicks on products with characteristics a, b and c, and a, b and c are rare compared with other product characteristics, then X is looking for a product with a, b and c. The fourth recommendation algorithm is one of *personalization*. This algorithm is similar to that of similarity because it also works from a content analysis of descriptions and product images. Here, however, the uniqueness of the product is less important than the recurrence of consumer action. For example, in the case of a road bike website, if a consumer repeatedly clicks on black bikes for men, the personalization algorithm will predict that the consumer is interested in black bikes for men, even though these two features are not unusual in comparison with the other available products. This logic is based on the following inference rule: If consumer X clicks repeatedly on products with characteristics a, b and c, and a, b and c are recurrent in terms of previously clicked products, then X is looking for a product with a, b and c. The fifth recommendation algorithm is an algorithm of *complementarity*. This algorithm is a hybrid form derived from algorithms based on content, collaborative filtering, similarity and personalization. According to the consumer's navigation, its aim is to remember those products receiving the highest prediction from the viewpoint of the collaborative filtering, similarity, and personalization algorithms; its second aim is to remember those products that are least similar to the reference products (i.e. corresponding to the product information page viewed by the consumer; see the content algorithms). This logic can then be exposed as follows: If consumer X clicks on product A, and if products B, C, D, E and F have the best prediction scores with the collaborative filtering, similarity and personalization algorithms, and B and C are less similar to A (see the content), then X may be interested in B and C. The *learning* algorithm then takes over the hybridization of the five algorithms presented previously. It is this algorithm that will determine a fairly sustainable and widely applicable winning combination of the five recommendation algorithms discussed above and according to:

- The commercial performance criteria of conversion rate (i.e. turning visitors into customers) and number of clicks by users on recommendations.
- Observations the agent makes in real time about the behavior of consumers visiting the site;
- The products available in the online catalog.

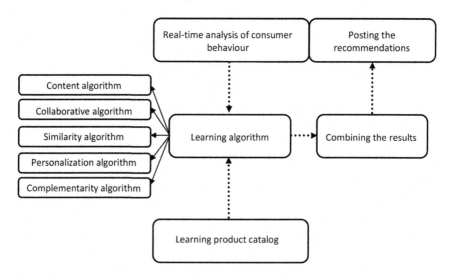

Figure 4.1 Cognitive architecture of the DataCrawler recommendation agent

Setting: the similarity algorithm based on scarcity and the strategy of up-selling

It is important to note that DataCrawler's recommendation agent rarely works completely autonomously. Indeed, according to the results obtained for a long period of learning, online vendors benefitting from these services generally prefer to define activation parameters for recommendations manually, based on algorithms that have historically produced the best results, particularly with a view to reducing the time it takes to load recommendations.

The five online stores we examined were using a special design strategy of the DataCrawler recommendation agent. This strategy highlights the similarity algorithm based on scarcity, and proposes, where possible, the upper range of goods (i.e. the more expensive) to the product of reference. This strategy is called up-selling. According to the DataCrawler recommendation agent designers, this strategy holds a better conversion rate and elicits more recommendation clicks in all the e-commerce sites in which it is implemented.

Use of the DataCrawler recommendation agent

In this third section, we propose an empirical examination of the performativity of DataCrawler's recommendation agent. We will study the uses that consumers make of the recommendation agent compiled from analysis of results obtained through the method of recording eye movement and clickstreams. In doing this, we wish to test the hypothesis of performance of serendipitous effects by the DataCrawler agent by examining the practical uses consumers make of it.

The recommendation agent incites exploratory reading of product information pages. In general, the method of analyzing eye movement with areas of interest (AOIs), as shown in Figure 4.2, demonstrates that the 38 participants allocated significant attention to the propositions coming from the recommendation agent (AOI d), compared with other product AOIs, as shown in Figure 4.3.

More specifically, DataCrawler's recommendation agent (AOI d) has an average duration of fixation (DFd) of 7,626 milliseconds per clickstream, putting it in third place on the scale of the observed AOIs (see Figure 4.3). Note that this difference is statistically significant ($p < .05$).

In addition, in terms of description, the recommendation AOI has a non-negligible centrality in terms of the visual scan that participants make of the product information pages. DataCrawler's recommendation agent (AOI d) has the largest transition percentage for the third (21.4%), fifth (21.1%), sixth (16.8%), 11th (11.4%) and 19th (5.4%) AOIs observed in the same visual scan. Thus, Figure 4.4 highlights the level of centrality of the recommendation AOI (d) compared with other areas of interest. Note that the horizontal axis represents the sequence of AOI observed during the same visual scanning (AOI 1, ..., AOI 20) and the vertical axis shows the transition percentages for each area of interest observed (PTa, PTb, PTc, PTd, PTe and PTf).

Figure 4.2 Presentation of product information pages AOI: AOI a-image, AOI b-title, AOI c-price, AOI d-recommendation, AOI e-description and AOI f-search

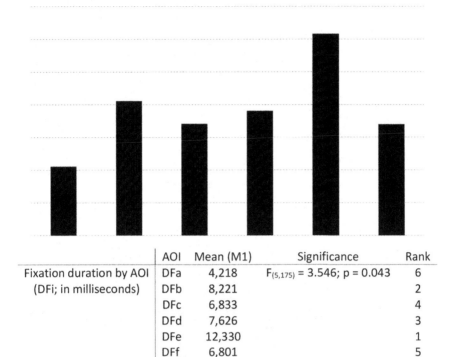

	AOI	Mean (M1)	Significance	Rank
Fixation duration by AOI	DFa	4,218	$F_{(5,175)} = 3.546; p = 0.043$	6
(DFi; in milliseconds)	DFb	8,221		2
	DFc	6,833		4
	DFd	7,626		3
	DFe	12,330		1
	DFf	6,801		5

Figure 4.3 Average AOI fixation duration (DFi) per clickstream

As we can observe in Figure 4.4, the average visual scan of the product information pages that participants make is mainly articulated around the AOIs price (c), recommendation (d), and title (b). Furthermore, it appears that the recommendation AOI (d) has a rather high general level of centrality because it is in fourth position in terms of average transition percentages for the first 20 observed AOIs (see Figure 4.4).

Consequently, on the descriptive as well as the statistical levels, the recommendations proposed by the DataCrawler agent have the effect of significantly attracting participants' attention. More precisely, the recommendations lead participants to adopt strategies for exploratory reading of product information pages. These strategies manifest themselves in transition patterns articulated around price (c), recommendation (d) and title (b) AOIs. These patterns generally indicate that participants do indeed find the recommendations proposed by the DataCrawler agent, since they observe them significantly and compare them with the reference product.

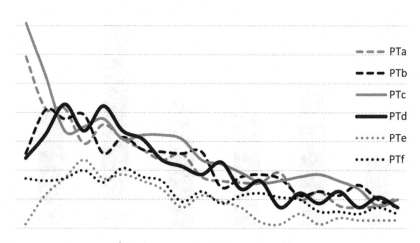

AOI	PTa	PTb	PTc	PTd	PTe	PTf	End
AOI 1	29.6	12.9	35.4	12.1	0.7	8.6	0.7
AOI 2	20.7	20.4	26.4	16.1	5.7	8.2	2.5
AOI 3	20.7	18.9	16.8	21.4	8.6	8.6	5
AOI 4	14.6	19.6	17.5	16.8	11.8	10	9.6
AOI 5	17.9	12.9	18.9	21.1	8.6	7.9	12.8
AOI 6	15.4	15.7	15.4	16.8	9.3	10.4	17.2
AOI 7	13.6	13.6	16.1	15.4	8.2	8.9	24.2
AOI 8	11.8	13.2	16.1	11.8	6.8	8.2	32.2
AOI 9	12.9	12.9	15.4	10.7	3.6	4.6	40
AOI 10	8.9	13.2	11.8	9.3	5.7	6.4	44.6
AOI 11	8.2	7.1	11.1	11.4	4.6	4.3	53.2
AOI 12	7.9	8.9	9.6	6.8	3.6	5.7	57.5
AOI 13	7.9	9.3	7.9	8.2	1.1	6.1	59.6
AOI 14	9.6	8.6	8.2	3.6	0.7	5.4	63.9
AOI 15	5	5.7	8.9	6.1	2.5	5	66.8
AOI 16	6.4	6.4	9.3	4.3	0.7	2.9	70
AOI 17	3.9	5.7	8.2	6.4	1.8	2.9	71.1
AOI 18	3.6	7.5	6.8	3.6	1.4	2.5	74.7
AOI 19	3.9	5	3.9	5.4	1.4	3.6	76.7
AOI 20	5.4	3.6	5	3.6	1.4	2.5	78.6
Mean (M1)	11.39	11.05	13.43	10.54	4.41	6.13	43.04

Figure 4.4 Transition percentages per AOI (PTi) for all product information pages observed

Intensity of recommendation agent use affects clickstream depth

Before examining the role of the intensity of use of the recommendation agent on consumer clickstream forms, we should point out that Figures 4.5, 4.6 and 4.7 were constituted from navigation data collected from five of DataCrawler's website partners. In addition, these figures were performed using the ANCOVA test with the number of open nodes as a covariant (i.e. clickstream; T). The number of open nodes is a confounding variable, in the sense that the number of recommendation clicks significantly increases with the number of pages viewed during the clickstream. Hence, in order to eliminate the effect of this covariant, the estimated marginal means (M2), shown in Figures 4.5, 4.6 and 4.7, are calculated with the ANCOVA model, with T = 9.33. In addition, for each of the conducted ANCOVA, we have selected the clickstreams that contain more than two open nodes (considering that it is necessary to open at least two pages of a website in order to observe one of the suggestions made by the DataCrawler recommendation agent). We have selected a total of 20,172 clickstreams.

The vertical axis of the graph presented in Figure 4.5 represents the number of homepages (PA), product lists (LP), and product information pages (FP) observed (see the three curves). The horizontal axis of the same graph represents the number of recommendation clicks (CR) performed during a single clickstream. We can see from this figure that the number of product information pages (FP) observed tends to increase linearly with the number of recommendation clicks (CR) performed during the clickstream, while it moves in the opposite direction to the number of product lists (LP). Note that these two effects are statistically significant ($p < .001$ in both cases). In turn, the number of homepages (PA) tends to vary slightly from the increase in number of recommendation clicks (CR). However, this variation is difficult to analyze given that its magnitude is very low and its evolution non-linear (see Figure 4.5).

In summary, the results presented in Figure 4.5 show that, in general, the more consumers click on the recommendations by the DataCrawler agent, the less they tend to observe product lists and the more they tend to observe product information pages. Remember that this effect is independent of the number of open nodes during the clickstream. Therefore, we can say that the more consumers rely on the DataCrawler system, the deeper their clickstream (i.e. they thoroughly explore a greater number of goods; Amadieu et al., 2008). Indeed, while product lists also allow for exploration of different consumer goods (the results of a query), this exploration is still relatively superficial, considering the scant information available on products in this commercial space. In this sense, the more intensively the consumer uses the DataCrawler recommendation agent, the less superficial their search.

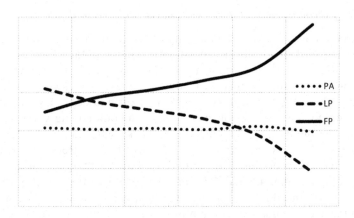

Number of homepages (PA)				
Number of recommendation clicks (CR)	Population (N)	Mean (M1)	Estimated marginal mean (M2)	Significance
$CR_{(0)}$	18,307	0.34	0.36	$F_{(5,20165)} = 11.882$; p = 0.000
$CR_{(1)}$	1,062	0.30	0.18	
$CR_{(2:3)}$	569	0.52	0.29	
$CR_{(4:5)}$	127	0.57	0.14	
$CR_{(6:7)}$	56	1.02	0.55	
$CR_{(>7)}$	51	0.71	-0.14	
Number of products lists (LP)				
$CR_{(0)}$	18,307	4.99	5.52	$F_{(5,20165)} = 131.480$; p = 0.000
$CR_{(1)}$	1,062	6.87	3.74	
$CR_{(2:3)}$	569	8.65	2.68	
$CR_{(4:5)}$	127	12.55	1.51	
$CR_{(6:7)}$	56	11.34	-0.68	
$CR_{(>7)}$	51	16.82	-5.51	
Number of product information pages (FP)				
$CR_{(0)}$	18,307	1.99	2.44	$F_{(5,20165)} = 136.343$; p = 0.000
$CR_{(1)}$	1,062	7.00	4.40	
$CR_{(2:3)}$	569	10.31	5.36	
$CR_{(4:5)}$	127	15.81	6.66	
$CR_{(6:7)}$	56	18.43	8.45	
$CR_{(>7)}$	51	32.51	13.98	

Covariants in the model are evaluated using the following values: T = 9.33

Figure 4.5 Evolution of the number of homepages (PA), product lists (LP) and product information pages (FP) observed according to the number of recommendation clicks (CR) performed during the clickstream

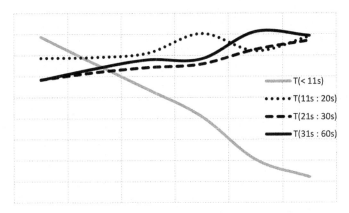

Number of nodes observed in less than 11 s ($T_{(< 11s)}$)				
Number of recommendation clicks (CR)	Population (N)	Mean (M1)	Estimated marginal mean (M2)	Significance
$CR_{(0)}$	18,307	2.33	2.87	$F_{(5, 20165)} = 119.191$; p = 0.000
$CR_{(1)}$	1,062	4.73	1.61	
$CR_{(2: 3)}$	569	6.34	0.38	
$CR_{(4: 5)}$	127	10.10	-0.90	
$CR_{(6: 7)}$	56	9.04	-2.96	
$CR_{(> 7)}$	51	18.51	-3.78	
Number of nodes observed between 11 s and 20 s ($T_{(11s: 20s)}$)				
$CR_{(0)}$	18,307	1.68	1.87	$F_{(5, 20165)} = 8.220$; p = 0.000
$CR_{(1)}$	1,062	3.07	1.91	
$CR_{(2: 3)}$	569	4.32	2.11	
$CR_{(4: 5)}$	127	7.12	3.03	
$CR_{(6: 7)}$	56	6.66	2.21	
$CR_{(> 7)}$	51	11.16	2.89	
Number of nodes observed between 21 s and 30 s ($T_{(21s: 30s)}$)				
$CR_{(0)}$	18,307	0.76	0.84	$F_{(5, 20165)} = 62.712$; p = 0.000
$CR_{(1)}$	1,062	1.66	1.18	
$CR_{(2: 3)}$	569	2.34	1.42	
$CR_{(4: 5)}$	127	3.28	1.58	
$CR_{(6: 7)}$	56	4.13	2.28	
$CR_{(> 7)}$	51	6.14	2.71	
Number of nodes observed between 31 s and 60 s ($T_{(31s: 60s)}$)				
$CR_{(0)}$	18,307	0.75	0.83	$F_{(5, 20165)} = 112.929$; p = 0.000
$CR_{(1)}$	1,062	1.84	1.36	
$CR_{(2: 3)}$	569	2.71	1.79	
$CR_{(4: 5)}$	127	3.52	1.83	
$CR_{(6: 7)}$	56	4.96	3.12	
$CR_{(> 7)}$	51	6.35	2.93	

Covariants in the model are evaluated using the following values: T = 9.33

Figure 4.6 Evolution of the consultation time of open nodes (T(is)) according to the number of recommendation clicks (CR) performed during the clickstream

Intensity of use of the recommendation agent affects clickstream relevance

Figure 4.6 allows us to see different dependent relationships between intensity of use of the DataCrawler recommendation system and time spent per open node.

The first relationship is as follows: the number of nodes observed in less than 11 seconds (vertical axis; T(< 11s)) tends to decrease with an increase in the number of recommendation clicks (CR) performed during the clickstream (see Figure 4.6). This relationship, which is more or less linear, is the most statistically interesting since it has the highest significance compared with the other curves ($F(5,20165) = 119.191$; $p < .001$). The second dependence relationship is represented by the curve T(11s: 20s). This curve shows that the number of nodes observed between 11 and 20 seconds tends to increase in a rather non-linear way with an increase in the number of recommendation clicks (CR) performed during the clickstream. The non-linearity of the curve makes it difficult to interpret. In addition, the statistical significance of this curve is the lowest compared with that of the other curves ($F(5,20165) = 8.220$; $p < .001$).

The last two dependency relationships are shown by the T(21s: 30s) and T (31s: 60s) curves. T(21s: 30s) shows that the number of nodes observed between 21 and 30 seconds tends to increase linearly with an increase in the number of recommendation clicks (CR) performed during the clickstream (see Figure 4.6). Thus, although this relationship is not the most significant in terms of description, T(21s: 30s) has a non-negligible statistical significance compared with that of the other curves ($F(5,20165) = 62.712$; $p < .001$). T(31s: 60s) shows that the number of nodes observed between 31 and 60 seconds also tends to increase with an increase in the number of recommendation clicks (CR) performed during the clickstream. This increase is fairly linear until the sixth and seventh recommendation clicks (CR). At that point, the curve shows a slight relationship reversal (see Figure 4.6). Note that T(31s: 60s) is provided with the second highest statistical significance of all curves ($F(5,20165) = 112.929$; $p < .001$).

Therefore, in general, the results presented show that the more consumers tend to click on recommendations suggested by the DataCrawler agent, the less they tend to open nodes observed for a period of less than 11 seconds, and the more they tend to open nodes observed for a period of 11 seconds or more. In other words, knowing that the average load time of a page on the relevant sites is just over three seconds, we can say that the more consumers tend to click on recommendations, the less they tend to open nodes that they do not really examine: in less than eight seconds, the page processing can only be superficial. While an increase in intensity of use of the recommendation system tends to have the effect of increasing the depth of the clickstream, it also therefore tends to decrease its level of irrelevance. In other words, it is apparent from Figures 4.5 and 4.6 that the more extensively consumers use the recommendation agent, the more product information they tend to explore. In general, this then has the effect of improving the subjective interest that consumers have in the different pages that make up their clickstream.

Intensity of use of the recommendation agent affects commitment to the purchase process

Figure 4.7 shows three curves with the number of nodes opened more than once (T+1), the number of different product categories (CD) observed, the number of cart clicks (CP) on the vertical axis, and the number of recommendation clicks (CR) performed during the clickstream on the horizontal axis.

We see that the number of nodes opened more than once (T+1) tends to increase in a non-linear way with an increase in the number of recommendation clicks (CR) performed during the clickstream. Specifically, this increase begins from the second and third recommendation clicks, to the fourth and fifth recommendation clicks. The upstream and downstream of these two threshold values show that the curve T+1 is relatively flat (see Figure 4.7). In addition, the statistical significance of this curve is the lowest compared with the other curves ($F(5,20165) = 10.155$; $p < .001$). Conversely, the number of different product categories (CD) observed during one clickstream tends to decline sharply and linearly with an increase in the number of recommendation clicks (CR; see Figure 4.7). We can then see that, unlike the number of different product categories (CD) observed, the number of cart clicks (CP) increases more or less linearly with the number of recommendation clicks (CR) performed during the clickstream (see Figure 4.7). While this increase appears relatively low at the descriptive level, its statistical significance is substantial ($F(5,20165) = 44.022$; $p < .001$). This last observation is especially so since the binary logistic regression model predicts that a consumer is almost 1.5 times more likely to click on their cart each time they click on a recommendation (odds: 1.474; $p = 0.000$).

Regarding clickstream analysis, we can say that the more heavily consumers tend to rely on the DataCrawler recommendation system, the more they tend to perform more redundant and less diverse clickstreams, and the more frequently they interact with their cart. These three results show that increasing the intensity usage of the recommendation system tends to have the effect of reducing the diversity of alternatives considered by consumers (i.e. getting them to clarify their choice) while simultaneously enrolling them in the buying process. In this sense, these results generally show that the more consumers rely on the DataCrawler system, the more they tend to enter into what professionals call the "conversion tunnel" – that is, the buying process.

Discussion

The DataCrawler recommendation agent is a device that produces serendipitous effects in digitalized markets. From the standpoint of its design, it has the effect of driving consumers to discover and explore the products that have not been the subject of prior research but which are nevertheless of interest to them. The purpose of DataCrawler's recommendation agent is to tie

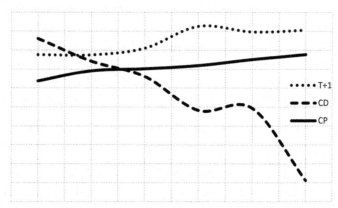

Number of pages opened more than once (T+1)				
Number of recommendation clicks (CR)	Population (N)	Mean (M1)	Estimated marginal mean (M2)	Significance
$CR_{(0)}$	18,307	1.46	1.76	$F_{(5,20165)} = 10.155; p = 0.000$
$CR_{(1)}$	1,062	3.52	1.75	
$CR_{(2:3)}$	569	5.46	2.10	
$CR_{(4:5)}$	127	9.46	3.25	
$CR_{(6:7)}$	56	9.73	2.96	
$CR_{(>7)}$	51	15.63	3.05	
Number of different product categories observed (CD)				
$CR_{(0)}$	18,307	2.39	2.61	$F_{(5,20165)} = 99.711; p = 0.000$
$CR_{(1)}$	1,062	2.72	1.42	
$CR_{(2:3)}$	569	3.09	0.61	
$CR_{(4:5)}$	127	3.39	-1.18	
$CR_{(6:7)}$	56	3.91	-1.07	
$CR_{(>7)}$	51	4.37	-4.89	
Number of cart clicks (CP)				
$CR_{(0)}$	18,307	0.35	0.37	$F_{(5,20165)} = 44.022; p = 0.000$
$CR_{(1)}$	1,062	1.03	0.91	
$CR_{(2:3)}$	569	1.24	1.02	
$CR_{(4:5)}$	127	1.59	1.19	
$CR_{(6:7)}$	56	1.95	1.51	
$CR_{(>7)}$	51	2.57	1.77	

Covariants in the model are evaluated using the following values: T = 9.33

Figure 4.7 Evolution of the number of pages opened more than once (T+1), different product categories (CD) observed and cart clicks (CP) performed according to the number of recommendation clicks (CR) performed during the clickstream

consumers to one or more available goods of the e-commerce site visited. Thus, in general, the recommendation agent involves an aspect of performativity because it tends to stimulate a certain disposition to serendipity among consumers.

The analysis of eye movement showed that the recommendation agent leads consumers to discover and compare various alternatives to the reference product they are looking at. Furthermore, clickstream analysis shows that the more consumers rely on the DataCrawler agent, the more their clickstreams tend to be deep and relevant. In other words, the recommendation system allows consumers to adopt a more fluid and intuitive navigation by avoiding going back and forth between product information pages and product lists. Moreover, it also limits the number of irrelevant web pages that consumers consult during their clickstream. Thus, DataCrawler's recommendation system tends to relieve the search for information activities undertaken by consumers in terms of information search activities, serving to formalize their need for information in order to launch product queries (for example, through keywords or clicks on one of the items included in the website menu). By delegating a part of the decision making to the recommendation agent, consumers can benefit from the reduced cognitive load involved in the search for information activities while enjoying effective help with the exploration of consumer goods available on the site.

Finally, clickstream analysis also shows that the more the consumers rely on the DataCrawler recommendation system, the further they enter into what professionals call the "conversion tunnel." Indeed, it is clear that the more frequently consumers use the recommendation agent during their clickstream, the more they tend to specify their choice, that is to say, they consider alternatives in similar categories which tend to be more and more redundant. At the same time, the more they rely on the recommendation agent, the more frequently they tend to interact with their cart, which is a good indicator of interest or commercial attachment. Therefore, by delegating a part of the decision making to the recommendation system, consumers are driven to compare similar categories of product (which are subject to a certain redundancy), which has the effect of favoring their involvement in the purchasing process. Note, however, that in reference to the up-selling strategy included in the setting of the version of DataCrawler's recommendation agent that we studied, we do not know whether or not the intensity of its use leads consumers to buy top-quality (i.e. more expensive) products.

We would now like to emphasize some limitations of these results, which must be understood as mainly exploratory. The studies of eye movement and navigation history were carried out on very different populations and with very different methods. As we pointed out above, the first study was carried out with a sample group of students from Montreal University, whereas the second study was carried out in situ on a population with unknown characteristics. We have thus combined two very different types of material without being able to control the bias effects that could be due to the specificities peculiar to each population. This leads us to point out a limitation that seems particularly significant. In the work we have just presented, we do not take account of the moderating effects that different individual variables can have on the performance of the DataCrawler agent. Yet, the age, level of expertise and level of receptiveness to advertising and advice are very likely to significantly modify the serendipitous effects we have endeavored to show in this chapter. Moreover, we think it would be extremely interesting to complement the studies we have carried out in order to have a better understanding of the advantages and drawbacks of the serendipitous effects produced by the DataCrawler agent with regard to the navigation strategies of consumers. Indeed, although we have found that these effects facilitate the exploration and comparison of products available on the site, they may also be detrimental to informational research carried out with fairly precise objectives (see Vayre et al., 2016). We would also find it appropriate to try to achieve a better understanding of the extent to which the serendipitous effects produced by the DataCrawler agent are subjectively considered helpful in navigation by consumers.

Conclusion

Similar to the way in which the Pricing of Options Theory developed by Black, Scholes and Merton tends to bring about economic rationality in those who employ it (MacKenzie and Millo, 2003), the DataCrawler recommendation agent materializes the representations of its designers. With reference to the work of Bruno Latour (2006) and Madeleine Akrich (1987), the agent portrays a scenario of use that has the ability to prescribe: it performs a certain disposition towards serendipity in consumers. One of the main advantages of our trifurcate approach in research methods is thus that it allows us to identify and quantify this performativity. Thanks to the combination of methodological approaches used, we have been able to better understand how, at an inter-psychological level (Tarde, 1973), certain big data commercial applications play a role in facilitating the existence of exploration of digitalized markets.

More specifically, the observations and interviews that we carried out regarding the design of the DataCrawler agent have given us a better understanding of how, from the point of view of its designers, the agent must allow the economicization (Akrich, 1989) of consumers' exploration activities. Its physical layout and cognitive architecture must evoke in consumers patterns of comparison and exploration of products that were not previously part of their search in such a way as to engage them more fully in an economic sense. We have seen that the action plan proposed by the DataCrawler agent is thus designed to provoke serendipitous effects to serve the financial interests of online vendors. Furthermore, we note that these serendipitous effects are reminiscent of the famous "dream of automatic serendipity" discussed by Rouvroy and Berns (2013).

Analysis of eye movement and clickstream data has therefore allowed us to better detect empirically how the DataCrawler agent produces in practical terms its programmed usage scenario. By making the way consumers read product information pages concretely visible and measurable, the eye movement study allows us to quantify concrete usage of the DataCrawler agent during their information research activity. Using this method, we have been able to show that by suggesting products to consumers that are likely to interest them, the agent leads them to adopt strategies of exploratory reading of product information pages by encouraging a comparative approach. The clickstream data study has allowed us to complete that of eye movement in the sense that this study makes possible the quantification of the effects associated with use of the DataCrawler agent. Thanks to this method we have, in effect, been able to pinpoint how, by anticipating consumers' information needs, the agent allows frequent users a more thorough experience of the site since they do not have to start their search over and select an item from a new product list. What is more, we have seen that the DataCrawler agent allows these same consumers to carry out more relevant searches by saving them from opening nodes observed in a superficial manner. Finally, by proposing products that are similar to the consulted product, the agent pushes consumers who use it most to specify their choice in the sense that it leads them to consider a narrower range of products while leading them into the conversion tunnel earlier.

In this way, the DataCrawler agent highlights a certain disposition towards serendipity in consumers which characterizes new forms of cognitive and relational framework (Mallard, 2009) established by commercial technology in the digital age. It would appear, in fact, that one of the primary interests of our work is in illustrating the way certain automatic marketing technologies aim to direct consumers by personalizing their digital environment to maximize its usefulness (Cardon, 2015a), rather than disciplining them by trying to constrain their behavior. Rather like Thaler and Sunstein's (2008) "nudges," the serendipitous effects produced by the DataCrawler agent are soft incitements aimed at guiding – never imposing – consumer behavior. From a socioeconomic point of view, such incitements are therefore debatable since, unlike the nudges that interest Thaler and Sunstein (2008), they are aimed less at improving an individual decision than at increasing online vendor sales. Of course, the serendipitous effects may have positive aspects from the point of view of consumers: the DataCrawler agent may allow some to discover new and interesting products. Moreover, this is why recommendation agents are often considered to be double agents, serving the financial interests of online vendors while improving the navigation experience of consumers (Haübl and Murray, 2006). It nevertheless seems to us that the role of the DataCrawler agent is in reality less double than it might appear in that all the recommendations it makes are the result of its learning aimed at optimizing online vendors' sales figures. There are many other ways of designing the way in which such technology learns. For example, it would be entirely possible to configure the DataCrawler agent to learn to recommend products not in the interests of maximizing online vendor profits, but in limiting consumer disorientation. Nor is it impossible that such learning would also allow it to improve e-commerce sales. What is more, the agent follows an up-selling strategy which makes the serendipitous effects it produces controversial from the point of view of consumers since they consist in suggesting goods that are much more expensive than those consulted.

To conclude, we would like to highlight that by recommending products to consumers that are likely to interest them, the DataCrawler agent simply shows them the "route," and not the "scenery" (Cardon, 2015b): we should remember, once again, that through its suggestions, the paths it marks out for consumers must maximize the economic utility of their searches. It could equally be true that, paradoxically, by provoking serendipitous effects, the DataCrawler agent fails to encourage serendipity in consumers in the sense intended by Merton and Barber (2004). In fact, as these two authors show, it is often on the edge of the path, somewhere among all the "useless" elements that make up the scenery, that the greatest source of serendipity is found.

References

Akrich, M. (1987) "Comment décrire les objets techniques?," *Techniques and Cultures*, 9: 49–64.
Akrich, M. (1989) "La construction d'un système socio-technique. Esquisse pour une anthropologie des techniques," *Anthropologie et Sociétés*, 13(2): 31–54.
Amadieu, F., Bastien, C. and Tricot, A. (2008) "Les méthodes on-line 1: analyse des parcours," in A. Chevalier and A. Tricot (eds) *Ergonomie des documents électroniques*. Paris: Presses Universitaires de France, pp. 251–270.
Austin, J.L. (1962) *How to Do Things with Words*. Oxford: Oxford University Press.
Baiocchi, M.C. and Forest, D. (2014) "'L'usager comme autorité cognitive': Perspectives théoriques sur les systèmes de recommandation," *Les Cahiers du numérique*, 10: 127–157.
Bobadilla, J., Ortega, F., Hernando, A. and Gutiérrez, A. (2013) "Recommender systems survey," *Knowledge-Based Systems*, 46: 109–132.
Callon, M. (1998) *The Laws of the Markets*. Oxford: Blackwell.
Cardon, D. (2015a). *Le bazar et les algorithmes: à propos de l'espace public numérique. Les entretiens du nouveau mande industriel*. Paris: Centre Pompidou.
Cardon, D. (2015b). *À quoi rêvent les algorithmes. Nos vies à l'heure des big data*. Paris: Seuil-La République des idées.
Cochoy, F. (2011a). *De la curiosité. L'art de la séduction marchande*. Paris: Armand Colin.
Cochoy, F. (2011b). "Le 'calqul' économique du consommateur: ce qui s'échange autour d'un chariot," *L'Année sociologique*, 61(1): 71–101.
Cochoy, F. (2011c). *Sociologie d'un "curiositif": smartphone, code-barre 2d and self-marketing*. Lormont: Bord de l'eau.
Gibson, J.J. (1966) *The Senses Considered as Perceptual Systems*. Boston, MA: Houghton Mifflin.

Granovetter, M.S. (1973) "The strength of weak ties," *American Journal of Sociology*, 78(6): 1360–1380.

Haübl, G. and Murray, K. (2006) "Double agents: Assessing the role of electronic product recommendation systems," *MIT Sloan Management Review*, 47(3): 8–12.

Hutchins, E. (1995) *Cognition in the Wild*. Cambridge, MA: MIT Press.

Kessous, E. (2012) *L'attention au monde. Sociologie des données personnelles à l'ère numérique*. Paris: Armand.

Latour, B. (1994) "Une sociologie sans objet? Remarques sur l'interobjectivité," *Sociologie du travail*, 36(4): 587–607.

Latour, B. (2006) "Portrait de Gaston Lagaffe en philosophe des techniques," in B. Latour (ed.) *Pandites leçons de sociologie des sciences and des techniques*. Paris: La Découverte, pp. 15–24.

Licoppe, C. (2006) "La construction conversationnelle de l'activité commerciale: 'Rebondir' au téléphone pour placer des services," *Réseaux*, 1(135–136): 125–159.

Licoppe, C. (2010) "Présentation. Un tournant performatif? Retour sur ce que 'font' les mots et les choses," *Réseaux*, 5(163): 9–10.

Lynch, C.A. (2001) "Personalization and Recommender Systems in the Larger Context: New Directions and Research Questions," Second DELOS Network of Excellence Workshop on Personalisation and Recommender Systems in Digital Libraries, Dublin, Ireland.

MacKenzie, D. and Millo, Y. (2003) "Constructing a market, performing theory: The historical sociology of a financial derivatives exchange," *American Journal of Sociology*, 109: 107–145.

Mallard, A. (2009) *Tome 1 – Le cadrage cognitif et relationnel de l'échange marchand: analyse sociologique des formes de l'organisation commerciale*. Toulouse: Université de Toulouse Jean Jaurès.

Martin, F.-J., Donaldson, J., Ashenfelter, A., Torrens, M. and Hangartner, R. (2011) "The big promises of recommender systems," *AI Magazine*, 32(3): 19–27.

Merton, R.K. and Barber, E.G. (2004) *The Travels and Adventures of Serendipity: A Study in Sociological Semantics and the Sociology of Science*. Princeton, NJ: Princeton University Press.

Mille, A. (2013) "De la trace à la connaissance à l'ère du Web. Introduction au dossier," *Intellectica*, 1(59): 7–28.

Muniesa, F. (2014) *The Provoked Economy: Economic Reality and the Performative Turn*. London and New York: Routledge.

Nageswara, R.K. and Talwar, V.G. (2008) "Application domain and functional classification of recommender systems: A survey," *Desidoc Journal of Library and Information Technology*, 28: 17–36.

Ochi, P., Rao, S., Takayama, L. and Nass, C. (2010) "Predictors of user perceptions of web recommender systems: How the basis for generating experience and search product recommendations affects user responses," *International Journal of Human-Computer Studies*, 68: 472–482.

Olmo, F.H. del and Gaudioso, E. (2008) "Evaluation of recommender systems: A new approach," *Expert Systems with Applications*, 35: 790–804.

Parisier, E. (2011) *The Filter Bubble: What the Internet is Hiding from You*. New York: The Penguin Press.

Park, D.H., Kyeong Hyea, K., Il Young, C. and Jae Kyeong, K. (2012) "A literature review and classification of recommender systems research," *Expert Systems with Applications*, 39(11): 10059–10072.

Pickering, A. (1995) *The Mangle of Practice: Time, Agency and Science.* Chicago, IL: University of Chicago Press.

Poirier, D., Fessant, F. and Tellier, I. (2010) "De la classification d'opinions à la recommandation: L'apport des textes communautaires," *TAL*, 51(3): 19–46.

Rouvroy, A. and Berns, T. (2013) "Gouvernementalité algorithmique et perspectives d'émancipation. Le disparate comme condition d'individuation par la relation?," *Réseaux*, 1(177): 163–196.

Strahm, M., Kicka, M. and Baccino, T. (2008) "Les méthodes on-line 2: mouvements oculaires," in A. Chevalier and A. Tricot (eds) *Ergonomie des documents électroniques.* Paris: Presses Universitaire de France, pp. 271–288.

Tarde, G. (1973) *Ecrits de psychologie sociale.* Textes choisis and présenté par A.M. Rocheblaye-Spenlé and J. Millet. Toulouse: Privat.

Thaler, R. and Sunstein, C. (2008) *Nudge. Improving Decisions about Health, Wealth, and Happiness.* New Haven, CT: Yale University Press.

Vayre, J.-S. (2014) "Manipuler les données. Documenter le marché. Les implications organisationnelles du mouvement big data," *Les Cahiers du numérique*, 10(1): 95–125.

Vayre, J.-S., Larnaudie, L., Dufresne, A. and Lemercier, C. (2016) "Effet distracteur des agents de recommandation et stratégies de navigation des consommateurs: le cas de l'agent de DataCrawler," *Revue des Interactions Humaines Médiatisées*, 17, 1.

5 Extending the mind

Digital devices and the transformation of consumer practices

Rebecca Jenkins and Janice Denegri-Knott

Introduction

Artificial intelligence that can change the way we live is less of a future possibility and more a present reality. Social robots that help the elderly, play children's games and learn from their environment in order to adapt and interact with humans are some of the latest breakthroughs (Honigsbaum, 2013). Such technological developments may make some people feel uneasy – perhaps a car's cruise control function or robot vacuum cleaners are more familiar robotic technology advances that rest more comfortably with people. Even less extreme but much more common technological advances see the use of digital devices and software applications being adopted by many and integrated into their everyday lives. For instance, wearable technology and fitness and weight loss apps that track performance, set goals and provide progress reports were amongst the most popular smartphone apps of 2015 (Techradar, 2015). GPS on smartphones is offered via map apps such as Google Maps, so there is little need to know where you are going or prepare a journey in advance or even be able to read a map accurately. Apps such as Timehop remind users of specific memories once posted on social networks, providing personalized material to reflect on and be nostalgic about. In relation to consumer practices, a wide variety of applications are routinely used via smartphones, tablets and laptop computers, and are consequently changing the way people engage in practices and the ways they consume more generally. For instance, 100 million monthly active users of Pinterest search, pin and share things they desire (*Fortune*, 2015) and can make purchases of these objects via the site. Nearly 50% of people reported using their smartphones while shopping for food and a third use their smartphones to find recipes as a matter of routine (Allrecipes.com, 2013). What these examples tell us is that there is a growing delegation of everyday practices to digital technology.

In this chapter we explore the growing digitalization of consumer practices from a perspective of how human and non-human actors come together in configuring such practices. We draw on practice theory – an accepted and growing area of work in consumer research – to introduce the foundational concept of human–non-human hybrids. We then focus particularly on the ways in which consumers' cognitive abilities are apparently extended by and externalized to digital technologies and use the concept of the extended mind (Clark and Chalmers, 1998) to develop this line of thinking. In particular, we focus on consumers' knowledge, imagination and memory related to a given practice or consumption object. To do this, we draw on data from a large, ongoing study related to digital virtual consumption conducted over the last eight years, which enables us to consider how digital devices and the various platforms and software applications that are accessed through them are integrated in and consequently shape consumer practices. We identify the kinds of new work that is required from consumers in terms of using digital technology – i.e. developing skills, knowledge, competence and a commitment to their use. We also consider the implications of this for practice and for the consumption experience.

Digital devices as consumer mind extensions

Our starting point is that know-how is central to carrying out any practice. Know-how or competence is best understood as distributed between the practitioner, other people, her tools and her materials (Watson and Shove, 2008). This translates into functioning human–non-human hybrids (Latour, 1993), companion species (Haraway, 1991) or co-agents (Michael, 2000) through which interconnected expertise and skills embodied in humans and embedded in non-human companions (Dant, 2005) coalesce in practice. Thus – and to borrow from Watson and Shove's (2008) example of fast-drying paint – painting, like other practices, is something achieved in the "doing" that brings together disparate and fragmented forms of knowledge (in the human, in the paint, the brushes and their relation to the door being painted). Knowledge scattered across these points is actively woven together.

A consumer using digital devices to construct desire for an object, or seeking knowledge to carry out practices, like cooking or motoring, is a very different consumer, with a new repertoire of capabilities and skills. This does not mean that the consumer has become less skilled, but rather that a redistribution of skills between people and technology taken place in practice. In this redistribution, the non-human companion, whether it is the shopping cart (Cochoy, 2008), the freezer (Hand and Shove, 2007) or the digital device, comes to absorb some of the competence and knowledge, and therefore agency, previously embodied in the individual carrying out the practice. If we accept that possibility – that consumers and artefacts are best approached not as discrete entities but rather as hybrids – then the suggestion that digital devices and consumers form a hybrid cognitive system is palatable. After all, what is scattered across material artefacts and instruction manuals that spell out how properly to use these in practice is written about at the level of knowledge. Watson and Shove (2008) write about "hybridised and distributed knowledge systems", and Dant (2005) differentiates between embodied human knowledge and embedded non-human knowledge, and those captured in instruction manuals. How do we describe, then, the knowledge captured by the digital device?

We use the concept of extended mind as a framework to answer this question and to deliver a more fine-tuned understanding of the ways in which consumer practices are digitalized. The premise of Clark and Chalmers's (1998) work on extended mind recognizes that humans make use of and rely on various external sources to enhance their cognitive abilities, which consequently inform and transform the practices in which they engage. As a simple example, when I use a mobile phone to call someone, I do not need to remember the telephone number – the phone does that for me by saving the name and number in a list of contacts. In this way, much cognitive work is "delegated to manipulations of external media" (Clark and Chalmers, 1998, p. 8). When the mind is linked with an external entity (by entity our focus here is on digital devices and the software applications accessed through them), there is a two-way interaction which creates what Clark and Chalmers (1998) regard as a coupled system, and this, they argue, creates a cognitive system in its own right. So long as the external resources are available when needed, they are coupled with the individual in a reliable manner. According to their thesis, digital devices (i.e. an external entity) are just as much part of cognition as the brain itself, to the point that if the device is not accessible, the behaviour (or practice) cannot be performed with the same level of competence. To return to the earlier example, if my mobile phone battery has died, I cannot call a particular person because I do not know the telephone number as a result of having come to rely heavily on the phone.

In the marketplace, apps are sold on this very basis. For instance, Evernote is marketed as an app to "organise your life's work" (Evernote, 2015). It saves everything you need to do, buy and remember, across your devices. The app does everything for you, but there needs to be a successful, reliable pairing between app and user for the cognitive system to work effectively. That is, the app needs to be there and work when required, such that it becomes "part of the basic package of cognitive resources" that one uses in everyday life (Clark and Chalmers, 1998, p. 11). The phone and its apps that are used and relied upon are an extension of the mind. What may seem like action-based tasks, such as using a pen and paper to help with long division or rearranging Scrabble tiles on a tray or accessing an app via a smartphone, are, from this perspective, regarded as part of cognition rather than action (Clark and Chalmers, 1998). In terms of consumption-based contexts, we can see how desiring practices are delegated to digital devices, for instance when saving objects in an online wish list, one no longer needs to remember or think about what they desire as it is safely stored for them (Denegri-Knott and Molesworth, 2013). Ideas for what to purchase are provided by website recommendations based on previous browsing and purchase behaviour. Likewise, inspiration for how to decorate or what to cook or sew is provided via desirable images that have been stored and shared on platforms such as Pinterest.

What becomes apparent is that not only does an app or device need to be readily available, but the user needs to develop particular skills, knowledge and competence in using it (and in the case of Evernote, across a variety of devices) to allow for effective pairing to occur. Accessing the app or entity is not enough. When it comes to digital devices and software, we note a shift in focus where the individual must also become a competent user of technology. Indeed, paired or coupled systems are regarded as fragile, as they can easily become uncoupled (Clark and Chalmers, 1998).

We want to consider how digital devices and their software applications become part of the package of cognitive resources in relation to consumer practices and the implications of this for consumers and for consumption. In the following sections we focus on particular ways in which digital devices/ software applications extend the mind, in terms of knowledge related to particular practices and their role in relation to imagination and memory. In particular we focus on the level of commitment in practice and consider the issues arising in terms of a shift from practice/consumption to becoming a competent and committed user of the technology itself.

Methods

We draw on data from a large, ongoing study of digital virtual consumption undertaken with avid digital technology users living in the south of England. The most recent study was of 29 enthusiastic home cooks who use digital devices in the practice of cooking, conducted in 2014/15. The second was a study of 20 wish-list users, undertaken by student research assistants in 2012, which considers the role of software-based shopping aids such as Amazon wish lists, eBay auction watch lists and Google shopping lists in terms of how these website functions interact with the imagination and subsequent consumer desire and actualization. The third was a study of 40 avid eBay users, conducted between 2008 and 2010. All participants were self-selected and recruited through personal referrals.

In line with existing work that documents and explores consumer practices we conducted interpretive in-depth interviews (Watson and Shove, 2008; Denegri-Knott and Jenkins, 2016). We gained a highly contextualized description of consumers' experiences with and usage of digital devices by concentrating our data collection and interpretation on these experiences, and meanings consumers attributed to them (Creswell, 2007; Goulding, 2005; Thompson et al., 1989). Our primary interest was in understanding the intersection between consumer practices and the use of technology with the aim to appraise how digital devices were integrated into everyday practices like meal preparation or consumer orientated practices such as managing wish lists and using eBay for inspiration for things to buy. As such, participants demonstrated their use of technology and how they engaged in a specific practice, which enabled us to capture the connection between those two. Following interpretive research conventions, the sample for each study was relatively small since the aim was to attain variation in experiences (Creswell, 2007; Thompson et al., 1989), not to attain a statistically representative sample or produce generalizable theory.

Most of the interviews were held at respondents' homes, with a handful taking place in coffee shops and on our university campus. The in-home context was useful as it gave insight into the broader ecology of digital devices, material objects and people implicated in practices narrated by our respondents. Throughout the interview process, all informants had access to a digital device. This was important, as it allowed participants to refer to recent and more distant experiences as well as to show interviewers processes followed. We asked grand tour questions (McCracken, 1988) to generate biographical data and a broader understanding of the context in which experiences with digital devices took place.

On average, interviews lasted approximately 70 minutes, with individual interviews ranging from one hour to three hours in length. In total approximately 100 hours of data were recorded. Each interview was transcribed verbatim and read carefully and repeatedly by an interpretative group of researchers to develop theory. Data interpretation took place by way of a hermeneutical circle involving a part-to-whole reading, made up of individual interpretation of interviews at an ideographic level and cross-case analysis (Thompson et al., 1989). Descriptive accounts of these experiences were derived from this exercise. This was followed by syntheses via which global themes were articulated and built upon for theoretical elaboration (Goulding, 2005; Spiggle, 1994).

A series of steps were taken not to compromise the authenticity and trustworthiness of interpretations (Thompson et al., 1989; Thompson and Haytko, 1997; Hogg and MacLaran, 2008). Researchers contributing to this project formed an interpretative group responsible for the data interpretation, which facilitated the bracketing process, thus limiting overt biases in the data interpretation (Hogg and MacLaran, 2008). During the interview process participants were asked if experiences captured were accurate and they were given the opportunity to read the finished work and provide commentary. Email exchanges followed interview sessions with some respondents with whom we continued to discuss emergent themes, and this helped us in re-thinking and fine-tuning interpretations.

Findings

In the following section we consider three specific ways in which digital devices, and the software applications accessed through them, extend the mind when it comes to consumer practices: knowledge, imagination and memory. A productive way to better understand such a relationship is to approach both consumers and devices as part of a cognitive system where consumers' cognitive abilities are extended. Furthering practice-orientated studies in consumer research (Warde, 2005), we draw attention to how the cognitive or knowledge-based elements in practices – general understandings, explicit rules and principles, and level of commitment (Schatzki, 1996) – are redistributed in consumer–digital device cognitive systems. Where other studies have shown teleo-affective structures and level of commitment as having a driving force in how practices are carried out (Schatzki, 1996; Watson and Shove, 2008), here we show how non-human agents in practice (like a digital device) have a role in moderating the level of commitment. In effect, we show how digital devices are experienced as absorbing consumers' commitment to carrying out practices – in particular with respect to the acquisition and storage of know-how in practice. We conclude that in addition to the redistribution of skill and competence in human–tool hybrids in practice already identified in the literature (Watson and Shove, 2008; Hand and Shove, 2007), commitment too is redistributed.

In concluding, we discuss the consequences of the integration of digital devices in practice and consumption and consider how new practices are required and developed in terms of the individual becoming a competent user of digital devices and associated software applications, such that the use of digital devices becomes a practice in and of itself requiring its own set of skills, competence, knowledge and commitment. Finally we consider this as a refocusing of desire, from desire for goods or desire to be a competent practitioner to a desire for being a competent user of digital devices and applications.

Extended knowledge

Digital devices are both epistemic objects of consumption and mind extensions. As knowledge projects for consumers they make accessible knowledge that is ontologically liquid, meaning that it is in a state of flux and ill defined, and thus inciting consumers to initiate acts of discovery (Knorr Cetina, 2001; Zwick and Dholakia, 2006). As mind-extending devices, they appear to both absorb and extend some of the cognitive work implicated in practice.

For example, many of our home cooks reported that they had substantially expanded the repertoire of meals they now cooked on an everyday basis as well as how they had increased the complexity of the meal projects they took on as a result of integrating digital devices in the practice of cooking. Carmen, who lives with her boyfriend and does most of the cooking in the household, described herself as an adventurous cook. She told us that a weekly vegetable box delivery often provided new, exciting ingredients that required her to research ways of using them, locating new recipes online and experimenting. Home cooks would also use their devices to find out about certain ingredients, to find out what to substitute for an ingredient, and to help with more technical aspects of food projects. Self-professed "cowboy cook" Rosie explained how she had dabbled with infused oils in the past, but locating online resources meant she could do it "properly". This resulted in great success – making flavoured oils that were balanced and would last – including how to sterilize the bottle, quantities of ingredients and preserving the final product. Knowledge is extended because digital devices and their extensive applications provide more resources to make use of, thereby enhancing cognitive ability and the practice itself, such that they become just as much part of the cognitive process as the brain itself (Clark and Chalmers, 1998).

Digital devices also offer help with specific knowledges and skills that our home cooks were lacking. For instance, one participant told us about how YouTube provided her with the means to de-shell scallops:

> He brings me fresh scallops and I didn't know how to open them or what to do with them so watched some videos on YouTube showing me how they are going and how they open them. You know, just getting some thinking from it.
>
> (Rina, 35)

Here the digital platform enables Rina to gain knowledge but also learn a new skill and enhance her kitchen repertoire.

Our participants often retold the time spent trying to find a useful instructional video, or accurate information on how to spot fake merchandise, as enjoyable. Albert, an engineer we interviewed alongside his wife, lived in a large bungalow in the countryside. He had a keen interest in tractors and refurbishing motorhomes, and had spent many hours "figuring out the value of these things" and "how best to renovate them". Alongside specialist magazines and visits to dealerships, Albert and his wife had learned much about motorhomes by monitoring eBay listings. Even in situations when they were unsuccessful with their bidding, Albert told us that he thought he had made progress because he:

> Was still building up my own knowledge about what was good and what was bad. So it was like, well, it looks good and I think I'd be happy with it but I'm not sure so the bid was still low. But then as I started to build up my experience of what was good and what was bad and what we needed as well ... We realized very quickly that there are very few motorhomes that look the same, there is no standard unit, every one of them is completely different. So just going and thinking, yes, I want the bed here or I want the kitchen there and we'd have to fold that out and put it back, and all of that stuff, we just realized there is so much out there.

Albert and his wife soon realized that there was no standard unit and that aspects like kitchen placement and multifunctional furniture were important. In building a better understanding of what was needed in order to complete a project (refurbishing a motorhome, cooking or completing a collection), we noted how commitment to carrying out a practice also meant commitment to becoming more skilled at "extending their mind". In effect, the alignment of consumer and device in consumer–digital device cognitive systems is maintained by the object-orientated practices linking consumers to their devices. To borrow from Knorr Cetina (2001, p. 185), it is because as epistemic objects, digital devices offer partial glimpses that imply what is missing and "suggest which ways to look further through the insufficiencies they display". Doing this is, as previous studies on epistemic objects indicate, an affectively charged affair, because it produces an intense desire to explore (Knorr Cetina, 2001; Zwick and Dholakia, 2006).

Albert and other participants like Steve, who collected luxury watches, become more knowledgeable about the product categories they were interested in. Effort and time expended in doing so often meant that the search for knowledge eclipsed or at least competed with our participants' commitment to completing practice-related goals (cooking a meal, completing a collection). Take Dom, for example, who was collecting figurines on behalf of his future mother-in-law and in the process became very skilled at finding rare items at bargain prices. We interviewed him in a dining room that housed an impressive collection of up to 500 *Camberwick Green* figures that were neatly displayed in two cabinets. He told us how much he enjoyed researching ways to find figurines at bargain prices:

> I found this American website, this sounds so sad and anorak-y. I found this American website, you'd put what you were searching for so like Camberwick Green. So you'd put Camberwick Green into this American search engine. It would then search the English eBay but it would search it for spelling mistakes because obviously with eBay whatever you type that's what it looks for. When you did this thing with this other website it was searching for maybe 500 variations of the words Camberwick Green.

He told us how he felt when "finding them, especially if they were spelt wrong", and how he missed it "because it was exciting and he was very good at it".

Extended imagination

Inspiration for objects of desire is acknowledged as something that can be generated externally, for instance from the media, via observation of other people, through the Internet and various platforms associated with it. Studies acknowledge the role of magazines (Belk, 2001; Stevens and MacLaran, 2005), catalogues (Clarke, 1998), window shopping, television and film (Belk et al., 2003) as resources inducing desire, stimulating the imagination and, in turn, actual consumption. Our studies of digital virtual consumption, technology users and imagination indicate that digital devices and platforms take this further. They do not simply provide inspiration to intensify desire but extend the imagination by way of taking on some of the cognitive work that is required by the consumer in order to locate objects of desire, to fuel desire, and to find inspiration for a particular consumer practice. Beyond offering fodder for the imagination, digital devices become consumer mind extensions – becoming the default go-to device to find inspiration, even doing some of the desiring work that was the domain of consumers, as they become human–digital device hybrids.

For many of our participants their digital devices are seen as extensions of their imagination – extending their cognitive ability. For example, in our study of home cooks, digital devices provide ways to get ideas for what to cook, whether it is finding inspiration or fulfilling a pre-existing desire for a particular dish. Many of the cooks told us that they look to digital devices for inspiration; specifically, they used food-based smartphone apps, YouTube channels and Internet searches for recipes and meal ideas, often based on particular ingredients they had available or needed to use up, and then let the device determine what to cook. For instance, one keen cook described her own ideas for using up a butternut squash in a soup as "quite boring", and so delegated to Google to locate more interesting and inspiring dishes for the ingredient, where she found a recipe for a curry instead.

The notion that the Internet offers more exciting options was particularly salient when cooking for other people and wanting to showcase cooking skills. For example, new food blogger Sarah, who had recently moved in with her boyfriend, described her cookbooks as "for us in the week" because they have a number of chefs and recipes that they like and rely on, but when trying something new she defers to the Internet, which offers more variety so she can weigh up her options:

> I use the Internet when I want to try something new that I thought of. So if I was looking for inspiration for something, I wouldn't go to our cookbooks, I would go to the Internet and just do a search and look at lots of different things. A lot of the time it will come down to how easy it is and what ingredients are in it and if I have got it already or if I have to make a special trip somewhere to go and get it. So I like to look at the options. I wouldn't say I go onto one website and that's it, unless it's a really amazing recipe. I do like to look at lots of different things.

Beyond delegating to the Internet to find greater inspiration, it is also apparent that certain platforms offer the user suggestions based on previous behaviour and searches. For instance, one participant told us about his use of YouTube videos, describing them as "quite smart" because of the suggestions they provided for him: "every time I use YouTube I usually watch the videos YouTube have suggested to me" (Jim, 24). Jim does not have a particular ingredient or occasion in mind but gets inspiration from YouTube based on his use of the site's channels, thereby potentially providing even greater inspiration that is not constrained by any initial thought, food or other criteria.

In relation to looking for inspiration and igniting the imagination, it is evident that the universe of potential things to desire is experienced as significantly expanded and continuously unfolding. As noted previously, here digital devices as both epistemic objects of consumption and mind extending become knowledge projects for consumers, making knowledge accessible and inciting acts of discovery (Knorr Cetina, 2001; Zwick and Dholakia, 2006). In being open ended and complex, digital devices and their associated software platforms mean there are always more or different things to be found and desired. Because the digital devices never stop signalling the possibility that new information, tutorials or item images are about to be found, this ignites cycles of revelation for consumers, and these cycles produce a sense that the mind is being extended. In consumer–digital device cognitive systems, the ability to imagine is redistributed in ways that, as we show in our examples below, are experienced by our participants as enhancing the amount of resources to feed into consumers' imagination but also consumers' skills to imagine.

Often the digital device is awarded agency in shaping what consumers want. Clarissa, one of our participants, reported feelings of intoxicated excitement upon discovering a multitude of sewing patterns she could find on eBay. When we interviewed Clarissa, she was living in a semi-detached home with her children. She had purchased a bundle of sewing patterns and was in the midst of sorting them out on a kitchen table when we first arrived. She told us how she got carried away, finding an incredible array of variety from international sellers which ensured there was always something new and different to look at. As Clarissa later told us, when she had struggled to visualize what an Indian outfit looked like, eBay had "shown her". The platform device did this by producing results to a search for Indian outfits: "I found out by looking at Indian clothing. I could actually identify which outfit I was looking for." She later explains:

> I wasn't looking for saris, I was looking for this type of [peshawari] or whatever outfit. So then I can go back up and search on [peshawari] and then it brings up all these different outfits. There was just nothing that I thought "that's really nice". It was beautiful embroidery on polyester and I thought that just doesn't feel right.

Note in these narratives how Clarissa, Sarah and Jim experience their digital devices as enhancing their ability to see what a peshawari looks like and what meal to prepare by creating clearly discernible and comparable choices that can be returned to. Choices are returned to, studied, evaluated and compared, such that the ability to imagine is enhanced, as a result of the time they have invested in searching online.

The redistribution of imagination in consumer–digital device practices produced different states of commitment and affect. Some participants remarked on how, in awarding the device agency in looking and finding things to buy, their commitment to acquiring them had been reduced. One of our participants, reflecting on the contents of his Amazon wish list, remarked on how over time, jeans, T-shirts and other items stored had become "boring to him". Others, like Dom, had stopped his obsessive use of eBay searching through the listings. Instead, the search itself had been delegated to the device. He told us: "I set up these alerts on eBay for each of the codes of each piece. So eBay would then email me or send me a message when something was listed." This, Dom told us, made it too easy and too mechanical an operation to hold his interest over time. This distribution of agency within the consumer–digital device cognitive system meant that only the device was entrusted a key role in finding new figurines to add to the collection, but also the fun associated with the search, often highlighted in the literature on consumer desire and imagination (Belk et al., 2003; Campbell, 1987), cut short. Over time this seemed to reduce commitment to the object of consumption but also the practice of searching.

This example illustrates how digital devices begin to take on some of the work that was previously considered to be done by the consumer in relation to desiring practices (see Denegri-Knott and Molesworth, 2013). Less agency is required from the consumer because websites and software locate better objects or projects and make consumers desire more because they provide options the individual had not thought of. If we consider Pinterest, this platform constantly provides new things for users to desire – whether it is an object to purchase, a style to recreate, a recipe to cook or a craft to make. It becomes a repository for things one desires, but also provides continuous inspiration for more ideas, for more projects, for more things to desire. The individual no longer needs to keep a scrapbook of cuttings from various sources but can simply "pin" things that are presented, such that it too does desiring and indeed remembering for us, efficiently storing ideas and objects that can be returned to (or not), which leads us now to consider the notion of extended memory.

Extended memory

When we refer to extended memory, we acknowledge the role of digital devices in terms of the storage, safe keeping and retrieval of things we desire – objects we want to own, or projects we want to complete. In a consumer–digital device cognitive system, consumers' ability to store and retrieve information, instructions, images and tutorials was experienced as being extended. For active externalists (see Menary, 2010; Clark and Chalmers, 1998), the external memory embedded in digital devices and consumers' internal memory complement one another in carrying out cognitive tasks in practice. In this way digital devices are experienced as taking on some of the work previously carried out by other consumer-cognitive systems, like a consumer manually writing up a wish list or referring to a cookbook. The operation of successful consumer–digital device cognitive systems is reliant on information retrieved from the digital device being endorsed more or less automatically.

This being the case, consumers must ensure that know-how embedded in the digital device is easily accessible (Menary, 2010; Clark and Chalmers, 1998), and this is reliant on easy retrieval of stored know-how.

Participants talked about objects and recipes being safe once stored on a digital device. In relation to the practice of cooking, participants tended to bookmark recipes, create folders to store recipes in, collect recipes on Pinterest and sometimes print them out to keep a hard copy in a folder. In relation to consumption objects, individuals added items to their online wish list or shopping basket, where it would be kept for later consideration or purchase. By storing objects of desire or practice-related content electronically or online, consumers use such devices as an extension of their memory – they are relieved of the need to remember for themselves. In terms of cooking, with the sheer volume of recipes available and used by our cooks, this was felt to be a necessary part of the practice, to the point that there was no desire to memorize recipes or even to memorize which website a preferred or successful recipe came from; instead we note a conscious delegation of memory to device. Adventurous cook Carmen explained how she bookmarked recipes she particularly enjoys, and now has a "huge long list under Food Folder", which she has kept to go back to because "I'm terrible really. I just won't remember kind of what I need to put in it or what I need to do, so as long as I have got it there I'm kind of safe and then I can add a few bits to it" (Carmen, 35).

For some, more involved practices were engaged in. One participant, Pamela, a self-taught cake decorator, likes to take photos of her cake-decorating projects, which she started when her daughter was small, to remember the projects she has achieved. Originally she started a hard-copy album for cakes that pre-date digital photography. She showed us how she now saves them to her iPad and has a Dropbox account created especially to back up and organize different folders related to her cooking, baking and cake-decorating projects. Pamela also describes how this was a solution to the problem of not remembering where she found certain recipes:

> [W]hen I created it, it links to my iPhone. I keep recipes as well as photos on Dropbox. Where I've been finding recipes online I then couldn't find them so I started taking photographs of them and saving the photos and it's backed up to the Dropbox.

Aspects of remembering are performed in conjunction with digital devices – the iPhone, iPad, laptop and apps like Dropbox – such that these have become a requisite part of the consumer–digital device hybrid. They have become part of what Clark and Chalmers (1998) refer to as the cognitive resources that individuals bring to bear on their everyday life. This conscious delegation of memory to devices changes the practice of cooking and consequently the specific things that individuals need to remember. No longer do we have to remember recipes, but where they are stored, how they are stored and be able to source them when required. For many, this was locating bookmarked web pages or recalling particular websites that certain recipes were on: this was one of the ways in which our home cooks extended their memory capability. Remembering or memory changes with the integration of digital devices and becomes about accessing stored information and using specific digital tools, rather than remembering content, details and specifics.

For practices like producing wish lists, our participants often spoke about their digital device as "remembering" for them. Albert, the motorhome enthusiast, felt that his engineering background conferred on him a disciplined approach to his eBay-ing. He described his use of eBay as fastidiously efficient. He kept all his past searches and items he had been monitoring – this for him was important, even if items had been sold because it gave him "a bit of history":

> A lot of those have actually sold but it still gives me a bit of history. So if I see something else I could think, well, I'll definitely watch this and see what the thing's sold for. That helps me judge what I can sensibly bid for something else that comes up.

Curiously he also felt comforted by the fact that he did not have to think about items individually, as they were stored in his "My eBay" area. Over time, Albert felt that he had been a little bit relaxed in carrying out his research and this ultimately ended in him purchasing a Smart car quite impulsively.

In these examples we can see digital devices extending memory. We also observe less commitment to actively remembering know-how in carrying out practices. The functions offered by the devices and platforms become extensions of one's mind, enhancing cognitive abilities, prompting memory, but we also observe a delegation of cognitive function to device here (Clark and Chalmers, 1998). The result of this is that the human agent is then freed up to engage in other activities – the burden of consumer desire or of commitment to practise is delegated to the device, only to be "picked up" again by the brain when the consumer is free to do so. This seems to transform the teleo-affective structure (Schatzki, 1996) of desiring practices, making the affective component less salient, and altering the focus from end purposes to being more task or project orientated.

Consequences and implications for the extended mind

Integration of digital devices/software applications changes the nature of cognition required to engage in a range of everyday practices. In extending knowledge, consumers need to know how to use devices, sites and apps. They do not need to retain this information necessarily, but know where to look for it and how to find it, and this in itself requires specific skills and a commitment to extending the mind. At times, extending knowledge becomes more important than the practice or end goal, and it is digital devices and their associated apps and platforms that enable this to be the case.

The extended imagination also relies on knowing where to look, what keywords to use, how to navigate sites and platforms like Pinterest, Google Images, YouTube and food blogs. In helping consumers locate objects of desire, fuel desire and find inspiration, digital devices become the go-to devices, relied upon because they produce more exciting options than one can imagine alone. In prompting and inspiring, digital devices extend imaginative skills providing ever more options and opportunities for desire and imagining. They can also ease the burden of desire as they take on some of the cognitive work previously carried out by consumers when they are awarded agency, which results in a reduction in commitment on behalf of the individual as imagining and desiring are redistributed to the digital device (Denegri-Knott and Molesworth, 2013).

The extended memory relies on specific ways of storing and retrieving. The nature of memory, or remembering, changes in that consumers do not need to remember content or information but how to access it. There is a clear redistribution of memory here as the external digital device takes on some of the work that the internal (human) memory used to do – as such, there is less commitment to actually remembering. Of course, the sheer volume of objects and projects available via digital devices potentially requires this development in memory as the endless possibilities could not otherwise be effectively managed.

In extending knowledge, imagination and memory, it is evident that the use of digital devices becomes a practice in itself, requiring skill, competence and knowledge. Skills are required to manage and maintain wish lists, to set up and use auction-sniping software effectively, and to store countless recipes so that individuals do not need to think about objects of desire or future meal projects. This results in new practices being required and developed in order to become a competent user of digital devices and their associated platforms, as well as a commitment to these new practices.

Moreover, we can notice a refocusing of desire – a desire to master the use of apps, the desire to become a more competent wish-list user, eBay-er or practitioner; the consumer–digital device cognitive system needs to be worked at and maintained. It also broadens desire – for example, cooking becomes not only about producing nice meals but learning new techniques, learning about new ingredients and impressing other people. The need to acquire and develop skills and competence to access content (to access the extended imagination, the extended memory or extended knowledge) when needed means technology introduces a broadening of what consumer practices may mean. There is also a redistribution of commitment when "work" (imagining, remembering, knowing) is delegated to or distributed between human and non-human agents. Whereas a scrapbook may be a curation of the things one desires to remind, to obtain pleasure from, to fuel desire and to compensate (act as surrogate experience), digital devices and platforms invite us to curate and store more things than we might ever want or be able to actualize. Such platforms and devices act as a holding place for our desires, and a consequence of this is that the focus of desire shifts from the object to the platform – that is, rather than simply desiring to be a better cook and searching for recipes and foods to make, we may locate other related artefacts, such as health and nutrition information such that Pinterest, for example, broadens what it means to cook. The practice is transformed as new cycles of discovery emerge (Knorr Cetina, 2001).

Conclusions

We have explored particular ways in which the mind is extended via the integration of digital devices and their associated software applications in everyday consumer practices. Such integration changes the nature of cognition and consequently changes consumer behaviour (Clark and Chalmers, 1998). Overall, our work contributes to a finer understanding of the cognitive dimension of consumer practices. Whereas other work tends to be more focused on the social and cultural (for example, Molander's (2011) work on motherhood), our approach provides us with an enhanced understanding of cognitive tasks and projects, and the relationship or pairing between user and technology that form part of these. Conceptually, our work makes a contribution in terms of integrating the concept of extended to the study of practices. As we have shown in this chapter, while this framework is well established in philosophy, it provides consumer researchers and practice sociologists with a new vocabulary to deal with the growing digitalization of consumer and other everyday practices. Although it may be argued that this is a narrower focus than other approaches, such as practice theory or actor-network theory (ANT) would consider – for example, ANT would look at broader networks of actants – it does enable us to bring into sharper focus how the cognitive dimension of practice is coupled to digital devices.

There are, of course, other aspects of the extended mind that might usefully be considered in consumption studies regarding the role of external entities, which we have not been able to do here but see value in future research exploring. First, given the fragile nature of consumer–digital device cognitive systems (Clark and Chalmers, 1998), there is potential work to be done on the consequences of failed systems. That is, what happens when internal (cognition) and external features (digital devices) are not effectively aligned, such as when the external features are not available or are removed; when a recipe is no longer available, when an object of desire is no longer for sale, or when a website or app cannot be accessed? This is particularly prevalent when we consider extended memory. Some of our cooking participants talked about bookmarking and making hard copies of digital recipes (saving, printing, writing down), indicating a potential fear of being without them, not being able to locate them, and not wanting to forget them. If the digital sources are not available, what happens to practices (skills, knowledge, competences)?

What are the behavioural and indeed emotional implications for consumers? How do practices change or adapt as a result? What coping mechanisms do consumers have when such experiences occur? If, as Clark and Chalmers (1998) state, we have come to rely on external entities so heavily – to the point where the brain may even have evolved as a result – how do we cope when they are not available and the consumer–digital device hybrid fails?

Second, Clark and Chalmers (1998) also highlight the socially extended mind in terms of other people and our networks being part of an extended cognitive system. Social networking sites and apps that we have considered here as digitally based mind extensions might be usefully explored in terms of this. For instance, YouTube, Pinterest, blogs and reviews are all based on information or experiences that other people have provided and shared, of which the individual makes sense. These form part of "socially extended cognition" – when other people (their beliefs, knowledge, experience) act as an external feature. Digital devices potentially open up a much larger socially extended cognition, and understanding how consumers navigate, understand and make use of this could shed new light on our understanding of social networks for consumption and consumer practices.

References

Allrecipes.com (2013) Allrecipes surveys thousands of cooks worldwide to capture global digital food trends. Available at: press.allrecipes.com/press/allrecipes-sur veys-thousands-of-cooks-worldwide-to-capture-global-digital-food-trends/ [accessed: 23/06/2014].

Belk, R.W. (2001) Speciality magazines and flights of fancy: Feeding the desire to desire. In Groeppel-Klien, A. and Esch, F.-R. (eds) *European Advances in Consumer Research* Vol. 5. Provo, UT: Association for Consumer Research, pp. 197–202.

Belk, R.W., Ger, G. and Askergaard, S. (2003) The fire of desire: A multisited inquiry into consumer passion. *Journal of Consumer Research* 30(3): 326–351.

Burawoy, M. (1991) The extended case method. In M. Burawoy, ed., *Ethnography Unbound*. Berkeley: University of California Press, pp. 271–287.

Campbell, C. (1987) *The Romantic Ethic and the Spirit of Modern Consumerism*. Oxford: Blackwell.

Clark, A. and Chalmers, D. (1998) The extended mind. *Analysis* 58(1): 7–19.

Clarke, A.J. (1998) Window shopping at home: Classifieds, catalogues and new consumer skills. In Daniel Miller, ed., *Material Cultures: Why Some Things Matter*. London: UCL Press, pp. 73–99.

Cochoy, F. (2008) Calculation, qualculation, calqulation: Shopping cart arithmetic, equipped cognition and the clustered consumer. *Marketing Theory* 8(1): 15–44.

Creswell, J.W. (2007) *Qualitative Inquiry and Research Design: Choosing Among Five Approaches* (second edn). Thousand Oaks, CA: Sage.

Dant, T. (2005) *Materiality and Society*. Maidenhead: Open University Press

Denegri-Knott, J. and Jenkins, B. (2016) The digital virtual dimension of the meal. In Capellini, B., Marshall, D. and Parsons, E. (eds) *The Practice of the Meal*. London: Routledge, 107–122.

Denegri-Knott, J. and Molesworth, M. (2013) Redistributed consumer desire in digital virtual worlds of consumption [in special issue: Virtual Worlds]. *Journal of Marketing Management* 29(13–14): 1561–1579 (doi:10.1080/0267257X.2013.821420).

Evernote (2015) evernote.com.

Fortune (2015) fortune.com/2015/09/17/pinterest-hits-100-million-users/ [accessed: 03/03/2016].

Goulding, C. (2005) Grounded theory, ethnography and phenomenology: A comparative analysis of three qualitative strategies for marketing research. *European Journal of Marketing* 39(3/4): 294–309.

Hand, M. and Shove, E. (2007) Condensing practices: Ways of living with the freezer. *Journal of Consumer Culture* 7(1): 79–104.

Haraway, Donna (1991) *Simions, Cyborgs and Women: The Reinvention of Nature.* Oxford: Routledge.

Hogg, M.K. and MacLaran, P. (2008) Rhetorical issues in writing interpretivist consumer research. *Qualitative Market Research: An International Journal* 11(2): 130–146.

Honigsbaum, M. (2013) Meet the new generation of robots. They're almost human … *The Guardian*, 15 September. www.theguardian.com/technology/2013/sep/15/robot-almost-human-icub [accessed: 29/09/2015].

Knorr Cetina, K.D. (2001) Post-social relations: Theorizing sociality in a post-social environment. In Ritzer, G. and Smart, B. (eds) *Handbook of Social Theory.* London and Thousands Oaks, CA: Sage, pp. 520–537.

Latour, B. (1993) *We Have Never Been Modern.* Hemel Hempstead: Harvester Wheatsheaf.

McCracken, G. (1988) *The Long Interview.* London: Sage.

Menary, R. (2010) *The Extended Mind.* Boston, MA: Massachusetts Institute of Technology.

Michael, M. (2000) *Reconnecting Culture, Technology and Nature: From Society to Heterogeneity.* London: Routledge.

Molander, S. (2011) Food, love and meta-practices: A study of everyday dinner consumption among single mothers. In Belk, R.W., Grayson, K., Muñiz, A.M. and Jensen Schau, H. (eds) *Research in Consumer Behavior* Vol. 13. Emerald Group Publishing Limited, pp. 77–92.

Schatzki, T. (1996) *Social Practices: A Wittgensteinian Approach to Human Activity and the Social.* Cambridge: Cambridge University Press.

Spiggle, S. (1994) Analysis and interpretation of qualitative data in consumer research. *Journal of Consumer Research* 21(3): 491–503.

Stevens, L. and MacLaran, P. (2005) Exploring the "shopping imaginary": The dreamworld of women's magazines. *Journal of Consumer Behaviour* 4(4): 282–292.

Strauss, A. and Corbin, J. (1998) *Basics of Qualitative Research: Techniques and Procedures for Developing Grounded Theory.* Thousand Oaks, CA: Sage.

Techradar (2015) www.techradar.com/news/phone-and-communications/mobile-phones/top-210-best-android-apps-2013-693696 [accessed: 29/09/2015].

Thompson, C.J. and Haytko, D.L. (1997) Speaking of fashion: Consumers' uses of fashion discourses and the appropriation of countervailing cultural meanings. *Journal of Consumer Research* 24(1): 15–42.

Thompson, C.J., Pollio, H.R. and Locander, W.B. (1989) Putting consumer experience back into consumer research: The philosophy and method of existential-phenomenology. *Journal of Consumer Research* 16 (September): 133–146.

Warde, A. (2005) Consumption and theories of practice. *Journal of Consumer Culture* 5(2): 131–154.

Watson, M. and Shove, E. (2008) Product, competence, project and practice. DIY and the dynamics of craft consumption. *Journal of Consumer Culture* 8(1): 69–89.

Zwick, D. (2006) The epistemic consumption object and postsocial consumption: Expanding consumer-object theory in consumer research. *Culture, Markets, and Consumption* 9(1): 17–43.

Zwick, D. and Dholakia, N. (2006) Bringing the market to life: Screen aesthetics and the epistemic consumption object. *Marketing Theory* 6(1): 41–62.

6 Promoting ethical consumption

The construction of smartphone apps as "ethical" choice prescribers

Lena Hansson

Introduction

Along with the advent of the Internet and digital technologies and even more intensively since the entrance of the second wave of Internet, commonly referred to as Web 2.0, non-governmental organizations (NGOs) and social movements concerned with ethical issues (such as human welfare, animal welfare and environmental welfare) have been taking advantage of information and communications technology (ICT) to communicate, educate and inform about corporate practices, products and campaigns, thus engaging consumers in their causes and trying to make them more ethically orientated on the market (Graham and Haarstad, 2011; Lekakis, 2013). However, although conscious consumers want to stay informed, the abundance of available information makes even the most knowledgeable consumers uncertain and insecure about how to behave ethically (Boström and Klintman, 2009). So consumers' quest for information about ethical issues is not always followed by a change in consumption patterns or a move towards more ethical choices (see Lekakis, 2014). This aligns with many consumer behaviour studies reporting that although consumers seem increasingly interested in ethical consumption, a change in consumption behaviour is much less apparent (Carrington et al., 2010; De Pelsmacker et al., 2005; Carrigan and Attalla, 2001). Furthermore, consumers may be concerned about more than one ethical issue (Low and Davenport, 2007; Connolly and Shaw, 2006; De Pelsmacker et al., 2005), increasing the complexity of behaving correctly and choosing the right products on the market. Could the arrival of new mobile technology such as smartphones and other handheld electronic communication devices together with software applications, so called "apps", change this? Such devices have become ubiquitous in the lives of their users (Goggin, 2011, p. 152; Shankar et al., 2010, p. 112), and allow market actors to communicate and interact with consumers at any time and wherever they are, and consumers are in turn given new capabilities to go about their consumption practices tracing product information, calculating and comparing products (Cochoy, 2008; Licoppe, 2008).

More recently, smartphone "apps" aimed at assisting consumers to make more "ethically" informed decisions concerning consumption have appeared on the market, such as GoodGuide (rating products), Boycott, Cruelty Free (promoting non-animal-tested products), Seafood Watch (informing about fish and seafood), and iRecycle. There are also a number of fair trade apps, such as GoFair. Do these kinds of digital devices have the capacity to make consumers engage in ethical consumption?

Three of this kind of smartphone app, the Fairtrade app, GreenGuide, and Shopgun which appeared on the Swedish market between 2012 and 2014, will be looked at more closely and analysed as "market devices" with the aim of understanding how they shape and promote ethical consumption.

A large body of previous research on ethical consumption has focused on the individual consumer perspective and consumers' behaviour (e.g. De Pelsmacker et al., 2005; Carrigan and Attalla, 2001), motivations and attitudes (e.g. McEachern and McClean, 2002) and decision making (e.g. Gregory-Smith et al., 2013; Young et al., 2010; Shaw et al., 2006), and more recent studies on the social and cultural aspects of ethical consumption (Pecoraro and Uusitalo, 2014; Moisander, 2007; Barnett et al., 2005). This chapter will focus on the role that market devices may play (Cochoy, 2011; Callon et al., 2007) in ethical consumption and contributing to a socio-materialized understanding of ethics and ethical consumption, a more uncommon approach in studies of ethical consumption (for exceptions, see Sörum and Fuentes, 2016; Fuentes, 2014b; Hobson, 2006).

In line with this, the purpose of this chapter is to examine and describe how ethics is "built in" or constructed in the smartphone apps and how this influences ethical consumption. Ethical consumption "carries a plurality of ethical stances that range from environmentalism to solidarity to fair trade to health to community support" (Cherrier, 2007, p. 321). However, ethics is also understood as something engineered into technological objects since they can be designed to "persuade" consumers to act in particular ways and even change their behaviour, i.e. what Guthrie (2013) refers to as "smart technology", giving them a moral dimension. Both understandings of ethics are embraced in this study and how "ethics" is being incorporated into the smartphone apps is studied empirically through an "object ethnography" (Carrington, 2012), and a cross-case analysis is carried out to distinguish and understand the specific ways these devices configure ethics, both in terms of what ethical aspects are considered and what it means to behave in an "ethical" way. The analysis discloses how these "ethical" smartphone apps are scripted to work as ethical choice prescribers and the implication of this for ethical consumption is discussed.

Next, the theoretical framework that this chapter draws on will be discussed, followed by a description of the method and the collected empirical material. I then present the findings and thereafter discuss it, and end with some conclusive remarks about the impact ethical smartphone apps can have as digital mobile devices for the shaping and promotion of ethical consumption.

Theoretical framework – market devices and the scripting of ethics

In an attempt to understand the role that smartphone apps can play in enabling and enhancing ethical consumption, these apps will in this chapter be conceptualized as "market devices", i.e. as "material and discursive assemblages that intervene in the construction of markets" (Callon et al., 2007, p. 2). The concept implies that it is not just human actors that are involved in the construction of markets, but as much non-humans such as material objects, technology, tools and other "market things" (Cochoy, 2011). Moreover, market devices can be ascribed agency; they act or they make others act (Callon et al., 2007). That is, they come to work as market actors, but, depending on their assemblage or how they are constructed, they act or do things differently. Employing this approach in the study of ethical smartphone apps makes it possible to emphasize the socio-material (including technical) aspects of the configuration of ethical consumption, but also the diversity of possible configurations (Callon and Muniesa, 2005). So how the app will act depends on its construction.

I will draw on the literature of socio-technical "scripting" (Latour, 2002; Akrich, 1992) to analyse the construction of ethical smartphone apps as market devices. When developed and designed, objects and devices are inscribed with ideas about their meaning and use based on the views of users, that is, materialized in the objects as prescriptions that shape actions, i.e. what the objects allow or forbid the actor to do and what they anticipate (Hansson, 2007; Ingram et al., 2007; Latour, 2002; Akrich, 1992). These actions can be referred to as "scripts" and, as they are embedded in an object, they can be "read" and interpreted as text (Carrington, 2012). Jelsma (2003) explains the reading of scripts as the reading of a text in which the author guides the reader in a specific direction. In a similar way, a user of a device is directed or encouraged to perform certain actions. Devices can thus be argued to be inscribed with what can be called "morality" or ethics, i.e. how to behave, since they can be designed to "persuade" us to act in a certain way and even change our behaviour and make decisions for us (Guthrie, 2013; Verbeek, 2006). It is this notion that is of particular interest in this chapter, since I want to explore how ethics is inscribed and thus materialized in the smartphone apps studied – that is, both in terms of how they are designed or constructed to prescribe consumers to act in specific ways, and what kind of ethical aspects are inscribed. Ethics in relation to consumption encompasses a wide array of issues related to human welfare, animal welfare and/or environmental welfare (Miele and Evans, 2010; Connolly and Prothero, 2008; Low and Davenport, 2007; De Pelsmacker et al., 2005).

Drawing on a socio-material approach to marketing practices, Fuentes (2014b) argues that products are also inscribed with specific moralities. Illustrated by the example of the "Save the Arctic Fox" T-shirt from the Nordic Nature Shop, Fuentes describes how a specific environmental morality, in this case biological diversity, is created and attached to this object through a process of socio-material scripting involving marketing practices of display-ing, attending and selling. In this way, products are constructed as green or ethical and linked to a "specific set of understandings and ideas of right or wrong" (ibid., p. 110). In a similar way, ethical product labels can be under-stood as being inscribed with specific certification standards, like Fairtrade, that link this specific ethical world to the labelled product (Neyland and Simakova, 2009). This chapter will depart from the understanding that "what counts as ethical is by no means stable or straightforward" (ibid., p. 785), since ethics is configured in different ways depending on whose perspective is used as a frame in the development and marketing of products.

Being inscribed with particular ethical issues, products can become quali-fied as "ethical" and "singled out" as market choices to consider in the mar-ketplace. Reijonen and Tryggestad (2012) use the concept of "qualification" (see Callon et al., 2002) to analyse how the quality of environmental friend-liness can be constructed with the help of visual image and text signs, what they call "inscription devices", to qualify it as an important property to con-sider for market actors. The qualification of products is carried out in a pro-cess that includes a number of "calculative" tasks, as explained by Callon and Muniesa (2005). For products or entities to be qualified, they first need to be detached from other contexts, classified, sorted or listed to make them com-parable, and then displayed. The properties such as function, aesthetics, ethics, quality, etc., used to compare or qualify products become in the next step a basis for an evaluation or calculation from which a result can be cal-culated and obtained, such as prescriptions of choice, price, etc. According to Mallard (2007), qualification foregoes choosing, and prescription supports the calculation of choice. The calculation can, according to Callon and Muniesa (2005), range from a more qualitative judgement of "qualculation" to a more quantitative (or numeric) "calculation" depending on the task of the market device and within which space the calculation takes place.

Cochoy (2004, 2008) has advanced the understanding of calculation within retailing and consumption, describing how the framing and making of con-sumer choice take place in stores and where the act of calculation is dis-tributed among several actors (producers, marketers, retailers, consumers) and material settings, such as packaging, signing, marketing, shopping lists and the shopping trolley. He introduces and adds new concepts to that of "calculation" to explain the different ways the shopping trolley is used and takes part in making consumer choice in relation to other material settings such as shopping lists, packaging, etc. ("qualculation") and other people involved in the shopping ("calqulation"), calculations that are based on more qualitative judgement (Cochoy, 2008). As a market device, the shopping trol-ley can be viewed as a "calculative space" (Callon et al., 2002), and so can the smartphone apps studied in this chapter. The concepts of qualification, qualculation and calculation will be used to explain how smartphone apps as market devices take part in the making of market choice for ethical consumption.

Method – an object ethnography of smartphone apps

The study in this chapter is based on an "object ethnography" (Carrington, 2012) of three smartphone apps – the Fairtrade app, the GreenGuide app and the Shopgun app – and includes digital observations and interviewing. At the time of the study, these smartphone apps were among the best known on the Swedish market in terms of use and attention given in media and by users on social media. The apps were chosen to consider some of the diversity of ethical consumption, since this encompasses many different "ethical" issues that consider human welfare, animal welfare and environmental welfare (Miele and Evans, 2010; Connolly and Prothero, 2008; Low and Davenport, 2007; De Pelsmacker et al., 2005). Moreover, as will be outlined in the analysis in the next section, the architecture and construction of the apps also varies in terms of how they are organized and what functions and content are included.

Adopting an object ethnographic approach was motivated by the focus on an artefact (Carrington, 2012), in this case smartphone apps constructed in socio-material networks and consisting of software, i.e. code, that becomes materialized as an application through a smartphone.

The chapter draws on three kinds of collected material. First, *interviews* were carried out with representatives of the owner organizations behind the apps: with the communications manager at Fairtrade Sweden, the owner of the Fairtrade app, which works to increase the supply of and demand for fairtrade-labelled products in order to enable producers to improve their working and living conditions (Fairtrade, 2014a); the department manager for consumer issues at the Swedish Society for Nature Conservation (SSNC), Sweden's largest NGO focusing on the environment (Naturskyddsföreningen, 2014) and owner of GreenGuide; and the founder of Consumentor, the economic association that developed the Shopgun app as a tool for sustainable consumption (Consumentor, 2014), and one of its engineers.

The *interviews* provided an understanding of the context in which the apps were developed and evolved around questions about the idea of the app, the design of the app, the imagined user, and how the app was marketed. The interviews were carried out between May 2013 and January 2014 and lasted between 75 and 120 minutes. They were all recorded and then transcribed.

Second, in addition to the interviews, the owners' *websites* and the *platforms for downloading apps* (iTunes and Google Play) were observed, and web pages were sampled to study the descriptions and marketing of the three apps studied.

Third, *observations* of the smartphone apps were made and documented through hundreds of "screenshots" (of the interfaces) taken when going through the apps in a systematic way to gain an understanding of the overview of the apps, their structure and menus, functions and content.

In the analysis, a close *"reading"* of the smartphone apps and their "scripts", i.e. actions that are prescribed by the material layouts (Jelsma,

2003), was conducted in order to examine how ethics is "constructed" or "built into" these smartphone apps. This technique is based on the premise that all artefacts contain scripts embedded in the artefact during the design process and that can be read and interpreted by a user (Carrington, 2012; Verbeek, 2006; Akrich, 1992), and thus also by researchers. Also the interview transcripts and the website screenshots "read" to interpret the relation between the scripts of the apps and the owners' intentions and expectations of the use and meaning of the apps, i.e. the inscriptions based on the owners' consumer images and views on ethical consumption.

In the first rounds of analysis, several consumer images emerge in the smartphone apps. There is a *conscious consumer* who is somewhat aware and interested in ethical issues; an *information-seeking consumer* who needs or wants information; closely related to the heavily inscribed *choosing consumer*, who in the model of consumers as decision makers requires information about options to make the "right" decision (Connolly and Prothero, 2008). In addition, a *social and cultural consumer* is visible and prescribed to participate in ethical consumption, and displaying as well as sharing the engagement with others on social media (for a more extended view on this see Sörum and Fuentes, 2016, and in this volume).

Since I am interested in examining how ethics is being incorporated into the smartphone apps, I chose in the second rounds of analysis to study more narrowly how the inscription of the choosing consumer, as the most prevailing consumer image in the smartphone apps, comes to prescribe how to act, i.e. as scripts of "choosing" in an ethical way. Furthermore, a cross-case analysis of the scripts of the smartphone apps discloses the specific ways these devices qualify and calculate market choice.

In the findings, the descriptions of the inscriptions and scripts of the smartphone apps are primarily based on the "readings" of the screen shots. In addition, accounts from interviews and the owner organizations' websites are included when needed to illustrate the intended meanings and use of the apps.

Findings – unfolding smartphone apps as "calculative" market devices

The focus of the findings is to disclose how the image of the "choosing consumer" comes to script what to choose and how "to choose" ethically. Furthermore, the concepts of "qualification", "qualculation" and "calculation" (Reijonen and Tryggestad, 2012; Cochoy, 2008; Callon and Muniesa, 2005) are used to demonstrate how ethical choice is created through an act of qualification and prescription of choice.

The findings are presented in three parts. In the first part, it will be described how the "choosing consumer" is embedded in the apps. In the second part the ways in which products and practices are qualified as "ethical" in the smartphone apps are described, and in the third and last part, the prescription of "ethical" choices is outlined.

How to be or become an "ethical" consumer – the choosing consumer

In the interviews, all the owners reflect in different ways that it is not easy for consumers to act ethically on the market, even if they wish to, and this is the reason why they developed the smartphone apps. Also, consumer studies of "ethical" behaviour report that even knowledgeable consumers do not feel sure how to behave ethically (Boström and Klintman, 2009) and this might be the reason why an interest in ethical consumption does not result in more ethical choices (see Lekakis, 2014; Carrington et al., 2010).

The idea that the apps should help consumers make ethical choices is reflected in the way the owners talk about their apps. Fairtrade Sweden, the owner of the Fairtrade app, argues for the app like this:

> how does one get Fairtrade into consumers' everyday life when they stand in front of the shelf in-store choose correct [products].
>
> (Fairtrade Sweden, owner interview)

This is further reflected in the promotional texts on the organizations' websites. On the SSNC's website, the GreenGuide app:

> think it should be easy to choose correctly – and who likes the idea of a green world to leave behind to the grandchildren.
>
> (Naturskyddsföreningen, 2014)

And Consumentor promote Shopgun as follows:

> your purchase choices make a difference, and together we have power to change!
>
> (Shopgun, 2014)

Thus, the image of a "choosing consumer" comes out strongly. Choice is assumed to be one of the core values for consumers and consumerism (Gabriel and Lang, 2006). The abundance of choice in contemporary societies, or what Mick, Broniarczyk and Haidt (2004) refer to as "consumer hyperchoice", leads to time-stressed consumers who experience information fatigue, indecisiveness in the quest to keep up with all choice possibilities. However, for consumers searching for "ethical" products, it is rather a problem of finding the right choice in stores, a lack of relevant information and handling contradictory information about ethical issues, which makes even well-informed and knowledgeable consumers uncertain and insecure about how to behave ethically (Boström and Klintman, 2009; De Pelsmacker et al., 2005). This aligns with the image of the "conscious consumer", that is, a consumer who has some level of awareness and interest and who wants to engage in choosing the "right" products, which is also prominent in the talk about the apps. For instance, the GreenGuide app is viewed by the owner as an initiator for those consumers who are interested in environmental issues but have yet to take the step to act. The app should guide the consumer in how to do things in a positive way. The "easy step" may be "to move the hand on the shelf, to choose non-bleached instead of bleached", but does not require any fundamental change of behaviour (SSNC, owner interview).

The images of the conscious and choosing consumer support the idea of an individual consumer who needs information in order to make well-informed decisions about consumer choice. This is a common view of ethical consumption in much research (see for instance, Young et al., 2010; Carrigan and Attalla, 2001).

The images of a choosing consumer as presented above are inscribed in the apps and translated into prescriptions of how to act, i.e. as scripts of "choosing". This became very obvious in the analysis of the smartphone apps, and will be described more thoroughly in the coming sections.

The qualification of ethics

In order for consumers to act ethically and make the right choices, or for the smartphone apps to prescribe the same, products (and practices) must first be evaluated or classified as "ethical". How the smartphone apps are scripted to do this will be explained and discussed as a "qualification" process that is performed by the smartphone apps. The information incorporated in the apps, both as product information and expert advice, constitutes the basis for the qualification process. What ethical aspects are promoted differs between the smartphone apps since they are inscribed with different kinds of ethics.

The Fairtrade label as a qualifier

In the Fairtrade app, products are classified or qualified as ethical if they are certified and carry the Fairtrade label. The label stands as a guarantee for the product to live up to the requirements set by the Fairtrade Labelling Organizations International (FLO) group. This is an international umbrella organization that develops criteria and supports farmers and employees in countries with severe poverty, and consists of national labelling initiatives, Fairtrade Sweden being one of them (Fairtrade, 2015). The Fairtrade app thus frames and qualifies fair trade as defined by the FLO. However, the FLO's Fairtrade label is only one among many fair-trade labelling initiatives. Each has its own certification grounds, which means that the app thus inscribes a certain kind of "fairness" (Neyland and Simakova, 2009, p. 785).

All Fairtrade-labelled products are registered in an international Fairtrade product database that is technically linked to the app (Fairtrade Sweden, owner interview). The information that is displayed for specific products are: a visual image of the product if available, or only the Fairtrade label; the generic product name; the brand (manufacturer); the size available; the distributor; whether it is an ecological product or not (about 70% of Fairtrade products are double labelled); and whether it can be found in a store. For example, among the 55 products within the app's "flower" category find mixed bouquets, with roses.

Products are also evaluated through the use of the app's scanning function. When scanning a product's barcode, the product will be compared with registered products in the database in order to confirm whether it is Fairtrade-labelled or not, i.e. qualified as ethical or not. Furthermore, the app lists retail brands/stores (classified as to how big an assortment of Fairtrade-labelled products they carry in percentage terms), and the locations of cafés, restaurants, hotels and filling stations that serve Fairtrade-labelled products. Their geographic locations can be found using the GPS navigation function in the app, provided by Google Maps.

Algorithmic qualification of fairness, environmental friendliness and health

For a product to go through the qualification process in Shopgun, it must be registered with a unique GTIN (global trade item number) in the standardized international product database. The product information that is stored in the database is reachable via the app's free text search function or via the scanner function that "reads" a product's barcode (i.e. its GTIN). The information that is displayed through this task is the specific product and the brand/company – for instance, ecological milk. Linked to this is additional information in the form of external expert advice about a product.

The external advisers are specially chosen by Consumentor's mentor board (Shopgun, 2014), and both Fairtrade Sweden and SSNC along with "Swedwatch" and consumer associations such as "Conscious consumption" and "Sweden's Consumers" (Shopgun, 2014) are. Consumentor, the owner, is very careful to add its own advice since they do not consider themselves experts but rather "ordinary consumers" who care about ethical issues (Consumentor, owner interview).

Shopgun thus relies on external advisers for the qualification of products, that is, the information that is provided to evaluate a product based on its ingredients and information about the brand/company. The advice from external advisers in Shopgun is inscribed as "buying advice", and a product can be linked to a number of pieces of advice or recommendations depending on its ingredients (Figure 6.1).

Shopgun focuses on three ethical aspects – ethics (fairness), environment and health (no sugar and chemical ingredients) – that are used in the qualification of products. Products are qualified on the basis of how fair (ethics), green (environment), and/or healthy they are. This is "qualculated" with the help of an algorithm that counts the number of pieces of expert advice related to a specific product and its ingredients. The result of this calculation of the three ethical aspects, i.e. the weighted advice, is presented in a pie chart that displays the ethical qualification of a product. Depending on how many of the three aspects are considered in the calculation (which in turn depends on whether there is expert advice the ingredients in a product), the percentage for each aspect displayed will differ. Also, the weighted result is colour coded to resemble a traffic light, as was explained by the developer: a fair product signals green, less fair signals yellow and a non-fair product signals red.

Qualified expert advice for environmentally friendly everyday practices

In the GreenGuide app it is practices rather than products that are qualified, although practices involve the use of products. The qualification of practices in the app is performed by the professional experts at SSNC working with environmental issues such as sea and fishing; environmental toxins; agriculture and food; climate, energy and transport; and forests and conservation (Naturskyddsföreningen, 2014). Knowledge of these issues is inscribed in the app as expert advice about what practices to focus on and how to behave in an ethical way. The practices are categories in a number of areas such as how to "detox the kitchen", "clean the house", "act green at the office", etc. Moreover, what to eat is an "ethical" issue and advice is given in the "Fish chooser" about what to eat and what to avoid: "Let the eel keep swimming", because "since the 1950s 99 out of 100 eels have disappeared from European coasts. You can help us fight for the eel by turning down the eel on the Christmas table and in your sushi" (Fish chooser advice, the GreenGuide).

Thus, the expert advice qualifies what fish are ethical or not. All advice in the GreenGuide app is related to environmental issues and it is behaving in a more environmental friendly way that is inscribed in the app and qualifies products and practices as "ethical".

Traceability and transparency as a qualifying magnifier

Trust or trustworthiness from the owners' point of view is inscribed in the apps by using expert advice, internal in the GreenGuide app and external in Shopgun, and through label and producer stories in the Fairtrade app. For instance, the product databases used in the Fairtrade app and in Shopgun reveal information that is usually invisible to consumers, which increases market transparency when displayed in the qualification process.

Furthermore, so-called "producer stories" are inscribed in the Fairtrade app as texts with pictures of the producers and their crops, and through short movies. These stories are linked to products from specific regions or countries of origin. For Fairtrade Sweden, it is important that these are authentic stories, told by the producers themselves with their own "voices", and not stories told about them (Fairtrade Sweden, owner interview). In this way, they are supposed to play on the individual's ethical obligation to others (see e.g. Shaw and Shiu, 2002) so as to persuade consumers to buy more Fairtrade products.

The qualification of products (and practices) as ethical in the apps is strengthened by the inscriptions of traceability and transparency. This provides trustworthiness, something considered important since consumers' disbelief in the claims made is a risk in ethical consumption (De Pelsmacker et al., 2005).

Figure 6.1 Buying advice from an expert adviser

Figure 6.2 Product information and the result of the qualification calculation

Prescribing "ethical" behaviour

As was shown in the previous section, the smartphone apps qualify ethics in different ways and based on different ethical issues. In this section will be presented how from the qualification carried out, prescribe specific kinds of "ethical" behaviour; that is, how choice is constructed and prescribed.

Prescribing complex choice

The qualification act and the prescription of choice are closely related in Shopgun, and while the product information database plays an important part in both cases, so does the expert advice. In Shopgun, the expert advice is used in two different ways in the prescription of choice. First, it is used to "qualculate" whether a product is, and to what extent it is, "fair", "green" and/or "healthy", equivalent to the qualification process described earlier. The result, weighted and displayed as coloured slices in the pie chart, is also used to decide what product to choose: green (good); yellow (both good and bad); red (bad). Considering the number of ingredients a product may contain, the calculation of those in relation to the three core aspects of ethics, environment and health makes the complexity of choice obvious. However, the colour system scripts an easy way to choose the "right" product for the individual consumer, i.e. if it shows green, then it is just a matter of going ahead, or if it shows red, then do not buy it. However, this result conceals the complex "qualculation" that has been made to qualify the products in terms of the three aspects.

So, dependent on what layer of information is used for making a choice, the choice is more or less complex. The first layer displays the information as prescription in the pie chart. The user is thus given a signal of what is acceptable to buy and what is not, depending on the result. However, since the algorithm calculates on the basis of the three aspects, respectively, the signal system can give contradictory advice concerning ethics, environment and health. For instance, if a product calculation shows red for health, it is a bad choice, but it may at the same time show green for ethics, which indicates a good choice. So, if the consumer wants to know more about what ingredients the result is based on and the related advice on which the calculation is made, then they can read the expert advice displayed in the written text. This constitutes the second layer of information in the prescription phase.

Prescribing closed choice

For consumers to be acting ethically, they are in the Fairtrade app prescribed to search for and choose Fairtrade-labelled products, either in the product list provided in the app or by searching for products elsewhere, such as in stores. With the help of the scanning function, it is possible to scan a product's bar-code and see whether it is labelled and thus can be found in the product database. If a product is scanned that is not fair, i.e. not Fairtrade labelled, a message will turn up on the screen saying "Oops, Fairtrade-labelled (zero)". Fairtrade Sweden hopes that this message will make the consumer reject the product, or "make the consumer think twice" (Fairtrade Sweden, owner interview). Thus, behaving fairly is not just about choosing the "right" product, but equally importantly it is to avoid and not to choose the "wrong" products, i.e. non-labelled. Stores and cafés along with other establishments that have Fairtrade-labelled products in their assortment are also prescribed as good choices to visit, as they are qualified as "ethical".

Prescribing practices or open choice

The GreenGuide does not provide any possibility of searching for products, since it is inscribed with advice that does not prescribe specific products but rather some generic ones (such as what fish to choose or avoid) and it does not have a scanning function, unlike the other apps. This is because the owner is sceptical of the assumption that consumers would take the time and engage in scanning products in the store:

> Hello, wait a minute, what do consumers want to do, do they want to go around and scan things in the store? Well, maybe some do, but ... I'm imagining people, stressed out on a Friday evening, running around with their mobile phone in their hand and in-store ... with a list of things ...
>
> (SSNC, owner interview)

Instead, the focus of GreenGuide is on prescribing what practices and areas of consumption are troublesome and need to be addressed. The app includes advice about what products to choose or avoid, but also which ones to get rid of. The app thus prescribes ways to change one's everyday life so as to become more environmentally friendly. Although the app does not prescribe specific products it still comes down to choosing to carry out specific practices (which also involves choosing and using products) and to act in the "right" way.

The prescription of ethical behaviour – from open to closed choice

As was shown above, the product information databases are important actors in qualifying products but also in the prescription of choice in both the Fairtrade app and Shopgun. However, while the Fairtrade app only has labelled products to handle, approximately 4,100 products, Shopgun uses an open database system, and the scope of products is thus much wider in Shopgun and allows a greater variation of product choices for consumers.

However, choice is framed differently in the apps and thus prescribes particular ways of behaving in an ethical way. The GreenGuide app prescribes free or "open choice" as long as consumers act and consume in an environmentally friendly way and thus align their everyday practices to this quest.

The "qualculation" that is carried out can be defined as a qualitative judgement (Callon and Muniesa, 2005), since it is based on expert advice. The same goes for the Fairtrade app, although the "qualculation" is based on the standards set by Fairtrade and inscribed in the label.

However, the Fairtrade app prescribes a "closed choice", i.e. Fairtrade-labelled products that align with Fairtrade Sweden's overall goal, to increase sales of Fairtrade-labelled products for the good of their producers (Fairtrade, 2014a). The app does it in different ways, helping consumers to locate Fairtrade-labelled products; by scanning products, presenting the supply of products in different store chains, and navigating users to cafés and restaurants serving their products. An "ethical" consumer in the Fairtrade app is therefore someone who chooses Fairtrade-labelled products at all times.

Shopgun relies on product choice, but prescribes a "complex choice" since it is three-dimensional, evaluating environment, ethics and health, and does not provide a conclusive result. Instead, the choice is open in that the pie chart needs to be interpreted and each dimension possibly further evaluated. The calculation that takes place is "algorithmically formulated" and thus quantitative in nature (Callon and Muniesa, 2005), although based on qualitative information, i.e. expert advice similar to the GreenGuide app. Moreover, the script of choice is also flexible in Shopgun, since it is possible to make changes in the evaluation or calibration of the three aspects of ethics, environment and health in relation to preferences of what values are most important for an individual consumer. It is through the choice of products from the right producers or with the "right" ingredients that consumers become responsible for their own health and that of their next of kin, other people's situations and being kind to the Earth.

The way that choice is framed, from open to closed, indicates different levels of flexibility in the prescribed actions but also different degrees of force inscribed in acting in a specific way or making a specific choice (Jelsma, 2003). The open choice implies a weaker moral script and the closed choice a stronger one, i.e. to what degree it is forcing someone to perform it without the possibility to opt out. So, to conclude, the smartphone apps shape different "ethical" choosing consumers.

Discussion and conclusions: the shaping and promotion of ethical consumption

As the previous sections have shown, as market devices the smartphone apps frame and prescribe different ethics, i.e. particular ethical issues are inscribed and how to behave in an "ethical" way is prescribed. As a result, the apps are scripted to work as *"ethical" choice prescribers*. There are different kinds of what Mallard refers to as "consumerist prescribers" that aid in qualifying goods in the marketplace and "carry out a 'pre-computation' of the purchasing act: choose first, then (maybe) buy" (Mallard, 2007, p. 156). Thus, they disengage consumers from the commercial act in space and time. The smartphone apps can be discussed in relation to this kind of "calculative" market device, as they are intended to disrupt consumers' routine way of shopping and choosing "conventional" products, i.e. bad products. However, contrary to disengaging consumers from the commercial act, the smartphone apps can guide the consumers during the commercial act. By means of the scanning function, the Fairtrade app and Shopgun qualify scanned products through their barcodes and prescribe consumers to act on their calculated recommendations, select the "right" products on the shelves, i.e. choose ethical ones and reject "conventional" or unethical ones. In the best cases, they will counteract the market devices that guide consumers in stores to make certain choices, from assortment displays, product packaging, signage, promotions, salespersons, etc. In addition, the Fairtrade app also prescribes choice of stores, cafés, restaurants, etc., increasing the possibility of finding ethical products.

The GreenGuide is scripted to guide consumers towards more environmentally friendly practices in everyday life. Although the app does not calculate specific choices, it still involves choosing the "right" products (and avoiding "bad" ones) when carrying out a practice. Emphasizing practices might be a successful strategy, as Røpke (2009) argues that in order to afford sustainable consumption, one should target "practices", what consumers do with the products they buy, and no change is possible if these efforts do not fit in with consumers' everyday lives.

As market devices these "ethical" smartphone apps thus have the potential to guide consumers to make the "right" choices and act in an ethical way. The knowledge from the owners (NGOs and a consumer association) and their expert advisers is distributed to the smartphone apps when inscribed, and the competence required to make the right choices or behave "ethically" has been delegated to the smartphone apps. So, equipped with the smartphone apps, any consumer can become "competent" enough to act in the marketplace in an ethical way regardless of their level of knowledge and skills. Working as choice prescribers, these digital devices can disrupt consumers from making bad choices, i.e. choosing conventional products, instead directing them to ethical options. In this way, the smartphone apps make it easier to "choose correctly". Since, as Connolly and Prothero (2008, p. 141), state, "making the right choice involves a questioning of what is the 'right choice'", these market devices can reduce some of the complexity of engaging in ethical consumption (e.g. Fuentes, 2014a; Moisander, 2007) and ease some of the anxiety in choosing wrong or "bad" products among all available options, by saving time and effort.

Obviously, the smartphone apps' scripts imply that the way for consumers to act "ethically" is more or less merely through consumption and making individual and particular "ethical" consumer choices. This individualistic view of ethical consumption framed in the construction of the smartphone apps is also commonly found in research on ethical consumption which focuses on individual consumers' ethical decision making (Chatzidakis et al., 2012; Cherrier, 2007) and their consumption choices (Moisander et al., 2010; Rokka and Moisander, 2009). However, contrary to this view, what this chapter discloses is that ethical consumption is in fact not an individual consumer act in that market devices, in this case smartphone apps, are involved and take part in shaping ethical choice and promoting ethical consumption. They come to act as ethical agents on the market but do it differently dependent on what understanding of ethics and ethical behaviour has been "built in" and materialized. This materialization of ethics is built on the owners' and expert advisers' knowledge and view of ethical consumption, as well as on designs and technical constructions.

The market devices' roles as ethical market actors are made possible by digital technology, in this case the Internet, digital databases, scanning software, application software and smartphones, etc. As ubiquitous mobile and digital devices, the "ethical" smartphone apps can extract information and make it accessible instantly, but they can also prescribe ethical market choices, whenever and wherever consumers are. These characteristics make them go beyond the task of merely informing and promoting ethical consumption since they have the ability to "nudge" consumers to choose "ethical" options as the prescription of choice is "made by" the smartphone apps. Moreover, it brings them closer to consumers and their purchase decisions than ever before.

For promoters of ethical consumption such as NGOs, these new kinds of market devices ought to be very useful when the goal is to make consumers change their behaviour towards more ethical consumption, something that had proven harder than expected, even among consumers who might be interested in ethical issues (Carrington et al., 2010; De Pelsmacker et al., 2005; Carrigan and Attalla, 2001). For consumers it might be either positive or negative, depending on their level of engagement in and view of ethical consumption. Although it can be argued that these market devices have the possibility to extend consumers' abilities to make well-informed "ethical" market and consumption choices, delegating ethical judgements to them narrows the scope of ethical commitments as they at the same time govern the choices and the ways of engaging in ethical consumption. Since they promote ethical commitments based on consumption and to a great extent commercial choices, alternative modes of ethical behaviour or ways to express ethical commitments, such as engaging in community-supported consumption or resisting consumption altogether by downsizing (e.g. voluntary simplicity) (Cherrier, 2007; Barnett et al., 2005), are disregarded. However, in the end, whether ethical smartphone apps become important market devices in shaping and promoting ethical consumption or not depends on if and how consumers use them or follow the scripts. That is another story, and one not told in this chapter. It would be an interesting and valuable continuation of this study.

References

Akrich, M. (1992) The De-Scription of Technical Objects. In Bijker, W.E., and Law, J. (eds) *Shaping Technology/Building Society. Studies in Sociotechnical Change.* Cambridge, MA: The MIT Press, pp. 205–224.

Barnett, C., Cafaro, P., and Newholm, T. (2005) Philosophy and Ethical Consumption. In Harrison, R., Newholm, T., and Shaw, D. (eds) *The Ethical Consumer*. Sage, pp. 11–24.

Boström, M., and Klintman, M. (2009) The green political food consumer: A critical analysis of the research and policies. *Anthropology of Food*, S5.

Callon, M., and Law, J. (2005) On qualculation, agency, and otherness. *Environment and Planning D: Society and Space*, 23(5): 717–733.

Callon, M., Méadel, C., and Rabeharisoa, V. (2002) The economy of qualities. *Economy and Society*, 31(2): 194–217.

Callon, M., Millo, Y., and Muniesa, F. (eds) (2007) *Market Devices*. London: Blackwell.

Callon, M., and Muniesa, F. (2005) Peripheral vision economic markets as calculative collective devices. *Organization Studies*, 26(8): 1229–1250.

Carrigan, M., and Attalla, A. (2001) The myth of the ethical consumer – do ethics matter in purchase behaviour? *Journal of Consumer Marketing*, 18(7): 560–578.

Carrington, M., Neville, B. and Whitwell, G. (2010) Why ethical consumers don't walk their talk: Towards a framework for understanding the gap between the ethical purchase intentions and actual buying behaviour of ethically minded consumers. *Journal of Business Ethics*, 97: 139–158.

Carrington, V. (2012) "There's no going back." Roxie's iPhone®: An object ethnography. *Language and Literacy*, 14(2): 27–40.

Chatzidakis, A., Maclaran, P., and Bradshaw, A. (2012) Heterotopian space and the utopics of ethical and green consumption. *Journal of Marketing Management*, 28(3–4): 494–515.

Cherrier, H. (2007) Ethical consumption practices: Co-production of self-expression and social recognition. *Journal of Consumer Behaviour*, 6(5): 321–335.

Cochoy, F. (2004) Is the Modern Consumer a Buridian's Donkey? Product Packaging and Consumer Choice. In Ekström, K.M., and Brembeck, H. (eds) *Elusive Consumption*. Oxford: Berg, pp. 205–227.

Cochoy, F. (2008) Calculation, qualculation, calqulation: Shopping cart arithmetic, equipped cognition and the clustered consumer. *Marketing Theory*, 8(1): 15–44.

Cochoy, F. (2010) Reconnecting Marketing to "Market-Things": How Grocery Equipment Drove Modern Consumption (*Progressive Grocer*, 1929–1959). In Araujo, L., Finch, J., and Kjellberg, H. (eds) *Reconnecting Marketing to Markets*. Oxford: Oxford University Press, pp. 29–49.

Cochoy, F. (2011) "Market-things inside": Insights from Progressive Grocer (United States, 1929–1959). *Inside Marketing: Practices, Ideologies, Devices*, 58–84.

Cochoy, F. (2014) Consumers at work, or curiosity at play? Revisiting the prosumption/value cocreation debate with smartphones and two-dimensional bar codes. *Marketing Theory*, 15(2): 133–153.

Connolly, J., and Prothero, A. (2008) Green consumption. Life-politics, risk and contradictions. *Journal of Consumer Culture*, 8(1): 114–145.

Connolly, J., and Shaw, D. (2006) Identifying fair trade in consumption choice. *Journal of Strategic Marketing*, 14(4): 353–368.

Consumentor (2014) www.consumentor.org/om-oss/ [accessed 13-10-2014].

De Pelsmacker, P., Driesen, L., and Rayp, G. (2005) Do consumers care about ethics? Willingness to pay for fair-trade coffee. *Journal of Consumer Affairs*, 39, 363–385.

Fairtrade (2014a). www.fairtrade.se [accessed 13-10-2014].

Fairtrade (2014b). fairtrade.se/inspiration-material/mobilapp/ [accessed 13-10-2014].

Fairtrade (2015) fairtrade.se/om-fairtrade/internationellt/ [accessed 14-10-2015].

Fuentes, C. (2014a). Managing green complexities: Consumers' strategies and techniques for greener shopping. *International Journal of Consumer Studies*, 38: 485–492.

Fuentes, C. (2014b). Green materialities: Marketing and the socio-material construction of green products. *Business Strategy and the Environment*, 23: 105–116.

Fuentes, C. (2015) Images of responsible consumers: Organizing the marketing of sustainability. *International Journal of Retail and Distribution Management*, 43(4–5): 367–385.

Gabriel, Y., and Lang, T. (2006). *The Unmanageable Consumer*. Cambridge: Cambridge University Press.

Goggin, G. (2011) Ubiquitous apps: Politics of openness in global mobile cultures. *Digital Creativity*, 22(3): 148–159.

Graham, M., and Haarstad, H. (2011) Transparency and development: Ethical consumption through Web 2.0 and the Internet of things. *Information Technologies & International Development*, 7(1): 1–11.

Gregory-Smith, D., Smith, A., and Winklhofer, H. (2013) Emotions and dissonance in "ethical" consumption choices. *Journal of Marketing Management*, 29(11–12): 1201–1223.

Guthrie, C.F. (2013) Smart technology and the moral life. *Ethics & Behavior*, 23(4): 324–337.

Hansson, L. (2007) The Impact of Design. Allies Fighting Design Exclusion. In Brembeck, H., Ekström, K.M., and Mörck, M. (eds) *Little Monsters, (De)coupling Assemblages of Consumption*. Zurich: LIT Verlag, pp. 15–28.

Harrison, R., Newholm, T., and Shaw, D. (2005) *The Ethical Consumer*. London: Sage.

Hobson, K. (2006) Bins, bulbs, and shower timers: On the "techno-ethics" of sustainable living. *Ethics Place and Environment*, 9(3): 317–336.

Ingram, J., Shove, E., and Watson, M. (2007) Products and practices: Selected concepts from science and technology studies and from social theories of consumption and practice. *Design Issues*, 23(2): 3–16.

Jelsma, J. (2003) Innovating for sustainability: Involving users, politics and technology, innovation. *The European Journal of Social Science Research*, 16(2): 103–116.

Latour, B. (1992) Where are the Missing Masses? The Sociology of a Few Mundane Artifacts. In Bijker, W.E., and Law, J. (eds) *Shaping Technology/Building Society. Studies in Sociotechnical Change*. Cambridge, MA: The MIT Press, pp. 225–258.

Latour, B. (2002) Morality and technology. *Theory, Culture and Society*, 19(5): 247–260.

Lekakis, E. (2013) *Coffee Activism and the Politics of Fair Trade and Ethical Consumption in the Global North: Political Consumerism and Cultural Citizenship*. Springer.

Lekakis, E.J. (2014) ICTs and ethical consumption: The political and market futures of fair trade. *Futures*, 62: 164–172.

Licoppe, C. (2008) Understanding and Reframing the Electronic Consumption Experience. In Pinch, T., and Swedberg, R. (eds) *Living in a Material World*. Cambridge, MA: MIT Press.

Low, W., and Davenport, E. (2007) To boldly go … Exploring ethical spaces to re-politicise ethical consumption and fair trade. *Journal of Consumer Behaviour*, 6(5): 336–348.

Mallard, A. (2007) Performance Testing: Dissection of a Consumerist Experiment. In Callon, M., Millo, Y., and Muniesa, F. (eds) *Market Devices*. London: Blackwell.

McEachern, M.G., and McClean, P. (2002) Organic purchasing motivations and attitudes: Are they ethical? *International Journal of Consumer Studies*, 26: 85–92.

Micheletti, M., Follesdal, A., and Stolle, D. (2004) *Politics, Products, and Markets. Exploring Political Consumerism Past and Present.* New Brunswick, NJ: Transaction Publishers.

Mick, D.G., Broniarczyk, S.M., and Haidt, J. (2004) Choose, choose, choose, choose, choose, choose, choose: Emerging and prospective research on the deleterious effects of living in consumer hyperchoice. *Journal of Business Ethics*, 52(2): 207–211.

Miele, M., and Evans, A. (2010) When foods become animals: Ruminations on ethics and responsibility in care-full practices of consumption. *Ethics, Place and Environment*, 13(2): 171–190.

Moisander, J. (2007) Motivational complexity of green consumerism. *International Journal of Consumer Studies*, 31(4): 404–409.

Moisander, J., Markkula, A., and Eräranta, K. (2010) Construction of consumer choice in the market: Challenges for environmental policy. *International Journal of Consumer Studies*, 34(1): 73–79.

Naturskyddsföreningen (2014) www.naturskyddsforeningen.se/vad-du-kan-gora/gron-guide/app [accessed 13-10-2014].

Neyland, D., and Simakova, E. (2009) How far can we push sceptical reflexivity? An analysis of marketing ethics and the certification of poverty. *Journal of Marketing Management*, 25(7–8): 777–794.

Pecoraro, M.G., and Uusitalo, O. (2014) Conflicting values of ethical consumption in diverse worlds – A cultural approach. *Journal of Consumer Culture*, 14(1): 45–65.

Reijonen, S., and Tryggestad, K. (2012) The dynamic signification of product qualities: On the possibility of "greening" markets. *Consumption Markets & Culture*, 15(2): 213–234.

Rokka, J., and Moisander, J. (2009) Environmental dialogue in online communities: Negotiating ecological citizenship among global travellers. *International Journal of Consumer Studies*, 33(2): 199–205.

Røpke, I. (2009) Theories of practice – New inspiration for ecological economic studies on consumption. *Ecological Economics*, 68: 2490–2497.

Shankar, S., Venkatesh, A., Hofacker, C., and Naik, P. (2010) Mobile marketing in the retailing environment: Current insights and future research avenues. *Journal of Interactive Marketing*, 24(2): 111–120.

Shaw, D., Hogg, G., Wilson, E., Shiu, E., and Hassan, L. (2006) Fashion victim: The impact of fair trade concerns on clothing choice. *Journal of Strategic Marketing*, 14(4): 427–440.

Shaw, D., and Shiu, E. (2002) The role of ethical obligation and self-identity in ethical consumer choice. *International Journal of Consumer Studies*, 26(2): 109–116.

Shopgun (2014) www.shopgun.se [accessed 13-10-2014].

Sörum, N., and Fuentes, C. (2016) Materialiserad moral. Smartphone, applikationer och etisk konsumtion. *Kulturella Perspektiv*, 2: 6–15.

Valor, C. (2008) Can consumers buy responsibly? Analysis and solutions for market failures. *Journal of Consumer Policy*, 31: 315–326.

Verbeek, P.P. (2006) Materializing morality design ethics and technological mediation. *Science, Technology & Human Values*, 31(3): 361–380.

Young, W., Hwang, K., McDonald, S., and Oates, C.J. (2010) Sustainable consumption: Green consumer behaviour when purchasing products. *Sustainable Development*, 19(1): 20–31.

7 Tracing the sex of big data (or configuring digital consumers)

Magdalena Petersson McIntyre

The world's most dangerous meeting: event for e-trade

We are in a theatre at eight o'clock in the morning. The lights are dimmed and it feels like an evening event. A Harley Davidson motorbike is placed in the middle of the stage. Eighty per cent of the visitors are men. Most are young and wearing suits. Rock music is playing loudly. Probably Dee Snider from the band *Twisted Sister*, I presume; he is there to launch his new book. The contrast between the clean-cut visitors who are carrying laptops and exchanging business cards and the projection of anti-authoritarian glam rock is sharp enough almost to appear ironic. All the speakers in the presentational poster are men, except one, "Dessie", a young blogger whose picture stands out; while the male speakers are portrayed with face shots, Dessie is depicted lying down on top of a pink unicorn.

A curtain in the background shows the organizer's symbol, a skull, to emphasize masculinity and rock. Twitter flows on a large screen beside the stage. "I wanna rock" is now playing loudly. "Let's rock 'n' roll", the first speaker says, entering the stage. "Someone overslept", he explains, "but that is just rock 'n' roll." Everybody laughs. The so-called unofficial after-party is announced. "Why is it called the world's most dangerous meeting?", the speaker asks the crowd, only to answer himself: "Because we are here to challenge ourselves and our comfort zone. The world is changing." The moderator for the day, a middle-aged man, takes over and goes on to talk about the changing world. "It is nice to be in control, but our formerly safe place is now precarious. We must change, move with the new."

Dessie, sidekick to the moderator, is announced. "She writes a diary on the Internet." It works like a magazine, and she sells advertising space, the moderator explains. The audience seems interested. Dessie symbolizes consumers as well as young women wrapped up in a new form of entrepreneurship, I think. "You're kind of for sale too. That's good, that's what we like", the moderator continues, while looking at Dessie, thus framing the encounter with sexual overtones. Everybody laughs, but Dessie looks uncomfortable and out of place. "I would not use under-the-belt humour, that is not who I am", the moderator continues. Normality seems restored. When asked how she likes to pay for things she buys online, Dessie says she prefers to do it by invoice; not quite the correct answer in this crowd full of representatives from novel payment devices, and the audience now listens carefully. The moderator goes on to talk about the importance of challenging oneself. We should be like Eleanor Roosevelt, he says, who tried to do one new thing that she was afraid of every day. Someone from *The Guinness Book of Records* is going to come later on, we are also told, to witness the breaking of a record that is yet to be announced.

The description is an excerpt from a field diary written during participant observations at an annual trade fair for e-commerce called "the world's most dangerous meeting", in Gothenburg, Sweden, in 2013. The following chapter examines discourses on the digitalization of consumption based on field work conducted at some of the many trade fairs for e-commerce that pop up every year in different cities all over Europe. The sheer number of them seems to have some significance in itself. Such trade fairs are particular forms of events in which specific, and as the initial anecdote illustrates, gendered, versions of consumption, consumers and devices for consumption are produced and entangled.

Figure 7.1 Rock 'n' roll is the theme at "the world's most dangerous meeting" trade fair for e-commerce. The picture shows the moderators of the year (here 2015) surrounded by rock props and ready to introduce the next speakers from "Byggmax", a chain store for building supplies
(Photo: Author)

One important aspect of such trade fairs is to function as a market for market devices (Cochoy, 2011). New devices and perspectives are here presented to market actors in the field in order to convince them of the advantages of or need for change, particularly regarding the digitalization of retailing. The events summarized the present concerns that market actors in the e-trade industry had, together with suggestions on how those concerns should be tackled or solved, often with the use of technologies or devices that were marketed simultaneously.

Devices, but also trade shows in themselves, can be understood as "material-discursive", that is as producing determinate meanings and material beings while simultaneously excluding the production of others. Drawing on the work of feminist science scholar Karen Barad (2007), e-commerce can be understood as a phenomenon and boundary-drawing practice. Like scientific apparatuses, trade fairs measure and explain the world around us. They do not represent a neutral truth, but actively do something, make cuts in presentations and descriptions of contemporary life in order to promote particular scenarios. In this way, trade shows do not merely produce devices or stories of devices, they help produce subjects and remake structures, gender structures as well as business structures.

Digital devices, technologies and services were centre stage. Consumers, in turn, were the objects that could be traced and tracked with the use of various solutions. As argued by Cochoy and Smolinski (this volume, see also Cochoy, 2011), the study of consumption is not necessarily equivalent to studying consumers (see also Zwick and Cayla, 2011). Rather, the actions and identities of consumers are modified and enabled by "market things" such as objects, devices and technologies. Devices attract consumers but also give opportunities for surveillance and calculation by anticipating and mapping consumer choices (see Sörum and Fuentes, this volume).

During the fairs, the talks and lectures on how to understand the consumers of the future had large numbers of visitors. Some speakers gave clear definitions of what consumers are like nowadays. These were often similar and centred on a few different themes that will be developed below. Even though consumption and the inner lives of consumers have been extensively researched by the marketing trade (Zwick and Cayla, 2011), the understanding of consumption among market actors is often based on the principles of increasing sales. Thus, field work at these events entailed trying to understand consumers by observing what others said about them, others who wished to promote their own devices by presenting truths and facts about consumers. Thus, the chapter builds on studying the role played by consumer research in the performative enactment of consumer subjectivities (Cronin, 2000; Butler, 1990; Nixon, 2009). The focus is on how consumer subjectivities are constructed and how particular ways of understanding this market and consumption are both presented and gain ground.

Fairs

E-commerce is a growing field that is trying to establish itself as distinct from the physical form of retailing. An important function of trade fairs in general is to bring people together and to work to define a field, explain how it is different from other fields, or illustrate particular challenges or problems. Trade fairs may help keep a field together that in reality has little in common (Skov, 2006).

The idea of trade fairs as "field-configuring events" was coined by Lampel and Meyer (2008) and defined as "temporary social organizations, professional gatherings, technology contests, and business ceremonies that encapsulate and shape the development of professions, technologies, markets and industries" (p. 1026). Field-configuring events are settings in which people from diverse organizations and with diverse purposes assemble periodically, or on a one-time basis, to announce new products, develop industry standards, construct social networks, recognize accomplishments, share and interpret information, and transact business, they argue.

Another important aspect of fairs is their symbolic, ceremonial and dramaturgical function. As argued by Moeran and Strandgaard Pedersen (2011), fairs (and for them also festivals) have symbolic functions. Outside the normal course of trade exchange, fairs are temporarily as well as socially bounded. "Overtly, trade fairs are about exhibiting 'the new', be it an idea in its initial state or a finalized product, showing one's capabilities, and trading in a particular commodity" (ibid., p. 8). Or as Lampel and Meyer (2008) put it, field-configuring events bring together actors from different professions, organizations and locations in order to provide opportunities for interaction as well as ceremonial and dramaturgical activities. They are occasions for information exchange and collective sense making that generate social and reputational resources.

In spite of their significance, trade fairs have not received so much attention from scholars. There is, however, a body of literature on World's Fairs. According to Rydell (1993, p. 7), World's Fairs promoted the development of empire on the one hand and on the other the new-found unity between science, technology and the modern corporation as the key to building a better future after the depression in the 1930s. Comparison can be made with the trade fairs studied where the future was promoted as formed by digital technology and consumption, and globalization was promoted as an opportunity for business. Rydell (1993, p. 10) saw the fairs as striving to modernize America, as working on the creation of an "ever more perfect realization of an imperial dream world of abundance, consumption, and social hierarchy based on the reproduction of existing power relations of race and gender".

The descriptions of global business opportunities resulting from digitalization also contained a form of dream or fantasy dimension. If colonial empire was a key dimension in the World's Fairs of the past (Rydell, 1993), with ethnic groups and natives exhibited in their "natural" environment, the e-commerce trade fairs of today gave a somewhat similar representation of consumers. Consumers were analysed and exhibited (metaphorically at least), anthropologists invited to speak of consumer behaviour, often female consumer behaviour, and consumers were the group exposed to colonialism, from the human resources of whom money can be earned. There was also a global dimension to the content, and consumers in what was referred to as "emerging economies" (the Arab world, Africa) were described as particularly interesting, and free trade and borders intertwined with technologies and devices. The fairs work to convince visitors of the need for reform. A strong message was that computer science helps the e-trade industry and devices were presented as working in favour of business.

Setting and methodology

Between 2012 and 2015 I visited seven different trade fairs for e-commerce in Sweden and London, on 14 different occasions, of which Internet World and Scandinavian e-Business Camp were among the larger ones, with the aim of analysing the views of consumers and consumption that emerged as the retail industry was undergoing digitalization. Six of the seven trade fairs were in Sweden, and one in London.[1] They had slightly different profiles. Some were located in exclusive hotels and conference centres. One, cited above,[2] was at a theatre in an amusement park. Others were in purpose-built trade fair centres.

All were framed with elaborate entrances and stylish hostesses, staffed wardrobes, and long counters for registration, name tags and entrance tickets of varying prices (see Skov, 2006). Exclusive or trendy lunches were common and mingling was encouraged. Champagne toasts to celebrate the growth of e-trade were made along with presentations of charitable projects in Third World countries. Connections with successful businesses, media personalities and even members of royal families were mentioned by speakers, all creating a feeling of being at the centre of events, and maybe of value for money for visitors who had paid the often expensive entrance price. Panels or expert groups that commented live or on Twitter were standard. The latest technological news from Japan was often presented with delight. Some fairs had a format taken from the creative industries, with awards, prizes and gala dinners (Moeran and Strandgaard Pedersen, 2011; Entwistle and Rocamora, 2011), performatively enacting their own importance. Art and culture framed events with musical performances, exhibitions and the auctioning off of art works. Musicians and artists were presented as geniuses of branding and management. The number of visitors was mostly between 500 and 1,500. Many participants reappeared, and after a while I started to recognize both speakers and visitors.

Some of the fairs had a broad approach to digitalization;[3] others were directed at the e-commerce trade more directly. One was organized by Jet-shop, a provider of digital platforms for retailers,[4] and many of the visitors were their clients. Another was organized by a trade organization,[5] and yet another by an advertising agency.[6] I participated in an "inspirational journey" to London that a trade organization[7] had arranged, with field trips to companies in London (Ve Interactive and Burberry) that were considered to be at the cutting edge of digitalization. I also visited several public events and lectures organized by representatives of the e-trade industry during the duration of the field work. Very similar descriptions of the current predicament circulated at all these events. Altogether, it gave a good picture of the ways in which the present and the future were talked about in relation to e-commerce by representatives of the industry, or summarized a form of "buzz" (see Bathelt et al., 2004; Bathelt and Glückler, 2011).

While some were trade fairs in a more conventional sense with exhibition booths (Moeran and Strandgaard Pedersen, 2011; Skov, 2006; Lampel and Meyer, 2008), others borrowed the format and name of fairs so as to create a whole concept for an event. Although all were called fairs, some could more correctly be described as hybrid events or something in between a happening, an entertainment event and a trade fair. They copied the form of a trade fair, more than actually being one, focusing more on "inspiration" and opportunities of finding out "what is going on", than on making business agreements or transactions. The same speakers and themes appeared at all the different fairs and made up a form of background meaning-making or worldview of market actors in this field.

The arrangement was much the same. Market devices were promoted in two ways: with exhibitions of actual devices and with seminars or lectures. The fair space was divided into two parts, consisting of a large, or small, exhibition hall as one part where companies active in any kind of digital commerce exhibited their products in booths. Logistics, payment solutions and banks dominated this space. As put by Skov (2006, p. 779), "exhibitors are under the obligation of hospitality". Gifts such as sweets, pens, reflectors or mobile chargers, brochures and coffee were offered to visitors. Accepting a gift usually requires an obligation to listen to a sales pitch, and many fair-goers develop techniques for how to grab gifts without having to engage in conversation with exhibitors.

The second part consisted of seminars and lectures of varying content. Big rooms hosted well-known companies such as Twitter, Microsoft, Facebook and Google, and attracted large crowds. Smaller companies that provided different solutions for Web design, conversion and other infrastructure of e-commerce, as well as e-stores themselves, small and large, gave talks of varying content in the smaller rooms. All promoted the devices and services their companies offered, sometimes directly, at other times more subtly. At some of the events, the talks or conferences appeared to be the main act, and the exhibitions were limited or appeared dutiful or only available to sponsors. The talks and lectures often explained and gave context to the exhibitions, which is why I found them to be of particular significance.

Participating in these settings allowed observation of the sense-making and sense-giving processes that help shape this field (Lampel and Meyer, 2008).

The fieldwork has ethnographic, qualitative methods with thick descriptions as its basis. It can be described as a form of tracing, through which I, the ethnographer, like a bloodhound, tracked meaningful expressions of culture or circulation of cultural meanings (Marcus, 1998). Observing, looking and listening were my main tools. I wandered around in the trade fairs, and looked at exhibitors' products and presentations. I took notes, took pictures, collected documents and interacted with exhibitors. I read my notes over and over again looking for patterns in the descriptions, recurring themes, devices, people, perspectives and statements. Was there any superordinate logic to things? I slowly started to notice how specific descriptions of consumption, consumers and new "market things" recurred and were related to the challenges that the retail industry was said to face. Similarly, Skov (2006, pp. 776–7) writes, for example, of participant observations in fashion trade fairs in terms of a "city-like spectacle" that invites "deciphering gazes", and of the method as "serendipitous".

In my analysis, I focus on recurring utterances by market actors from different firms or organizations. I have not made any point of where, what speakers or companies the quotes or utterances come from. Rather, I have approached these things as a form of flowing cultural talk (Moisander and Valtonen, 2006), a shared meaning making or sense making that recurred in different fairs and from different speakers, a form of soundscape or buzz that framed the events, and summarized a form of analysis of the contemporary, taken from the starting point of digital devices for e-commerce (see also Favre and Brailly, 2016).

On the scene: revolution?

Many of the fairs had talks and lectures with a similar dramaturgy. Speakers began their talk by introducing words such as "change", "digital revolution" and "paradigm shift". Images of the Earth and the ability of the company in question to connect people all over the globe set the mood. Figures were used to show the breadth of the communication activities (millions, billions, etc., of tweets). Images of airports recurred, as did "globalization". Metaphors were taken from the natural sciences and companies' infrastructure; devices were described in terms of evolution, eco-systems, ecologies and DNA. Digital wallets were, for instance, described as "the next evolution in payments". Pulses, rhythms, streams and flows were other common words used to describe the workings of digitalization. Human evolution with images of evolving humans (male) also appeared. "The mobile landscape will evolve", was a typical statement. "Gateways" was another common metaphor. Movement, mobility and the future were other recurring features. Computer technology was related to breathing and thereby made into something organic. Technical development was presented as something natural, thus made into science.

Lectures on "big data" attracted the largest numbers of visitors. Big data was the concept that "everyone" seemed to want to learn more about or at least felt that they should. Big data is a term that has come to signify the methods by which the traces that people leave online can be saved and analysed in order to be processed to show connections and patterns (boyd and Crawford, 2012). In a consumption context, in contrast, it allows the possibility for market actors to be able to find and predict connections, purchases and taste preferences by targeting marketing, optimizing offers or reading the market, thus creating advantages for certain brands (see also Boullier, this volume).

Many speakers reported with delight the information that big data could provide for e-commerce. From following the digital trails that consumers leave behind, to seeing which sites they came from, whether they visited the site in question directly or linked there via another site, how many seconds they stayed on the pages, what they put into their digital shopping carts, what they bought (converted), whether they left any personal information, whether they had visited the site before, how they paid and what shipping options they preferred, and how much they spent. Big data was often described as the tool for making marketing personal, a way of breaking into the world of individual subjects, as revealing "the truth" about consumers. As described by boyd and Crawford (2012), the mythological dimension that deals with the general belief that big data provide truer, more objective and more accurate knowledge than was previously available, is widespread. Big data were often described as "amazing". Many talks focused on showing amazing and different possible applications to astound the listeners, to create an affective response that anything is going to be possible and that everything is going to change.

There was also a lot of talk about empowerment and democracy, individuality, collaboration, knowledge and power. We are heading toward flexibility, to reimagining the world. Many emphasized that personality and individuality will replace the market segments of the past. Messages about a brave new future were combined with ideas on how to reach customers in new ways. "Change your world for the better", also reappeared. Another common theme was "effectiveness". New technologies and devices were "so many times more effective than the old way". Another recurrent theme was stories of small firms fighting against the tide, only to achieve enormous success by focusing on their original idea.

Trade fairs of this kind can be seen as scenes for the display of contemporary culture, in particular digitalized culture. More importantly, they enact the future. The attempts by market actors to predict the future and capture the present were perhaps most successful in their mediation of emotions and affect, in their intensity and the thoughts and feelings they made possible, whether intended or something completely different (McFall, 2015). It was a dramaturgy staged to mobilize emotions, to create a reaction in visitors that would lead to action; the future is here, the digital revolution has begun, and we all have to change ourselves and our stores to keep up.

There were stories that were repeated so many times by different speakers at different fairs in their attempts to characterize the contemporary, that I began to wonder about their significance on a deeper level. One of these was the election of the last two popes and a comparison of pictures of the crowd waiting outside the Vatican, one year without and one year with smartphones. Another was the benefit of big data in forecasting a breakout of influenza, and a third story was about a dad in New York (at least that is where he lived most of the time) who did not know that his daughter was pregnant until free samples of baby supplies started turning up in their post around six months after someone had Googled "pregnancy". A fourth story was the full-season-at-once release of Netflix's TV series *House of Cards* as a response to how consumers like to watch. A fifth recurring story was about a shoe store in Brazil that gave timed offers to visitors in a shopping centre in order to make them run. The faster they showed up in the shop, the bigger the discount.

All these stories, which I heard many times and in slightly different versions during my field work, exemplified particular versions of technical devices and the relation to consumption. The first story exemplified technical revolution and rapid change, the second the benefits of big data in supplying medication for society, and the third has to do with the business opportunity of tracking consumers. The fourth concerned consumer power and the benefits of adapting to what consumers want. The fifth was about controlling consumer behaviour with targeted marketing, like making puppets dance. The ways in which these stories were presented also enacted particular versions of consumption and consumers, that consumer behaviour can be broken down into different search categories and predicted – the ultimate fantasy, perhaps, of any market actor (see also Czarniawska, this volume).

As discussed by Czarniawska (this volume), visions of the future can affect the present. They shape the future as much as they describe the present. Trade fairs staged and celebrated novelty. The future was presented as if it were already here. These stories became a form of folklore, mixed with science fiction. The reiterations have significance. As fair-goers hear them repeated, their performative effect is multiplied. They were stories about time, about the temporal aspects of technologies and devices, and about space, as they were located across the globe. They also illustrate the telling and choosing of stories to reflect particular scenarios. Taken together, they summarized quite well the depictions of the present that were enacted at the trade fairs.

Configuring digital consumers

I will now move on to suggest a model for how digital consumers were configured by speakers at the trade fairs, by making a comparison with an analysis of the emergence of self-service by Cochoy (2011). Cochoy describes the role that open display had in encouraging consumers to stop and to buy more.

In analysing the trade journal *Progressive Grocer* over the period 1929–59, Cochoy observes the roles played by what he calls four types of tightly intertwined innovations, for the development of new patterns of consumption.

Figure 7.2 DB Schenker, a company that handles logistics and deliveries, invites fair-
         goers to try their rock 'n' roll potential in their exhibition booth
(Photo: Author)

These were: the redistribution of furniture within the walls of the grocery store; a controlled "liberation" of consumers' lines of sight and trajectories; the invention of flexible display furniture; and the implementation of devices aimed at easing the movement of the consumer.

Just as observed by Cochoy regarding grocers at the beginning of self-service, speakers at the trade fairs showed a constant ambivalence between the promises of increased sales opportunities embedded in new technologies and the concerns of losing control over customers' actions that these simultaneously brought to the fore. In the sections that follow I have adapted Cochoy's model to digital consumption, but now with five different and tightly intertwined processes of change: 1) the expansion of physical boundaries; 2) new space and time for consumption; 3) new roles for consumers; 4) compensation for sensual displacement; and 5) attract and contain. However, compared with self-service, these processes of change are not as much within stores, as between them.

1 The expansion of physical boundaries

Many speakers talked about the importance of "omni-channel", a term that referred to the integration between the different outlet forms such as online sites, mobile sites and physical stores. These "channels" must be seen as one and the same without any glitches between them, they emphasized. The customer experience must be "seamless". Seamless sometimes also referred to making customers happy by delivering goods well, giving them "relevant" suggestions for what to buy next, and in general "making life easier". At the same time, many speakers also talked about the importance of bringing digital consumption sites inside the walls of physical stores, to make goods that are not in stock available to customers through online ordering. Consumers would thereby be encouraged to search for goods in stores and be given access to full stock as well as a choice of payment and delivery options.

Such a supply of devices for online activities in stores metaphorically expands the walls of the store, and may be seen as a response to market actors' concerns that consumers search for products in stores on their own devices, usually smartphones, only to find the right product in a competitors' store. Thus, the expansion of physical boundaries can be seen as a double process of on the one hand increasing choice, and on the other attempting to contain consumer choice within a particular store.

2 New space and time for consumption

Many speakers characterized digital consumption by talking about the new opportunities in search tools, applications and personalized marketing through which retailers now could contact consumers. Speakers enthusiastically emphasized the benefits of consumers now being able to shop 24 hours a day, from wherever they are, from home or on the go, as long as they have a device connected to the Internet. Consumers may even shop during times and in spaces that were previously separated from consumer activities, or while performing everyday and dull tasks, such as going to the toilet, as one speaker from Google pointed out to loud laughter from the audience. Customers' ability to see and read more about products and digitally access stock and goods that are not in store was also described as an opportunity to capture consumers.

These observations by speakers can be taken as examples of how digitalization maximizes visual access to goods, but also makes movement between competitors easier. As a form of continuation of open display, these aspects of digitalization have similarities with what Cochoy (2011) calls controlled "liberation" of consumers' lines of sight and trajectories. However, these transformations were not only met with delight at the fairs. As the opportunities increase for consumers to browse, continually be inspired by new goods and find the best price (see also Denegri-Knott and Molesworth, 2010), retailers' control of consumers' actions becomes increasingly difficult. Customers can move freely within stores, but also between competitors' stores. Individual retailers can no longer keep an actual look-out from behind the cash register. The alternative is to try to trace and track consumers' activities afterwards, and give a response in the form of automated suggestions for more goods, personalized discounts, or offer encouragement to fill the digital shopping cart and proceed to the digital cash register. "Geo-localized" offers through which the consumer receives an offer when they approach a given supply are another related example. Google analytics, for instance, offer methods for monitoring where the online visitors come from and who they are, how many buy and what they buy, facts that to some extent were previously observed by cashiers or grocers. Thus, the enthusiasm for big data can be seen in the light of a hope to compensate for the loss of personal contact brought on by digitalization. "Consumers shop while they are doing something else, today, and this can be observed with data from Google", was a typical statement that I heard many times.

Nevertheless, this form of control, too, has its limitations. New search possibilities mean that consumers may follow the goods, rather than the display of one particular store. The general development is that individual stores no longer represent particular brands or goods exclusively; they are just one of many possible outlets. The market for retail is not even just national, but stretches across the globe to low-price countries. Market actors at trade fairs generally described the development following on from digitalization as a threat, but some speakers also pointed to the opportunities of taking market share from "others".

3 New roles for consumers

Another general development of retailing is that upon the new space and time for consumption follow new roles for consumers, particularly regarding information. Store personnel or store owners no longer have control over information and reviews of products, even when such information is shared by stores themselves. Customer reviews have become part of many stores' online sites in which consumers speak to other consumers on store sites. Customers not only have direct access to goods, but also access to information about product quality as well as alternative models, colours or sizes. Customers can access brands' product information and connect with other consumers to share reviews, inspiration, product characteristics and value for money. Hence, information about products is no longer connected to the act of purchase in a retail outlet. The spaces of consumption have opened up, and consumers are increasingly involved in the circulation of goods and information. If the barrier in the form of a counter was removed with the introduction of self-service, digitalization removes barriers of other kinds, and communication about goods follows new paths of circulation. Information about the lowest price, about availability or better products, or even conditions of production, is open to all (see also Sörum and Fuentes, this volume). Thus, consumers take more active roles by getting involved in the supply side of consumption processes.

Speakers at the trade fairs often characterized contemporary retailing in ways similar to the above, but also expressed concern over the development and the fact that stores cannot control information. For retailers, the challenge was to get consumers to commit in the right way. Many talks were targeted at explaining to shop owners that they should not be concerned over consumers' bad reviews. Rather, honesty creates trust, it was argued, and shops or brands should be visible online and respond to consumers' concerns. Many pointed to the importance of "understanding your customer". To understand was usually presented as the equivalent of tracking data. Loyalty, connection and engagement were buzzwords. "Be like a friend – measure everything", was a recurring statement, and it might not need to be pointed out that friendship is usually not equated with measuring everything. New technologies, such as big data, were often presented as the solution to these challenges. With big data it becomes possible to really find out what the customer wants and make the customer stay and like being on one's site. Customers are insecure and need to be convinced, some argued, along with the statement, "customer first". Many speakers also stressed that customers should do the selling for you. "The trick is to empower other consumers to sell your product for you." Create "pull" instead of "push", they said. So-called social merchandizing (similar to self-marketing), such as customer comments, questions and answers, size recommendations, marking favourites and likes, and blogging were all brought up as examples of empowering the customer to sell for you.

Thus, with digitalization, shopping does not necessarily begin with what is on display on a store shelf, but places consumer choice at the centre, even if just symbolically. Consumers may search for the best match to their need or taste, or for the best value for money. In that respect, this is full circle back to before self-service, when consumers might have thought about what they wanted and then gone to ask the person behind the shop counter for it. However, with digitalization the consumer no longer needs to go to the store, and the counter is the search engine. It is no wonder that lack of inspiration is of major concern for market actors. Although the opportunities for market actors to visually expose consumers to products has multiplied manifold times with digitalization, the opposite is also true. When shopping on digital devices, consumers do not need to see products they do not intend to buy, thus reducing the opportunities for impulse buying.

4 Compensation for sensual displacement

The possibilities for browsing in digital stores are endless. However, goods can be seen, in digital form, but not touched unless paid for. As discussed by Cochoy (2007), consumers have increasingly been separated from goods during the development of retailing, particularly groceries, through the layers of packaging. Packaging prevents consumers from sensually experiencing products. With the digitalization of retailing, consumers are even more separated from goods, even goods such as clothes that can be felt and tried on in physical stores. Although the possibilities of contacting consumers digitally have opened up enormous opportunities to reach out, as acknowledged by speakers at the fairs, many also expressed great concern about how to tackle the loss of inspiration that follows if customers no longer go to stores. A related concern of many shop owners was called "showrooming", which is when customers go to physical stores to touch and try certain products that can be tested in stores, only to order online at a better price; or the concerns for how to handle the vast amounts of returned goods, or to stop consumers from returning goods.

Speakers presented different solutions for such concerns. Attempts to compensate for the lack of touch, smell and sense with digital devices were frequently mentioned. The development of mobile applications that convey the feeling of touching velvet was one such example. Other devices presented were applications for finding the right skin tone match for make-up shopping, or body measurement techniques designed to compensate for the loss of fitting rooms. Digital mirrors are another frequent application used for cosmetics and clothes e-shopping.

Thus, "just looking", a phrase so important for consumption patterns in the 19th and 20th centuries (Bowlby, 1985), has changed in meaning. Consumers may look as much as they like, but not touch. Customers may see all the possible versions, sizes, colours or cuts of a particular object online, but not actually touch or try it on. Looking loses some of its value when it cannot be controlled. Just looking is only a successful trick of the trade when it changes into acts of purchase within a distinguishable field. This loss of control is largely rhetorical. It is crucial to say that control has been lost in order to sell new control devices.

5 *Attract and contain*

Many fair-goers expressed thoughts that can be interpreted as concern for the loss of control over consumers' actions in which digitalization results. Although movement between goods and within stores was presented as opportunity, there was also concern that consumers' movements could not be contained within the individual store or chain. The movement is eased, but the concern of market actors is that it is eased too much.

As with the other four areas of opportunity and concern, a fair speaker presented solutions for how to embrace consumers' new ways of moving between goods and stores without losing control over their purchase power. These solutions primarily focused on attracting consumers to stores and then trying to contain them within. Loyalty cards, customer clubs, targeted offers and consumer registers are all responses to such concerns that have existed for a while. A more recent response was the calls for seamless customer experiences, which attempted to ease as well as control the movements of customers.

Cochoy (2011) describes the same techniques during the introduction of self-service, and what he refers to as increasing the mobility of customers in order to open up the range of their purchases. Open display with a controlled liberation of lines of sight and movement is now followed by the attempts to attract clicks and "conversion" – as speakers call it, to go through with a purchase; not, however, within individual stores, as during the time of the introduction of open display and self-service, but to attract traffic, clicks and "conversions". The omni-channel idea as well as the seamless idea must be seen in this light. They are attempts to ease and control the movements of customers. With digitalization, the increase of traffic to a store's site functions, as Cochoy puts it, to increase the mobility of customers in order to open up the range of their purchases, as do channels such as Facebook and Instagram or pop-up ads, which all extend the visibility and exposure of goods. These technologies are used to compensate for the loss of inspiration that many retailers fear follows on from digitalization. With regular updates, consumers may be attracted to things they do not necessarily seek. Inspirational images, price reductions and product news posted digitally transcend the previous spaces of consumption, such as store spaces, and reach consumers wherever they are. Retailers in the digital age may not promote material innovations such as the turnstile (Cochoy, 2011), but they nonetheless promote the removal of barriers in the form of complicated payment solutions in steps that make consumers hesitate. A "seamless" customer experience also refers to the removal of obstacles that stop the flow of purchase, which encourages and triggers customers to "convert" a purchase. Storing card and personal information and offering personal reductions and product suggestions are other examples of offering such seamless experiences. "How can you get consumers to press the [purchase] button?", was a question asked by many speakers, though few had any convincing answers. "It should be easy to buy more", was another frequent piece of advice. Another example was to send messages to consumers that contain information about the distance to a physical store, or as some speakers described it, "digital drives foot traffic".

The consumer is not stupid: she is my daughter

> The consumer is not stupid. She is my daughter.
>
> (Panel discussion with representatives from Microsoft, Seven Seconds and
> MobHappy, Internet World, London)

During these trade shows, presentations of payment tools, delivery logistics, safety, big data and opportunities of tracking consumers were entangled in the perceived challenges of the world of tomorrow. Mobile payments were presented with the allure of new technologies. The future society without cash was often described with delight. Utterances such as "it happens on Twitter", "you have to be where your customers are" or "this is in the DNA of social media" positioned speakers as holders of knowledge of how, when and where the crowd of consumers move. Terms such as "mobile ecosystem", "ecology", "DNA", "mobile landscape", "ecosystem for payment", were used to describe the digital world, turning it into an organic entity that could be conquered and mastered.

The future of e-commerce was also presented with and through human bodies of particular kinds, by (white) middle-aged male presenters dressed in grey suits. Stories about male heroes and risk-taking were prevalent in speakers' stories about firms' success. Men from different companies talked about solutions for the future and the importance of challenging oneself. Many presentations relied on overly masculine symbolism with the use of references to heavy metal, motorcycles and digital technologies.

This contrasted with traditional mail-order firms, or small independent clothes shops, of which many (women) in the audience were representatives. Large parts of the e-trade industry have evolved from mail order, a branch of retail generally targeted to women (Clarke, 1998; Casey, 2014; Hagberg, 2008). The symbols of playful masculinity must be interpreted as an expression of the attempt to shift the industry, making it more masculine and moving away from small-town mothers as the target group. Gender played a prominent role in the configuration of this field.

At one event, the CEO of Jetshop, an organizer and provider of digital solutions, "pre-launched" the company's new app for big data. The big data will be accessible to all, he explained, to look at all transactions, how many, what, men and women, where they live and what site they came from. Based on a sample of 690,000 purchases from 216 stores, they had found, he explained, that cards and invoices were the most popular methods; that men prefer cards and women invoices; that women buy the most around the 20th of each month when the Swedish child allowance is paid out. Women were often characterized as being more old-fashioned than men and not as technologically

Figure 7.3 Visitors at D-Congress 2015, here gathered under a green sign with the
words "Listen to your customers. You will profit from this" ("Lyssna på
dina kunder. Det tjänar du på")
(Photo: Author)

savvy. Men like price comparisons and women social media. The conclusion
to draw from this, the speaker said, was that "if I target women, I should use
social media".

During presentations, women were often presented as consumers, social
networkers, parents and frivolous shoppers. Images shown to illustrate "the
consumer" always depicted a (young) woman. Images of teenage girls frequently appeared to symbolize consumers, often with a smartphone in their
hands. Consumers were portrayed as a fickle crowd who need to be tracked,
traced and analysed, an uncontrollable mass, feminine, native, moving, and
like nature/natural. A mass that was addressed with comments such as "the
consumer isn't stupid; she is your daughter" (an update, of course, of the
classic marketers' line replacing wife with daughter), or with feminized
objects such as calling a red high-heeled shoe "a typical search". Thus, these
sense-making processes iterate discourses of nature as feminine and technology as masculine, and of consumers as a feminine crowd waiting to be
explored by male technicians and "e-tailers". "Nowadays, what young girls
are interested in is fashion. They socialize via fashion, not music", said
another speaker while presenting his company's digital solutions. On one
occasion, a woman dressed in undergarments and with a shopping bag and a

mobile phone was used to illustrate the future consumer, and this was typical. Change was in that sense in a way presented as feminine, and the past as masculine, the presentations were formed around how "we" (men in e-trade and related fields such as banks and delivery services) will change, and adapt to the future, by colonizing "them" (the women), and what they do on Facebook.

Above all, however, digital consumers were described as individuals. Thus, consumer choice was presented as not only involving products or services, but identities. Big data were often explained as the end of traditional segmentation. Marketing now has the opportunity to be completely individual, many argued. "Technology empowers consumers to be at their best", and the "business imperative for the future" should be to create opportunities for a choosy consumer, one speaker said. Gender segmentation was presented as the past; consumers should no longer be approached as representatives of categories of identity, but as individuals. Still, women often symbolized the irrational consumers. "My wife goes shopping without spending. Imagine what she is like online", said one man to illustrate the problem of abandoned shopping baskets. Gender continued to be the most frequent categorization of consumers, together with age groups, so the vision of the individual was perhaps mostly in the realm of science fiction.

New consumer subjects emerge as a result of new consumer technologies. Worth noting, however, is that so-called one-to-one marketing has been a distinct feature of earlier marketing practice, and is not tied specifically to big data. Rather, it is one of many examples of how existing practices are presented as new in the context of the fair, which is all part and parcel of emphasizing the importance of change and of the market devices presented. Presentations of new technologies were often contradictory when related to the understanding of (gendered) consumers. Gender was in one way never spoken of. It was not something that speakers addressed specifically; it was conceived of as an unproblematic fact. All the same, gendered statistics were often presented, and gender was the main segment when statistics were presented. Gender segmentation was on the one hand repeatedly described as obsolete with new technologies and big data, but when consumers were characterized, gender was always the most prominent category. The new world order seemed to have mysteriously disappeared, at least concerning gender.

Conclusion

Digitalization has brought a set of challenges to which retailers try to respond in different ways. The disruption of physical boundaries has resulted in technologies that attempt to contain consumers within stores. Likewise, the new spaces and times for consumption have made it increasingly difficult to control consumers' actions and have led to a number of concerns. Speakers said "consumers have the power today" – an old claim that is given new digitalized meaning. Big data, the tracking and tracing of consumers' activities as well as targeted offers are all technologies that are put to use to replace the change in control brought by digitalization. Market actors' interest in monitoring consumers' online activities is massive. The logic behind it is, however, not about preventing theft (Cochoy, 2011), but to stimulate more consumption, or to locate consumption in one's own store. New roles have emerged on the consumer side as well as the supply side. Market actors are encouraged to participate in online activities on their own sites or on Twitter or Facebook in order to influence consumers to engage in brands in ways that benefit these as much as possible. Price comparisons make customers into calculating subjects, responsible for finding the best prices, and conscious about price setting, and make consumers more active, shifting responsibilities to a greater extent from stores and to consumers. Furthermore, the distance from sense and touch in which online shopping results leads to a number of suggested solutions, devices and technologies to compensate for the loss. The loss of "inspiration" was considered to be one of the main challenges of digitalization. "Just looking", the practice of consumption so important for earlier generations of retailers for bringing customers into stores and creating desire for goods, changes in meaning when consumers now come to stores just to touch and try, but look and buy somewhere else online. Finally, technologies have emerged to attract consumers to stores as well as to keep them there. The consumer is encouraged to become even more active in digital shopping. However, consumers' activities cannot be controlled and contained. Stores have opened up, but have also lost power. Market actors try to compensate by increasing consumers' exposure to goods.

With these challenges and transformations, new ways of describing consumers emerge. The presentation of the digitalization of consumption at trade fairs relies on particular ways of understanding consumer identities. Digital consumers like choice; they want to be in control; they like genuine communication, simplicity and attractive packaging. They like to share, to shop when they like, and to be social about their consumption practices, and they expect quick delivery. These descriptions of contemporary consumers were typical and frequently recurring at the trade fairs.

Cochoy (2011) points to the liberal ideology inherent in the increase in consumer choice brought about by self-service. Added together, in the configuration of digital consumption at trade fairs, the power of the individual emerged as a strong cultural belief. Categorizations according to gender, age group or more traditional consumer segments were on the one hand described as obsolete, and on the other continued to be a fundamental part of presentations, pointing to contradictory circulations of ideas. "You" emerged as the most important subject of digital consumption, and individual marketing was described as the future. It is what "you" want that matters. Companies were advised by data experts to "try to understand everything about the consumer" in order to "segment and market differently". There was an iteration of a neo-liberal ideology of emphasizing individuality rather than collective identities. At the same time, presentations were filled with gendered meanings and attempts to depict consumers as representatives of different groups. The idea of "just looking", so important for earlier consumption patterns, has become a dilemma for market actors in digital consumption. In order to track, trace and anticipate consumer choice, a rational consumer who is not just looking but buying was needed in order to market the market devices of digital consumption. A trackable and traceable consumer must follow the patterns staked out by market actors, otherwise the market devices become obsolete, and that was perhaps the real challenge in market actors' attempts to depict digital consumers. When presentations of consumers are based on functions of devices, aspects that cannot be explained in relation to the same devices become irrelevant. That is perhaps why many honestly wondered why so many consumers fill their digital shopping carts, and then leave them "unconverted". Challenges for retailers are not so much movement within stores, as uncontrolled movement between them.

The ways in which consumers were configured by market actors took the idea of a rational consumer for granted. The techniques that were presented for how to track, trace and anticipate consumer choice relied on ideas of a consumer who follows the patterns that have been staked out. However, consumers might not be looking to buy; they might be just looking, like the wife who goes shopping without spending, quoted by the man above. Thus, the presentations expose a dilemma. Without a rational consumer who follows the paths staked out, these market devices that are presented become meaningless.

The solutions that were presented followed a predefined agenda: to characterize consumption in specific ways in order to promote particular technologies or devices. Thus, analysis of talks and presentations exposes the meanings that "market things" have for the emergence of markets as well as the importance of the meanings of expectations created and dispersed with new technologies. So, while the understanding of the consumer was greatly desired, it was at the same time elusive and in many ways just not there. Big data and consumption tools are not so much about finding the truth about consumers, as about attempting to control consumer behaviour. The many narratives of heroic entrepreneurs turned consumption into a passive act.

In this chapter, I have tried to understand digital consumption, not by studying what consumers actually do with devices, or by understanding consumers and devices as assemblages, but by understanding the mechanisms through which particular ideas of consumers come into existence. Studying these fairs gave access to processes through which specific truths about consumption and the effects they have were created. Devices are material-discursive and produce determinate meanings and material beings while simultaneously excluding the production of others. In this, the retail industry confirms its self-image. Fair-goers get confirmation of their worldview in which consumption is governed by market actors. This view is not challenged.

Notes

1 Internet World.
2 The world's most dangerous meeting.
3 Internet World and Webbdagarna.
4 Scandinavian e-Business Camp.
5 Distanshandelsdagen, later named Digital Handel.
6 The world's most dangerous meeting.
7 Svensk Digital Handel (Swedish Digital Trade).

References

Barad, K. (2007) *Meeting the Universe Halfway. Quantum Physics and the Entanglement of Matter and Meaning*. Durham, NC: Duke University Press.
Bathelt, H. and Glückler, J. (2011) *The Relational Economy: Geographies of Knowing and Learning*. Oxford: Oxford University Press.
Bathelt, H., Malmberg, A. and Maskell, P. (2004) Clusters and knowledge: Local buzz, global pipelines and the process of knowledge creation. *Progress in Human Geography*, 28(1): 31–56.
Bathelt, H. and Schuldt, N. (2010) "International trade fairs and global buzz, part i: Ecology of global buzz", *European Planning Studies*, 18(12): 1957–1974.
Bowlby, Rachel (1985) *Just Looking*. London: Methuen.
boyd, d. and Crawford, K. (2012) "Critical questions for big data", *Information, Communication & Society*, 15(5): 662–679.
Butler, Judith (1990) *Gender Trouble*. New York and London: Routledge.
Casey, Emma (2014) "Catalogue community: Work and consumption in the UK catalogue industry", *Journal of Consumer Culture*, 15(3): 391–406.
Clarke, Alison J. (1998) "Window shopping at home", in D. Miller (ed.) *Material Cultures*. London: UCL Press.
Cochoy, Franck (2007) "A brief theory of the "captation" of publics: Understanding the market with Little Red Riding Hood", *Theory, Culture and Society*, 24(7–8): 203–223.
Cochoy, Franck (2011) ""Market-things inside": Insights from Progressive Grocer (United States, 1929–1959)", in Detlev Zwick and Julien Cayla (eds) *Inside Marketing: Practices, Ideologies, Devices*. Oxford: Oxford University Press.
Cronin, Anne M. (2000) *Advertising and Consumer Citizenship*. London: Routledge.
Denegri-Knott, Janice and Molesworth, Mike (2010) ""Love it. Buy it. Sell it." Consumer desire and the social drama of eBay", *Journal of Consumer Culture*, 10(1): 56–79.
Entwistle, Joanne and Rocamora, Agnès (2011) "Between art and commerce: London fashion week as trade fair and fashion spectacle", in Brian Moeran and Jesper Strandgaard Pedersen (eds) *Negotiating Value in the Creative Industries: Fairs, Festivals and Competitive Events*. Cambridge: Cambridge University Press.
Favre, G. and Brailly, J. (2016) "La recette de la mondialisation: sociologie du travail d'un organisateur de salon", *Sociologie du Travail*, 58(2).
Hagberg, Johan (2008) *Flytande identitet: Netonnet och e-handelns återkomst*. Borås: Högskolan i Borås.
Lampel, J. and Meyer, A.D. (2008) "Guest editors' introduction", *Journal of Management Studies*, 45(6): 1025–1035.

Marcus, G. (1998) *Ethnography Through Thick and Thin*. Princeton, NJ: Princeton University Press.

McFall, Liz (2015) *Devising Consumption*. Abingdon: Routledge.

Moeran, Brian and Strandgaard Pedersen, Jesper (eds) (2011) *Negotiating Value in the Creative Industries: Fairs, Festivals and Competitive Events*. Cambridge: Cambridge University Press.

Moisander, Johanna and Valtonen, Anu (2006) *Qualitative Marketing Research*. London: Sage.

Nixon, Sean (2009) "Understanding ordinary women: Advertising, consumer research and mass consumption in Britain, 1948–1967", *Journal of Cultural Economy*, 2(3): 301–323.

Rydell, Robert (1993) *World's Fairs*. Chicago, IL: University of Chicago Press.

Skov, Lise (2006) "The role of trade fairs in the global fashion business", *Current Sociology*, 54(5): 764–783.

Zwick, Detlev and Cayla, Julien (eds) (2011) *Inside Marketing: Practices, Ideologies, Devices*. Oxford: Oxford University Press.

8 "Write something"

The shaping of ethical consumption on Facebook

Niklas Sörum and Christian Fuentes

Introduction and aim

Consumers are increasingly being urged to address recent environmental, social, ethical and economic issues: climate change; unfair trade; animal cruelty; and other potential future damages associated with consumption and product choice (Giesler and Veresiu, 2014). Furthermore, consumers are seemingly answering that call with the purchase of more ecological and fair trade-certified products, shopping for second-hand goods, monitoring their energy use, boycotting products and companies due to their irresponsible behaviour, and trying to reduce levels of consumption (Sahakian and Wilhite, 2014; Connolly and Prothero, 2008). Ethical consumption – the "conscious and deliberate decision to make certain consumption choices due to personal moral beliefs and values" (Crane and Matten, 2004, p. 290), in its diverse forms and practices – is a growing trend. With the development of the Internet in general, and social media platforms in particular (e.g. Facebook, Twitter, blogs), consumers enjoy the possibility of gathering around environmental, ethical and sustainability issues while interacting on a consumer-to-consumer (or citizen-to-citizen) level (Kozinets and Belz, 2010). Communities of interest commonly form around online forums for exchange of information and, as Merrick (2012) and Haider (2015) show, personal experience and advice are typically mixed with references to formal and expert information. Also, such digital tools support the formation of consumer subjectivities, projects and collectives around greener living, and thus act as facilitators for normalizing consumer efforts for more conscious consumption practices (Haider, 2015; Sahakian and Wilhite, 2014; Marres, 2012; Merrick, 2012; boyd, 2010). Haider (2015) and Nathan (2012) found that aspects of identity formation and normalizing of environmentally friendly living through connecting online have emerged as important in network communities, blogs, and social media platforms such as Facebook and Twitter. Importantly, not only dedicated environmental activist communities but also mainstream consumers and citizens engage in a variety of projects and are increasingly sharing, mobilizing, and involving themselves in social marketing and campaigning online (Haider, 2015; Albinsson and Perera, 2013; Langlois et al., 2009).

Against this background, this chapter investigates the shaping of ethical consumption in and by social media. Specifically, we ask how consumers construct ethical consumption through the use of the Facebook platform as the empirical setting of our study.

The main contribution of the chapter to this book lies in developing an empirically grounded, theory-based argument, disclosing how the materiality of shaping what ethical consumption means is socially and technically constituted. How ethical consumption is presented online arguably has an impact on the type of information or content that is made available on specific consumption-related issues and in turn plays a role in the forming of the issue at stake (cf. Rogers, 2013). As Haider (2015) argues, this is the case in how consumers talk about issues, such as the environment, in the blogosphere. Consequently, there is increasing importance within which different digital tools (like Facebook, Twitter, YouTube and Instagram) allow users to access information and conduct communication-related consumer activities. Furthermore, these platforms provide possibilities for consumer engagement and actively contribute to shaping how consumers frame common understandings, norms and values that form the foundation of ethical consumption, and in turn determine what ethical consumption content or information looks like; in other words, these tools shape the meaning and behaviour of ethical consumption.

The chapter's aim is twofold. First, it aims to show how the use of the digital platform contributes to shaping what is perceived as ethical or responsible consumption in a Western consumer culture context. Second, it aims to examine how practices of self-government, as inscribed in digital tools, disclose some of the power regimes that inform consumer practices of shaping the meaning of ethical consumption. To accomplish this, two theoretical concepts are combined: first, the Foucauldian concept of "technologies of the self" with particular reference to the notion of "governmentality" (see, for example, Rutherford, 2007; Foucault, 1997, 1991). Technologies of the self are techniques that allow individuals to work on themselves (bodies, thoughts and conduct) within and through systems of power and governmentality, for example, and are processes whereby concepts have entered into practices of governance and governing narratives that appear to regulate everyday human conduct (Foucault, 1997, 1991). Second, the concept of "affordance", as first introduced by James Gibson (1979), is used to examine how specific tools and their functions afford opportunities for particular consumer actions and make others less probable (see also Haider (2015) and Marres (2009) for recent applications of the concept). The concept of affordance allows for a closer investigation of how technology has shaped ethical consumption in this particular context.

Understanding how technology shapes consumption is important because it addresses a "gap" in the field of ethical consumption research. Much research literature on responsible consumption emphasizes its diversity of forms and names, such as ethical consumption, for example (Barnett et al., 2011), or political consumption (Micheletti, 2003), green consumption (Fuentes, 2014), sustainable consumption (Pecoraro and Uusitalo, 2014), and fair trade (Barnett et al., 2011). Responsible consumption is often conceptualized as individual consumers working to change or resist the habits of consumerism as part of building their own moral consumer selves at a micro-level, but in a smaller number of cases, it has also been analysed at the collective level as part of changing governance and shared ethical responsibility (Barnett et al., 2011; Micheletti, 2003) or as cultural practices (Sahakian and Wilhite, 2014). In sum, they often disclose the ethical dimensions of the personal that also touch on social matters.

Recently, and important from the point of view of how we theorize the shaping of ethical consumption in this study, Noortje Marres (2012) has highlighted what we can call the "device-ification" of participation and engagement in forms of responsible consumption. From a Science and Technology Studies perspective, Marres examines the role that objects have in the performance of public participation and how it matters for sustainable living. We propose that Facebook groups, aside from the content written about in them and the devices needed to produce and consume them, can be conceptualized as such devices. They are enrolled in performances of participation when used to enact and reflect on practices of ethical consumption (see also the chapters from Hagberg and Kjellberg, and Sjöblom, Broberg and Axelsson, this volume, regarding analysis of how technologies affect mundane consumer practices such as music consumption and sharing, and producing market campaign content). The material, infrastructural and technical dimensions of ethical consumption are often neglected in studies of ethical consumption, and research tends to emphasize individual behaviours and values (Chatzidakis et al., 2012; Shove, 2003; Heiskanen and Pantzar, 1997). The techno-cultural landscape of ethical consumption is changing with the introduction of digital devices (Sörum and Fuentes, 2016) and in this chapter we study not only consumers, but also the devices and infrastructure surrounding, enabling and shaping consumer actions and meanings. Through taking into account these "missing masses" (to paraphrase Latour, 2000), we contribute to a theoretically informed analysis of technologies and their impact on ethical consumption.

Sample and analytic methods

The arguments proposed in this chapter are based on an analysis of a selected Swedish-language Facebook group called "Conscious Consumption" (Medveten Konsumtion in Swedish). According to the description of the group, the aim of the group page is to engage people to think through: 1) how we consume; and 2) consuming more sustainably regarding nature, animals and humans. During the time of our study the group had almost 5,000 registered members. The idea of consuming less is also part of the group's philosophy. Reduce, Reuse, Recycle and Respect are mentioned as the four guiding pillars of the conscious consumption philosophy. The forum description also provides a short guide for members towards consumption, based on the advice that: 1) if you have to buy something, you buy second-hand or remade/redesigned; 2) if you buy something new, buy recycled products or ecologically labelled goods; and 3) consider the social justice aspect of consumption, for example, fair trade-certified goods and the fact that consumption in Sweden affects people in other parts of the world.[1] One reason why Facebook groups are a good way to examine online consumer issues is that they are dynamic objects of study that mirror the participatory aspects of social media. Consequently, studying a Facebook group is an appropriate way to study the formation of consumer issues and information practices among consumers within social media.

When selecting the group we wanted one that was active, as we were interested in real-time development of issues in a social media context. We wanted a group that attracted a large number of members, because it allowed a potentially higher degree of variety in terms of voices heard, information shared and practices made visible in the material, rather than a small-scale homogeneous group of friends.

To start our investigation, we collected the hyperlinks (URLs) posted on the Conscious Consumption Facebook group. We used a PDF copy of the Facebook group and pasted it into the Harvest program, available at wiki.digitalmethods.net/Dmi/ToolDatabase. We chose to collect data from the group from its launch in 2008 until September 2014. This gave us in total 473 pages of data. The program (tools.digitalmethods.net/beta/harvestUrls/) allowed us to extract URLs from text, source code or search engine results. It helped us to produce a clean list of URLs. We collected 1,271 links through the Harvest tool.

We first asked the tool to return an alphabetical list of URLs and then only to return the hosts as an alphabetical list. We used this tool to extract the number and character of the available URLs on the Facebook page as a first step in the analysis of the hyperlink network of the page. This made it possible to come up with an idea of what kind of hyperlink network we were analysing and what kind of resources members shared. Questions regarding this step of the analysis were whether the links showed diversity or homogeneity in terms of subjects and actors linked to the Facebook feed, and the total number of links, i.e. whether the page provided a large quantity of resources for members or not. This could provide us with some answers regarding the character of the hyperlink network of Conscious Consumption. From a reading of the results we collected, we saw that the network was diverse and linked to a large number of different actors.

A number of private blogs were shared with personal experiences of trying to live according to a conscious consumer lifestyle. Furthermore, scientific-leaning private blogs were also shared which included many references to scientific debates and formal sources regarding climate change, genetically modified organisms, environmental politics, etc. These appear alongside professional and organizational blogs, such as the think-tank Cornucopia, which is Sweden's largest independent blog focused on finance, the economy and the environment. Environmental association Swedish Society for Nature Conservation, fair-trade organization Fairtrade, watchdog organization Swedwatch, and lifestyle magazines like Camino are also linked. YouTube videos were also shared containing a variety of material, for example Vegan Society on sustainable agriculture and the nuclear power station in Fukushima after the meltdown. Mass media articles from Swedish newspapers (cf. www.dn.se, www.SvD.se) and other news aggregators like Swedish Television (www.svt.se and www.svtplay.se) share space with commercial actors like Swedish retailer Coop and toy store Ekoleko, which specializes in non-toxic children's toys. In sum, the Conscious Consumption Facebook page linked to a variety of different actors as well as digital platforms, and could be described as a heterogeneous forum in "socio-technical" terms. Diversity not only in terms of content but also in technology provided answers to questions about the shaping of ethical consumption on Facebook. For this chapter and in order to gain deeper insight into the site of engagement, we investigated more closely how and what users were commenting on, sharing and linking to, and how these activities were associated with specific forms of concerns and projects.

We then analysed data from the group lasting for approximately a year (from September 2013 to September 2014). Our analysis was inspired by nonintrusive digital observation methods as developed by Kozinets in netnographic research (Kozinets, 2010). Netnography allows for involvement in digital environments in order to disclose cultural practices, values, relations and meanings. In order to analyse the dataset, we used the nVivo software and coded the material after a first round of close reading. The codes emerged through ongoing reading and observing of the data file and we moved from the empirical data to more abstract themes of similarities, but were also informed by engaging with research literature and theory. Our interpretative analysis disclosed particular forms of consumer practices, allowing us to formulate initial themes: informing and advising; marketing of green alternatives and products; enrolment activities for campaigns, projects or consumer activism; awareness raising; promoting the self and the good life through visualization and publication; but also a wide range of group-directed activities like discussions about netiquette, welcoming and other forms of social networking practices, values and norms for interacting in the forum. In sum, all of these activities can be interpreted as contributing to the shape of the group or community. Through object- (platform-)focused readings of data and interactions we focused on technical specificities: use of sharing, liking, embedding of links, videos, pictures, etc. We analysed the use of Facebook as the result of interplay between technical code (information infrastructure; communicative practice; technical affordance), and political or consumer content or discourse. Constant comparative analysis was used to determine returning topics. They were then analysed through theoretical reading drawing from our theoretical concepts as analytical tools for organizing as proposed by Kozinets (2010).

Theorizing ethical consumption as technology of the self

One important theme that emerged during analysis with regard to the shape of ethical consumption and how to consume responsibly in contemporary Western society (which is also conditioned by the Internet in particular ways), was self-management or control in various versions. For example, a member would reach out to the group through writing about his or her concerns regarding what mobile phone to buy since it combined complexity in terms of ethics but also functionality and price. Such status updates exemplified how modern consumers employ technologies to expose feelings and experiences in order to interpret and understand the complex realities in which they exist, and situate themselves within them. These activities were related to versions of how to control purchases, how to consume the right products and how to avoid the wrong ones; they therefore illustrated how members collectively contributed to determining norms, values and meanings of ethical consumption. Personal experience and advice were often combined with references to formal and expert discourse. Arguably, consumers related to themselves and others in ongoing public ways and thus governed their conduct in accordance with expectations and norms by both following and maybe breaking, resisting or even violating them. Self-governance and control were identified as returning topics in accounts of ethical consumption or living in the study, but in many guises. Additionally, self-control was also often reported in forms of mundane projects, campaigns and activities, and expressed in ways that are provided by opportunities as well as restrictions of today's social media. How this was practised specifically, what it looked like and how we chose to conceptualize it are presented with empirical examples after the theoretical approach and are introduced considering the concepts of "technologies of the self" and "affordances".

According to research, contemporary consumers are asked to take responsibility to pursue ethically and environmentally conscious acts on the market and make good choices to improve themselves as well as the world (see Fuentes and Fuentes, 2015; Giesler and Veresiu, 2014). One tendency toward the internalization of this re-evaluation of consumption awareness is the increased amount of discussion of, for example, environmentally friendly living or ethical consumption on social media platforms (Twitter, Facebook, blogs). People online document personal decisions and share practices of greener projects, including, for example, shopping, information and eating practices. Importantly, these depictions and narratives become part of what Haider calls an "online ecology of information" (Haider, 2015, p. 5), presenting particular ways of living, i.e. which behaviours are considered more "ethical", for what reasons, and how to enact these in social practices (see also Cooper et al., 2012; Marres, 2012; Rokka and Moisander, 2009). Documenting one's consumption activities online, as we will show, becomes a form of self-management, scrutiny and confession that exposes them to others – and makes them public/visible to others' inspection, observation and feedback, and thus their control, affirmation and critique.

This close relationship between self-management and publicity/visibility on social media is important for the analysis of the shaping of ethical consumption on Facebook. We address it further below in a discussion about the technical characteristics of social media platforms such as Facebook through operationalizing the concept of affordance. The Foucauldian concept of "technologies of the self" and the related notion of "governmentality" have been introduced in research on how environmental discourses and practices inform the production of normalized subjectivities (see Rutherford, 2007) and can help us understand aspects of ethical consumption online. Technologies of the self, as defined by Foucault, are a series of techniques that allow individuals to work on themselves by regulating their bodies, their thoughts and their conduct within and through systems of power which often seem to be either "natural" or imposed from above. Governmentality, in the context of consumption, is processes whereby, for example, sustainability, ethics and responsibility have entered into practices of governance and underlying governing narratives as a form of governance that appears to regulate and, for example, "environmentalize" everyday human conduct according to individualized understandings of ethical or conscious consumption (Foucault, 1997, 1991). One part of the making of particular subjectivities is through technologies of the self or ways in which people work to become certain kinds of subjects through the application of techniques for improvement. This conceptualization of the formation of subjectivity as an improvement – a more virtuous subject – fits nicely with projects associated with how people engage in processes of becoming more aware of their consumption habits and choices. Following Foucault, Rose (1996) writes about the neo-liberal subject in relation to the notion of incompleteness. In order to become whole and reach completion, it is through the examination of conscience, processes of confession to experts, and the renunciation or rejection of particular behaviours that the subject's conduct can be improved or corrected, for the individual to find a path to self-fulfilment (Rose, 1996, p. 158). Thus, reminiscent of Foucault, practices and discourses that seem innocent have both disciplinary and productive sides to them (Foucault, 1991, 1982). What the technologies of the self provide, for example, is that in addition to positioning the subjects as autonomous and able to change their own lives, they inscribe desires visible in the various ways that many people want to be better and do better in the world.

Arguably, desire becomes the outcome of the intersection between communication technologies and consumers, as they co-constitute each other in an ongoing process of self-formation. These technologies for improvement are, at least in our study (see also, Rutherford, 2007), often broken down into manageable steps for easy application. Examples are the many "to do lists" or advice from environmental organizations on how to improve your consumption through eating vegan once a week, signing a petition, joining a campaign, or using cloth bags instead of plastic. Guides to greener, more ethical and healthier living are supplied in a variety of forms. Such strategies, directed at the consumer, associate environmental destruction and detrimental effects of over-consumption with the individual (hence the importance of Rose's critique of the neo-liberal subject). Responsibility for the environment and other people (producers) is shifted onto citizens or consumers rather than governments, industries and companies. Arguably, consumers are called to take on the responsibility – and proposed to have the ability – to save the planet or people in rather simplistic ways. Added together, this allows for the management, self-surveillance or self-control, and behaviour regulation that lay claim to particular kinds of subjectivity that those who are conscious about their consumption wish to have. A number of different concepts have been suggested over the years to frame the political character of the consumer, consumers' choices and everyday life practices, as they are relevant to ethical consumption. Arguably, ethical consumption often relates to decisions with moral dimensions and they are embedded in mundane, everyday practices. For example, in our data, intense ethical dilemmas can be stirred among consumers over the right toothpaste as well as how one ought best to celebrate Valentine's Day in a "conscious consumption" way (cf. Marres, 2012, for a discussion of the mundane character of many environmental projects). Thus, even though the matters at hand are in nature related to, for example consumers' concerns about environmental damage of a global economic structure, they become concrete in mundane practices of shopping, cooking, socializing, washing, commuting and so on (cf. Shove and Spurling, 2013).

Platform affordances and ethical consumption

On Facebook, the features of the platform seem suitable for individualized, ethical consumer actions, such as awareness-raising events, campaigns or petitions, or other homemade consciousness-raising activities (e.g. "things-to-avoid" lists), which are common in the marketing of conscious consumer lifestyles. Here we find examples such as EcoDay (annual grassroots campaign to promote awareness among consumers to consume more environmentally friendly and fair-trade products), the Veganist Easterfood folder (an awareness-raising campaign targeting shops and consumers regarding environmental, ethical and health benefits of vegan food), and Slaveryfootprint.org (campaign from an organization that developed a website and digital tool that allows consumers to visualize how their consumption habits are connected to modern-day forced labour).

Two platform architectural features are interesting here for our purposes. The first is the networked, interconnected members or followers of the page. This feature supports (affords) the "viral quality" of the platform: the viral distribution of content and updates. Second, it makes it easy for members to produce and share content with other connected members. Arguably, different digital devices ought not to be considered equal but also different. They differ in terms of what is technically possible and what is encouraged but also rewarded and punished. We understand devices are tools, used with cultural implications. This techno-cultural complex can be conceptualized through the notion of *affordance* (Gibson, 1979). Social media platforms provide different affordances or opportunities for action and make others more difficult. Twitter, for example, puts a technical limit on the length of text (140 characters). It might not decide content posted, but it does play a role in the emergent style of writing/interacting which is based on short messages. Similarly, Facebook updates or Instagram photos act according to certain prescribed rules. Thus, affordance helps us analyse how ethical consumption behaviour online is "device specific". According to Hutchby, the perception of communication technology affordances are not found within objects or subjects, but in the moment of action: "the uses and 'values' of things are not attached to them by interpretative procedures or internal representations, but are the material aspects of the things as it is encountered in the course of action" (Hutchby, 2001, p. 27).[2] How, then, are affordances made sense of in action, and how are they put in relation to each other, as Facebook also functions as an environment for other platforms? We will discuss these issues after presenting findings on some of the self-managing processes in our data.

Campaigns, projects and managing ethical consumption

Consumer actions as made possible by technologies affording easy sharing of information are used by consumers to accomplish a variety of goals, such as informing themselves about company practices, products, shops and brands, and boycott campaigns, enlisting fellow consumers in activist endeavours, and promoting their own sustainability projects. Common types of posts are those aimed at enrolling consumers in various sustainability campaigns and other project-based information. These posts are similar to social or viral marketing of products or services that circulate on social media. Notable examples are the ones mentioned above, EcoDay and Slaveryfootprint.org, but there are many more: Buy Nothing Day (an international day of protest against consumerism), Fairtrade Challenge (awareness campaign from the organization behind the Fairtrade certificate), Anti Scampi (a campaign from the Swedish Society for Nature Conservation to stop production and sales of tiger shrimp), Earth Hour (a worldwide movement and campaign for the planet organized by the World Wide Fund for Nature), and so on. Rather than commercial products or services, these posts are political: to promote eco- and fair-trade products and to raise environmental and ethical awareness; to end forced labour in production; to curb overconsumption; to stop production and sales of tiger shrimp for environmental reasons; and to save energy to protect the climate. The list is rather long and they share the trait of promoting simple actions focused on material objects – buy organic; do not buy products made by forced labour; do not buy anything for a day; buy fair trade-certified goods; do not buy tiger shrimp and complain when found on menus; and switch off lights when not in use – to introduce behaviour change and particular practices. Social marketing campaigns work, as Marres argues, to make broader issues visible, for example unsustainable production, overconsumption, forced labour and energy crises (Marres, 2012). These campaigns also function as points of reference for those attempting to engage in ethical consumption, by providing their actions with contexts and meaning. The posts in Figure 8.1 about the Buy Nothing Day campaign illustrate this.

Interestingly, in this post, members of the group instantly start discussing by relating their own conduct to others in public and observe their own as well as others' performance in accordance with expectations and norms by both following and transgressing them. In so doing, they illustrate the productivity of understanding such techniques as techno-cultural means for self-management. The initial post is a question directed to other group members regarding how they will celebrate the Buy Nothing Event that is followed by several re-posts by other members: 1) offering critique of the idea of a single day as a progressive means towards change; 2) remaining sceptical but also positive towards the potential of such easy steps towards large-scale change; 3) being an exemplar of a more radical reduction of consumption (buy nothing); 4) suggesting practical assistance like a Web page with guidelines for reduction of consumption levels; and 5 arguing that the event could work as an antidote to other over-commercialized celebrations like Mother's Day. Some members argue for reduction of consumption levels while others point to making particular product choices. At the extreme end, some members boycott the campaign altogether as part of ethical consumption. In sum, it adds to a process of social meaning making in a complex world. The tension within the process of shaping ethical consumption is represented by a continuous scale between a prescribed set of actions for attaining an ethical consumption standard (represented by the campaign) and an emergent normative strain of critique against any simple one-time consumer gesture that would save the world. Associating this type of activity with the process of self-management, Sauter (2014) discusses forms of public confession on Facebook as a modern form of confession that is a mode of self-writing, an old practice that has become part of sense making in complex societies based on digital platforms with built-in affordances for expected publicity (see also Foucault, 1997). As seen in the example above, "expected publicity" is part of consumers' handling of everyday complexity related to consumption and could spur both conflicting advice and reduction of dissonance through feedback and reciprocal affirmation. These activities do not end with projects, campaigns or posts linked to well-known official templates; people also design their own bottom-up projects and campaigns based on challenges that suit their particular contexts. For instance, the themes of a "simpler lifestyle" and "downshifting" occur on several occasions. In the posts in Figures 8.2 and 8.3, we

den 22 november 2013

Hur ska du fira En köpfri dag 30/11?

Gilla · Dela

4 personer gillar detta.

 Verkar det inte bättre med låg konsumtion alla dagar på året? En dags köpstopp räddar inte vår jord.

Jag är inte säker på att dessa dagar är av godo, jag tror att det finns en risk att många tänker att de gör något gott, ja rentav tillräckligt, för att de upphör med sitt destruktiva mönster en dag om året. Sedan kan de med gott samvete resa till Thailand årligen, äga två bilar, frossa animalier och konsumera heminredning med gott samvete alla andra dagar.

Eller vad tror ni?

........mber 2013 kl. 13:04 · Gilla

Jag tror det finns en poäng i det du säger, men jag tror också att det alltid kommer finnas möjlighet för människor att känna att man gjort något och därmed inte behöver göra mer.

Därför tror jag att det är bra att det finns en särskild kampanjdag mot överkonsumtion, ungefär som kvinnodagen kan ge extra uppmärksamhet för ojämställdheten.

den 22 november 2013 kl. 13:10 · Gilla

 handla inget
den 22 november 2013 kl. 14:59 · Gilla ·   1

Jag har gått och funderat på en idé om att göra en enkel hemsida med en text som uppmanar till att konsumindre på något slagkraftigt sätt. Den sidan kan man sedan tipsa folk om att surfa in på när man är inne på elektronikaffärer och testar t ex surfpl... Visa mer
den 22 november 2013 kl. 15:21 · Gilla ·   3

om/groups/medvetenkonsumtion/?ref=ts&fref=ts

(2) Medveten Konsumtion

 Vi har farsdag, morsdag, alla hjärtans dag mfl som uppfunnits för att vi ska konsumera - då tycker jag det är ett utmärkt sätt att uppmärksamma vårt slösande med en Köpfri dag! Jag låter bli att handla och går på fest istället
den 22 november 2013 kl. 16:58 · Gilla

climat earth day = buy nothing at all

Figure 8.1 A screenshot of a discussion illustrating the interactive nature of the medium

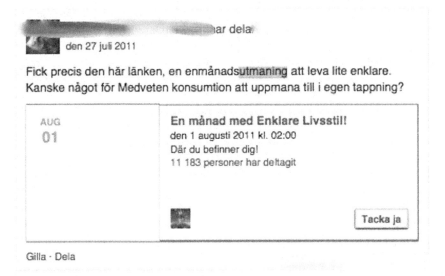

Figure 8.2 A screenshot of a member post with a link to the One Month with a Simpler Lifestyle project

Figure 8.3 A screenshot of a member post with a link to the 30 Days Challenge project

can read about two such projects, One Month with a Simpler Lifestyle, and the 30 Days Challenge.

The two campaigns share the features of being grassroots initiatives that include guidelines and suggestions for how to challenge participants to become more aware of shopping habits and more general everyday routines which at the same time shape and are shaped by contemporary norms associated with what conscious consumption is or ought to be. On the blog lammunge.blogspot.se/2011/08/en-manad-med-enklare-livsstil.html, we can read about one family that joined the One Month with a Simpler Lifestyle project through the advertisement in the Facebook group, and they published a photo of their dinner along with the goals of the project: consuming less; no imported products; and only natural and simple raw materials. The family states that they are living close to ideals stated in the campaign with self-produced lamb, cucumber, garlic, potatoes, courgette (zucchini) and so on, with one exception: they become dysfunctional without coffee! A possible violation of emergent norms for the totally conscious consumer is disclosed in this instance of self-scrutiny. A typical 30-day challenge would be the popular "things-to-do list", which included, for example, 30 days of vegetarian food, walking or biking to work, making one green smoothie a day, and a buy-nothing month with no new clothes or stuff. Both project campaigns include examples of people trying to introduce change by altering individual con-sumption habits (cf. avoid particular products, change a mode of transport, reduce energy consumption), and thus taking control over their lives in order to start living a more righteous, ethical and healthy life.

Arguably, such projects offer "a path to self-fulfilment" for the subject through step-by-step realization (see Rose, 1996, p. 158), and are mundane practices in the sense discussed by Marres (2012). In short, projects worked in order for people to better themselves and also visualize their improvement work through publishing their efforts and advice online through links on Facebook and other easily accessible platforms. Regardless of whether the campaigns or projects came ready-made and associated with social marketing campaigns such as Earth Hour and the Fairtrade Challenge, or as more-or-less homemade or grassroots as in some of the other examples, the information on the specific issues was connected with and located in material practices (cf. Marres, 2012). All them were firmly anchored in social contexts, giving them meaning and a technical environment that made it easy to share, comment on and access. Our results accentuate the project-like features of becoming an ethical or responsible consumer as observed in the digital platform context as well as some aspects of its technical reliance. Through revealing the impact of situated material practices on shaping ethical consumption, our results ques-tion abilities properly to theorize ethical consumption practices through excluding issues of their material constitution (see Hansson, this volume, for a similar argument; cf. Sörum and Fuentes, 2016).

Fluidity of technical affordance and ethical consumption

Some of the posts, projects and campaigns included links to Instagram and Twitter accounts, websites, other Facebook profiles (as seen in the examples above), and blogs. This observation disclosed something about the type of engagement that digital platforms afford. Here, we want to draw attention to some of the particular characteristics of digital platforms that were introduced above in the discussion about affordances, through examining some empirical examples.

A first example is two posts where a group member posted content for mobilizing members for the campaign EcoDay on the Conscious Consumption Facebook page. The first post includes a link to the Facebook page (profile) arranged for the event of EcoDay 2014. The campaign is an awareness-raising event to promote environmentally friendly and fair-trade products, and it is a private initiative. In the other post the advertisement on Facebook is accompanied by an imperative for members to take photos of the things they buy on EcoDay 2014 and to "hashtag" them with "#ecoday2014" on Facebook, Instagram and Twitter for others to see and to spread the word. Thus, people are encouraged to organize a photo with their fair trade- or eco-labelled products and to announce it on a special Facebook page, Instagram or Twitter account, where it is then made accessible together with all other EcoDay photos at the same time as the hashtag #ecoday2014 collected tweets of various EcoDay 2014 events (see Figures 8.4, 8.5 and 8.6).

Several campaigns, events and projects from different actors that connected to and were linked by members included names that started with a hashtag, for example #recycleheaven, #restfest, and #delandetsekonomi. The hashtag used for organizing tweets seems particularly suited for this type of engagement and is an example of what Rogers (2013) calls "natively digital objects", a form of object that is born online, exists online, and is shaped by the particular technical features of the digital context that afford tags to connect communities of interest and cross-communicate content across different platforms in a seamless fashion to increase their impact and visibility. Although seemingly individualized forms of consumer action, the sharing of digital content resonates with the concept of "networked publics" as introduced by Boyd (2010) to describe the dynamic features of technology affordance. Boyd argues that networked publics' affordances "do not dictate participants' behaviour, but they do configure the environment in a way that shapes participants' engagement" (Boyd, 2010, p. 39), and thus shape ethical consumption. Arguably, our observations also disclose how digital platform applications tend to become connected and become each other's affordances. This also gives content new meanings within different sets of affordances. Consider, for example, how a campaign like EcoDay 2014 gains different values and meanings as content is shared and commented on in different contexts, contributing to shape what conscious consumption could mean, include and exclude, and also attributes the potential of, for example, eco-labelled goods to become part of a campaign that disclosed one dimension of emerging conscious consumption practices. It has the potential as practised in the Facebook group to cross-connect content among connected consumers, accounts, profiles or people, and knit them into loosely attached communities of interest. Potentially it makes content easier to find as it is openly published and tagged.

den 25 april 2014 · 🌐

Ekologiskt/fairtrade godis till fredagsmyset var nytt för oss, hoppas också
att jag fann en ny favorit i hudvårdsserien Ros från Ekenäs naturprodukter
😊🌷

#ecoday2014 ♥

Dela

Figure 8.4 A screenshot of a member post including a photo of eco- and fair-trade candy
from a family's Friday night event, published on the EcoDay Facebook page

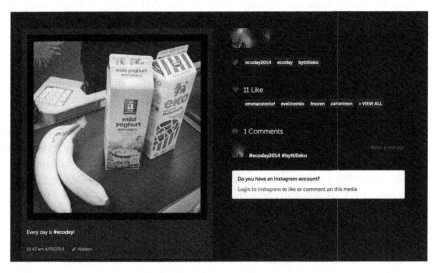

Figure 8.5 A screenshot from an Instagram account showing eco-milk and eco-yoghurt
hashtagged with #ecoday2014

Figure 8.6 A screenshot of a number of #ecoday2014-hashtagged images published on Instagram collected around a tweet

Shaping of ethical consumption through metavoicing

As Ellison and boyd argue, although commenting was there from the start of social media's implementation and use, it "became more central with the rise of media sharing and the popularization of updating" (Ellison and boyd, 2013, p. 154). Facebook's "status updates", Twitter's "tweets" and MySpace's "status and mood" are all examples of opportunities for action that social media implements to encourage its users to create and share content. "Write something", as found in this chapter's title, is a version of this feature encouraging member activity in Facebook groups and to incite creation and sharing of content. For one thing, links and followers or members and possibilities to engage with others' linked content are optional, but dependent on the fact that all members have access to published material as well as the technical incorporation of visible connections, in the form of other profiles. We offer an example in Figure 8.7, where a member asked fellow group members for advice on good websites with information about non-toxic fish that consumers can buy with a clean conscience.

The initial post that contains a question about non-toxic fish for food is followed by the suggestion to pay a visit to the Swedish Society for Nature Conservation's website or consult their smartphone app for further advice. The website and app include a recycling guide, a green guide (for information about ecological products) and a fish guide, among other things, equipping consumers with advice and expertise. Other members following the post as well as the initial posting member "liked" the comment and expressed

den ... september 2013 · Stockholm

Hej, finns det någon bra informationssida med sammanställning över vad för giftfri fisk man kan konsumera med gott samvete?

Gilla · Dela

gillar detta.

...gen tipsar jag om Naturskyddsföreningen. Deras hemsida och deras app Grön guide har massa bra information. Den gröna guiden innehåller en återvinningsguide, en frukt- och grönt guide och en fiskguide.
den 11 september 2013 kl. 23:42 · Gilla ·   3

Tack, den är jätte bra men jag hoppas även på att hitta en sida som är mer ingående. Vill veta vilka hav och varför,... Men tack snälla du för att du svarade.
den 12 september 2013 kl. 23:06 · Gilla

Finns det giftfri fisk kvar?
den 21 september 2013 kl. 15:27 · Gilla ·   1

Kanske inte. Är det så? Sorgligt tanke
den 22 september 2013 kl. 08:27 · Gilla

När jag tittar i backspegeln blir man mer än fundersam Som barn o tonåring bodde jag i en liten stad i småland-i samma hus fanns en "liten" fiskaffär-där fanns alla sorters fisk man kan tänka sig till oflatbart lågt pris.Fisk var vardagsmat.Nu är det en lyx att kunna köpa(om det ens finns) en fiskbit som inte heter sill eller odlad lax.Varför---Haven är snart utfiskade-man tar upp "rubb som stubb" fiskarna hinner inte reproducera sig,Insjöfisk dör p.g.a övergödning m.m Men vad gör vi gräsrötter--accepterar?Tycker det är fördj---gt Men mera då-----
den 22 september 2013 kl. 10:06 · Gilla ·   2

Vissst går det att engagera sig. I Naturskyddsföreningens Handla Miljövänligtgrupper har vi haft fisk som tema i två år (just i år är det ekologisk mat). Vi har bland annat ordnat möten, haft utställningar och stått i butiker och informerat om vilka fiskar man kan köpa med gott samvete och vilka man bör undvika.
den 22 september 2013 kl. 17:00 · Gilla ·   2

· 2

Figure 8.7 Screenshot of status updates assembled into a "thread"

appreciation for the initiated advice. Then the conversation opens up with a critique of the first suggestion and members start to question whether it is enough to follow these sorts of lists when it comes to fish consumption. Questions are raised about how one finds reliable information about what particular waters to avoid; whether there actually are any non-toxic fish left in the world; and then, finally, the discussion moves on to questions about political mobilization regarding the status of fish in terms of change through consumer awareness, markets or political channels. There was no consensus or agreement on the issue and a variety of solutions were suggested following the original post. Interestingly, several posts included references to people's private lives, personal life stories, memories and experienced difficulties regarding ethical considerations on an everyday life basis when faced with conflicting information or demands.

When published content assembled into longer conversations through feedback between different members of the group, "threads" were constructed into traceable discussions (cf. Hansson, 2009, p. 89). This opportunity for collective action disclosed another form of technique of the self whereby consumers managed themselves in public. This "threading" feature affords what we, following Majchzrak et al. (2013), call metavoicing; members did not simply voice their advice, opinion, campaign, project or piece of information, but added "metacontent" to the already existing online content. This activity took on different forms including commenting on someone's post, and "liking" a profile, post or other piece of content published. The analogue affordance on Twitter would be the re-tweet. Metavoicing disclosed how technical capacities contributed to shaping ethical consumption and knowledge sharing as a collective enterprise and it highlighted the decentralized nature of this process. Facebook allowed the shaping of ethical consumption to become a continuous process as members engaged in online conversations through "threads". Arguably, as much previous research on ethical consumers is based on the assumption of the decontextualized individual consumer seemingly burdened with the weight of making the right decision, our data show a complementary picture of a collective learning process and sharing experience that can expand on the notion of ethical consumers as individualized decision makers. Similar "collectivizing" mechanisms are found in other studies of how sociality grows and exists within social networks (Ellison and boyd, 2013).

Conclusion

Social media materially shaped what ethical content or information looked like, and our approach to studying ethical consumption online as the result of collective interaction and dynamics revealed the techno-cultural construction of an ethical set of rules of individual consumers and emergent collective norms, values and meanings growing from contributions and unplanned connections as members used the Facebook platform to share content, comments and "likes". Our results and approach are therefore different from much individually focused previous research on ethical consumption. Many early studies either defined or predicted responsible consumer behaviour based on assumptions understood in terms of measuring individual traits (see Kilbourne and Beckmann, 1998, for a critique of this approach). By emphasizing individual consumers, earlier studies tended to isolate consumers from their technical, cultural, social and historical settings (Dolan, 2002), both abstracting consumers and reducing the complexity of ethical consumption as a result. Thus, while a larger body of consumer and marketing research previously tended to emphasize individual choice more, recent work has focused on the collective strategies and actions of consumer communities (see for example, Moraes et al., 2012; Moraes et al., 2010). Interestingly, in these studies, collective efforts of members of sustainable consumer communities are dependent on and supported by physical place (Chatzidakis et al., 2012) and boundaries that seem important to the development of these communities. In their study of online environmental communities Rokka and Moisander (2009) make a contribution to understanding how digitalization affects ethical consumption, and suggest it is a major influence regarding possibilities of sustained practices of imagined global ethical consumer communities. In this chapter we further aspects of how digitalization shapes ethical consumption by introducing social media platforms as devices for participation and engagement with consumption. Similar to Hansson's results (this volume), we argue that technologies are not neutral mediators of consumption or at the mercy of consumers' intentions, but active agents of change in terms of providing paths of action and engagement that feed back into the practices, discourses, minds and bodies of ethical consumers (see also Hansson, this volume).

For our purposes, it is interesting to note that technical affordances informed the multiple processes of connecting with other profiles and users: the possibility to share content and the feature of publicness or visibility that we have discussed. As stated in our aim, we see these features as part of social media's role in processes of self-control and consumer governmentality where members write about the practicalities of ethical consumption. Our empirical examples can be interpreted as public accounts of consumers consciously challenging themselves to become better, more ethically aware, by avoiding certain products, diminishing consumption of particular goods, reducing one's environmental or social impact, social campaigning and projects, and more. Simultaneously, this endeavour made political dimensions of consumption explicit.

As stated in the introduction to this chapter, we have found a number of issues and products in our empirical data that stirred ethical dilemmas and which were aired collectively on Facebook: how to make a responsible choice of toothpaste, how to celebrate Valentine's Day responsibly, whether vegetarian diets are a good way to implement ethical consumption on an everyday level, and how to change one's transportation and energy consumption for a more environmentally conscious lifestyle, could all serve as examples. Practices and discourses that might seem innocent or benevolent have double implications, both disciplinary and productive sides to them, as we have shown with empirical examples (cf. Foucault, 1991, 1982). Buy-nothing periods, avoiding certain products or companies, keeping "to do lists" with concrete advice and so forth, in order to control consumption, were common activities in our data and facilitated paths for becoming an ethical consumer (cf. Rutherford, 2007). The technologies for improvement were often broken down into manageable steps for easy application. These projects were often but not always associated with various organizations' social marketing campaigns. Facebook was an important tool in this individualization as well as self-management of ethical consumption. In this sense, technologies of the self (Rose, 1996) positioned the subjects as autonomous consumers able to change their lives. This social media technology helped consumers manage the pressure that comes with the increasing individualization of environmental responsibility (Maniates, 2001), while simultaneously contributing to the individualization processes. These governmental techniques also inscribed desires (to do good; become righteous; become a moral person; a person in control of consumer passion) visible in the many ways that people expressed ambitions to do better and be better in the world. Importantly, its administration became visible, circulated, and was also documented and intended for a larger audience of like-minded people. Thus, seemingly individualized forms of consumer action also disclosed collective dimensions, and sharing of digital content complied with concepts like "networked publics" (Boyd, 2010), which points towards group or collective levels of engagement.

Paradoxically, what can look like an individualized form of consumer responsibilization also disclosed collective engagement, which is a result of the techno-cultural inscription of the device and the perceived affordances of the device on the part of community members. As such, the consumer networked public can be conceived of as both individual and collective at the same time. This characteristic of the platform and the community disclosed the "device-ification" of ethical consumption and how platforms materially shaped what ethical consumption looked like (cf. Marres, 2012). Desire for responsible consumption was the outcome here of the intersection between communication technologies and consumers, co-constituted in an ongoing process of self-formation. Following Sauter (2014, p. 829) and her argument regarding Facebook activity, we argue that the "techno-social hybridity of modern Western societies shapes practices of self-formation". This was arguably the case of self-writing consumers working to improve their ethical self-images online. In neo-liberal society, when consumers are (supposedly) controlling and disciplining their own conduct, working on their consumer selves through continual improvement, they also performed their attempts, conflicts, accomplishments, projects and failures in public and displayed this work in tandem with internalized rules or possible loss of such ethical standards. The public enactment of consumption projects and individualized forms of action for social change, we argue, are better understood taking into consideration the workings of socio-technical tools, i.e. devices, as aspects of control and self-management are inscribed in their configuration.

Thus, returning to our theoretical argument regarding technology's role in shaping conscious consumption, we conclude by arguing that theorizing technology from the point of view of affordance (Marres, 2012; Gibson, 1979) meant that a neglected source of influence regarding shaping of ethical consumption was disclosed. In this chapter, the missing *masses* of *ethical consumption* were brought to the fore and made part of the analysis – both through empirical examples and theoretical conceptualization – showing the important constitutive force they can have in the shaping of ethical consumption and ethical consumers.

Notes

1 Conscious Consumption also exists as a member association outside Facebook and works with the aim to increase knowledge about consumption and its consequences on the environment and people working in the industry. The Facebook group is not an extension of the association in the sense that it is a forum controlled by the association, but introduced by the association to trigger a discussion about consumption. From our analysis we can conclude that the Facebook group is not closely attached to any agenda coming from the association but lives a life of its own. The absolute majority of posts, comments, responses and other activities on the page come from Facebook group members and not from official association members.
2 Hutchby (2001) argues that any technology may be presented to the public as fulfilling specific needs in specific ways, but that in the end, it is the end user who defines and interprets the most appropriate use to which the technology can be put. To make this argument, Hutchby draws upon Gibson's (1979) concept of "affordances", arguing that each technology possesses an inherent range of possibilities, not all apparent at the time of production. When new people with new perceptions use the technology, new affordances, and new possibilities for its exploitation, will be realized. Central to our interpretation of affordance is that the concept claims that when actors enter a setting – for example, social media platforms – they perceive cues about what behaviours it affords and these perceptions shape behaviours without determining them. Because we are interested in *the execution of actions* rather than describing social media platforms or digital devices in terms of structural forms of modality, we chose not to use a concept like "modality".

References

Albinsson, P. and Perera, B. (2013) "Consumer activism 2.0 – Tools for change", in R. Belk and R. Llamas (eds) *The Routledge Companion to Digital Consumption*. New York: Routledge.

Barnett, C., Cloke, P., Clarke, N. and Malpass, A. (2011) *Globalizing Responsibility: The Political Rationalities of Ethical Consumption*. Chichester: Wiley-Blackwell.

boyd, d. (2010) "Social network sites as networked publics: Affordances, dynamics and implications", in Z.A. Papacharissi (ed.) *A Networked Self: Identity, Community, and Culture on Social Network Sites*. New York: Routledge, pp. 39–58.

Chatzidakis, A., Maclaran, P. and Bradshaw, A. (2012) "Heterotopian space and the utopics of ethical and green consumption", *Journal of Marketing Management*, 28(3–4): 494–515.

Connolly, J. and Prothero, A. (2008) "Green consumption: Life-politics, risk and contradictions", *Journal of Consumer Culture*, 8(1): 117–145.

Cooper, G., Green, N., Burningham, K., Evans, D. and Jackson, T. (2012) "Unravelling the threads: Discourses of sustainability and consumption in an online forum", *Environmental Communication*, 6(1): 101–118.

Crane, A. and Matten, D. (2004) *Business Ethics: A European Perspective*. Oxford: Oxford University Press.

Dolan, P. (2002) "The sustainability of "sustainable consumption"", *Journal of Macromarketing*, 22(2): 170–181.

Ellison, N.B. and boyd, d. (2013) "Sociality through social network sites", in W.H. Dutton (ed.) *The Oxford Handbook of Internet Studies*. Oxford: Oxford University Press, pp. 151–172.

Foucault, M. (1982) "The subject and power", in H.L. Dreyfus and P. Rabinow (eds) *Michel Foucault: Beyond Structuralism and Hermeneutics*. Chicago, IL: University of Chicago Press.

Foucault, M. (1988) "Technologies of the self", in L.H. Martin, H. Gutman and P.H. Hutton (eds) *Technologies of the Self: A Seminar with Michel Foucault*. Amherst, MA: University of Massachusetts Press, pp. 16–49.

Foucault, M. (1991) "Governmentality", in G. Burchell, C. Gordon and P. Miller (eds) *The Foucault Effect*. Hemel Hempstead: Harvester Wheatsheaf, pp. 87–104.

Foucault, M. (1997) "Self-writing", in P. Rabinow (ed.) *Ethics: Subjectivity and Truth – The Essential Works of Michel Foucault, 1954–1984*. New York: New Press, pp. 207–222.

Fuentes, C. (2014) "Managing green complexities: Consumers' strategies and techniques for greener shopping", *International Journal of Consumer Studies*, 38(5): 485–492.

Fuentes, M. and Fuentes, C. (2015) "Risk stories in the media: Food consumption, risk and anxiety", *Food, Culture and Society: An International Journal of Multidisciplinary Research*, 18(1): 71–87.

Gibson, J.J. (1979) *The Ecological Approach to Visual Perception*. Boston, MA: Houghton Mifflin.

Giesler, M. and Veresiu, E. (2014) "Creating the responsible consumer: Moralistic governance regimes and consumer subjectivity", *Journal of Consumer Research*, 41(3) (October): 840–857.

Haider, J. (2015) "The shaping of environmental information in social media: Affordances and technologies of self-control", *Environmental Communication: A Journal of Nature and Culture*, online first.

Hansson, N. (2009) "Network politics online. The Gothenburg social forum-process, IT and actor-network theory", *Ethnologia Scandinavica, A Journal for Nordic Ethnology*, 39: 82–98.

Heiskanen, E. and Pantzar, M. (1997) "Toward sustainable consumption: Two new perspectives", *Journal of Consumer Policy*, 20(4): 409–442.

Hutchby, I. (2001) *Conversation and Technology: From the Telephone to the Internet*. London: Polity.

Kilbourne, W.E. and Beckmann, S.C. (1998) "Review and critical assessment of research on marketing and the environment", *Journal of Marketing Management*, 14(6): 513–532.

Kozinets, R.V. (2010) *Netnography. Doing Ethnographic Research Online*. Thousand Oaks, CA: Sage Publications.

Kozinets, Robert V. and Belz, F.-M. (2010) "Social media for social change: Sustainability-based community in a sustainable world", Association for Consumer Research 2010 NA Conference, Jacksonville, FL, October.

Kozinets, R., Belz, F.-M. and McDonagh, P. (2011) "Social media for social change", in D. G. Mick, S. Pettigrew, C. Pechmann and J. L. Ozanne (eds) *Transformative Consumer Research to Benefit Global Welfare*, pp. 205–223.

Lammunge.blogspot.se (2011) lammunge.blogspot.se [accessed 23 June 2015].

Langlois, G., Elmer, G., McKelvey, F. and Devereaux, Z. (2009) "Networked publics: The double articulation of code and politics on Facebook", *Canadian Journal of Communication*, 34(3). Retrieved from www.cjc-online.ca/index.php/journal/article/viewArticle/2114.

Latour, B. (2000) "Where are the missing masses? – The sociology of a few mundane artifacts", in W.E. Bijker and John Law (eds) *Shaping Technology/Building Society – Studies in Sociotechnical Change.* Cambridge, MA: The MIT Press, pp. 225–258.

Majchrzak, A., Faraj, S., Kane, G.C. and Azad, B. (2013) "The contradictory influence of social media affordance on online communal knowledge sharing", *Journal of Computer-Mediated Communication*, 19: 38–55.

Maniates, M. (2001) "Individualization: Plant a tree, buy a bike, save the world? *Global Environmental Politics*, 1(3): 31–52.

Marres, N. (2009) "Testing powers of engagement: Green living experiments, the ontological turn and the undoability of involvement", *European Journal of Social Theory*, 12(1): 117–133.

Marres, N. (2012) *Material Participation: Technology, the Environment and Everyday Publics.* Houndsmill, Basingstoke: Palgrave Macmillan.

Merrick, H. (2012) "Promoting sustainability and simple living online and off-line: An Australian case study", *First Monday*, 17(12). Retrieved from journals.uic.edu/ojs/index.php/fm/article/view/4234.

Micheletti, M. (2003) *Political Virtue and Shopping.* New York: Palgrave.

Moraes, C., Carrigan, M. and Szmigin, I. (2012) "The coherence of inconsistencies: Attitude–behaviour gaps and new consumption communities", *Journal of Marketing Management*, 28(1/2): 103–128.

Moraes, C., Szmigin, I. and Carrigan, M. (2010) "Living production-engaged alternatives: An examination of new consumption communities", *Consumption, Markets & Culture*, 13(3): 273–298.

Nathan, L.P. (2012) "Sustainable information practice: An ethnographic investigation", *Journal of the American Society for Information Science and Technology*, 63: 2254–2268.

Pecoraro, M. and Uusitalo, O. (2014) "Conflicting values of ethical consumption in diverse worlds – A cultural approach", *Journal of Consumer Culture*, 14(1): 45–65.

Rogers, R. (2013) *Digital Methods.* Boston, MA: The MIT Press.

Rokka, J. and Moisander, J. (2009) "Environmental dialogue in the online community: Negotiating ecological citizenship among global travellers", *International Journal of Consumer Studies*, 33(2): 199–205.

Rose, N. (1996) "Governing "advanced" liberal democracies", in N. Rose, Andrew Barry and Thomas Osborne (eds) *Foucault and Political Reason.* London and Chicago, IL: UCL Press.

Rutherford, S. (2007) "Green governmentality: Insights and opportunities in the study of nature's rule", *Progress in Human Geography*, 31(3): 291–307.

Sahakian, M. and Wilhite, H. (2014) "Making practice theory practicable: Towards more sustainable forms of consumption", *Journal of Consumer Culture*, 14(1) (March): 25–44.

Sauter, T. (2014) ""What's on your mind?" Writing on Facebook as a tool for self-formation", *New Media & Society*, 16: 823–839.

Shove, E. (2003) "Converging conventions of comfort, cleanliness and convenience", *Journal of Consumer Policy*, 26(4): 395–418.

Shove, E. and Spurling, N. (eds) (2013) *Sustainable Practices: Social Theory and Climate Change.* London: Routledge.

Sörum, N. and Fuentes, C. (2016) "Materialiserad moral. Smartphone, applikationer och etisk konsumtion", *Kulturella Perspektiv*, 25(2): 6–15.

9 Digitalized music

Entangling consumption practices

Johan Hagberg and Hans Kjellberg

Introduction

It is difficult to ignore the development of music consumption when taking an interest in the digitalization of consumer culture. In relation to other products and services, music digitalized early through the introduction of compact discs (CDs), continuing with MP3 files, (il)legal downloading and the current proliferation of streaming (see e.g. Magaudda, 2011; Denegri-Knott, 2015; Werner, 2015). Given the rapid development of digital music consumption in recent years, it is not surprising that research has been extensive (e.g. Oakes et al., 2014; Kerrigan et al., 2014; Magaudda, 2011; Dholakia et al., 2015; Denegri-Knott, 2015; Fleischer, 2015; Werner, 2015). This body of work has explored music consumption in relation to various digital formats and attended to a variety of aspects including emotions, materiality and mobility. These studies exemplify in different ways what Oakes et al. (2014) explicitly stress, namely that music has become *ubiquitous* in contemporary society. Digitalization has arguably been an important driver of this ubiquity by contributing to make music increasingly mobile and by multiplying forms of distribution and listening.

This chapter is based on extensive interviews with Swedish consumers concerning the digitalization of music consumption. These interviews reflected many of the changes discussed in the literature, e.g. changes in how consumers bought, talked about and listened to music. The ubiquity of music was a prominent theme: the digitalization of music allowed it to be consumed in more situations and more often. However, the interviews also unearthed facets of digitalization that previous studies have not addressed to any great extent. Most importantly, they suggested that music consumption is increasingly integrated into other aspects of everyday life rather than being a "stand-alone" activity. As a consequence, music listening comes to intersect with a growing number of mundane activities. The specific intersection of music consumption and running has recently been explored by Kerrigan et al. (2014), but the wider issue of how music consumption is integrated with everyday activities remains largely unstudied.

Against this background, we address three specific questions:

1   With what other activities is digital music consumption integrated and how is music consumed in these situations?
2   How can we characterize the integration of music consumption and other activities?
3   How does this integration affect music listening?

Thus, our purpose is to identify activities with which music consumption intersects, delineate how music consumption is integrated with these activities, and explore how this integration affects music listening.

Based on our interview material, we identify and describe seven intersections between music listening and other mundane activities: exercising, walking/cycling, commuting, working, hanging out, being at home, and driving (see Figure 9.1). We do not suggest that these intersections were caused by or created as a result of digitalization. Many of them existed long before the introduction of the CD, which can be considered the first digital music technology with extensive impact. We do argue, however, that the digitalization of music has influenced these intersections, their occurrence and intensity. We identify and discuss four types of intersection patterns between music listening and these activities: parallel, integrated, discrete, and connected. Finally, we discuss how the digitalization of music and the increased intersection with other mundane activities transform music listening practice.

The chapter is organized as follows: first we discuss previous literature focusing on consumption practices and music. This is followed by a description of our method and interview material. Thereafter we describe the seven identified intersections between music listening and other mundane activities. We then present our analysis and propose a typology of activity intersections. Finally, we offer some concluding remarks about the transformation of music listening and how its intersection with other activities due to digitalization affects music listening.

Music consumption practices?

The "practice" concept is increasingly employed in studies of consumption (see e.g. Holt, 1995; Warde, 2005; Shove and Pantzar, 2005; Shove et al., 2007; Akaka et al., 2013; Hartmann, 2013; Fuentes, 2014; Kjellberg and Stigzelius, 2014; Hagberg, 2016). While there are many definitions of practice (see e.g. Schatzki, 2001; Reckwitz, 2002), most revolve around the idea that practices integrate a set of activities into recognizable, interconnected wholes. Most practice approaches view practices as co-constituted by material objects like tools, equipment and goods (see e.g. Schatzki, 2010; Halkier et al., 2011). These objects are regarded as essential for carrying out practices, although there are differences in exactly how material aspects are conceptualized in relation to practices, for example being part of, interrelated with or mediators of practices.

Our approach is closely related to actor-network theory in the sense that we view the material world as constitutive of practice (see Shove et al., 2012). We define a practice as a nexus of doings and sayings (Schatzki, 2001) quite similar to the notion of action nets (Czarniawska, 2004), but recognized as a relatively distinct entity. Such practices are constituted by: 1) routinized activities involving, 2) competencies, 3) objects, and 4) meanings (Shove et al., 2012). Through interaction among these elements, practices are integrated into larger complexes. Based on Araujo and Kjellberg's (2009) discussion of Reckwitz (2002), our conception of practice emphasizes the interrelation of *praxis* (action as opposed to theory) and *praktik* (routinized behaviour). While "a practice" constitutes a recognizable "block" of doings, sayings, entities and meanings, the instantiation of a practice, i.e. its performance, generates variation and may at times produce outcomes that do not pass as an instance of said practice (due to misfires, happenstance, errors, etc.).

Saren's (2015) recent critique of the notion of *consumption* in the context of music makes it important to specify how we use this term. In short, what is meant by consumption from our practice perspective? Depending on the starting point, consumption can itself be regarded as a (set of) practice(s), as implied by the consumption cycle of acquisition, consumption (use), possession and disposition (Arnould and Thompson, 2005), or as "not itself a practice but ... rather, a moment in almost every practice" (Warde, 2005, p. 137). Following De Certeau (1984), we equate consumption with use and specifically restrict our attention to the practice of *listening to music*, thus disregarding other instances of music consumption such as acquisition and collection. Thus, music listening is a music consumption practice that is constituted by activities (selecting songs, handling music players, plugging in earphones, etc.), competencies (knowledge of music styles, technical abilities), materials (smartphones, earphones, digital files), and meanings (nostalgia, party mood, affiliation to social groups). As Kerrigan et al. (2014, p. 152) say in relation to the case of running, "[t]he use of music and music devices can be viewed as part of a wider set of consumption practices". Thus, music listening can become interlinked with other activities, which directs attention to what these other activities are, how they are interlinked with music listening, and what the effects of these links are.

Methods

In order to explore the consequences of digitalization on music consumption, we designed an interview study focusing on Swedish consumers. Sweden is a country in which the digitalization of music has been particularly marked and where many popular digital music innovations have emerged, for example Kazaa, Pirate Bay and Spotify. Swedish consumers have quickly adapted to and shifted to new forms of music consumption: streaming services accounted for 83.9% of total music sales in Sweden during the first half of 2015 (IFPI, 2015). Arguably, this makes Sweden a good context for studying the consequences of digitalization on music consumption.

To design the study, we first conducted a literature review to identify different aspects of digital music consumption, including important shifts in digital music technologies and categories of music-related consumption practices. Based on this, we developed an interview guide that focused on previous and contemporary music consumption including one section asking respondents to list and elaborate on the three most important situations in which they listened to music. Using this guide, we performed extensive, semi-structured interviews with 15 Swedish music consumers from four different age groups. These groups were defined in relation to the three central digital music technology shifts: from vinyl to CD, from CD to MP3, and from MP3 to streaming. The duration of the interviews ranged from 29 to 103 minutes, with the average interview lasting 57 minutes. The interviews explicitly sought to trace practices by encouraging respondents to speak of their everyday music consumption and how it had developed over time. While this method has limitations for capturing finer details about the constitution of individual practices, it offers advantages in terms of identifying such practices and understanding their significance to individual consumers.

Each interview was conducted by one of the researchers, recorded and transcribed. The interview transcripts were read in their entirety by both authors, highlighting consumption-related themes and summarizing these per interview. A central observation from this reading was that most situations in which the respondents said they listened to music were not exclusively devoted to music. Instead, music was consumed in connection with the performance of other activities or engagement in other practices. Based on this observation, we systematically mapped the situations in which the respondents stated that they listened to music. From these situations, we selected activities which in principle could have been performed without listening to music, but where the respondent for some reason chose to listen to music.

This procedure led us to identify between four and nine situations for each respondent. In total, the respondents discussed 88 instances (situations) when they listened to music. Many of these were similar across the respondents. By sorting and aggregating them, we arrived at seven categories of activities where the respondents also consumed music: 1) exercising; 2) walking/cycling to work; 3) commuting by public modes of transport; 4) working; 5) hanging out; 6) home-based practices; and 7) driving. Each of these activities was recurrent, although the specifics of the situations differed between the respondents. For example, many respondents claimed they listen to music when they drive, yet the specific way in which music was consumed in this situation differed across the respondents.

We then compiled all interview passages related to the seven categories in separate text files. This involved browsing through printouts of the interviews as well as searching for specific keywords in the transcripts. Based on this material we drafted accounts of how these activities intersect with music listening, and how the digitalization of music influenced them. We did this jointly for the first activity intersection (driving to music), reading in parallel and then discussing the material to extract themes and identify interesting observations before drafting a first running text. We then analysed the remaining activity intersections in sequence, passing the documents between us.

Intersections of music listening in everyday life

Our respondents provide ample support for the claim that music is ubiquitous (Oakes et al., 2014). Several respondents spontaneously suggested that they "always" listen to music, and went on to elaborate on various everyday situations in which they consumed music. They gave few examples of listening to music as a stand-alone activity. Instead, the situations they considered most important for music listening were such that listening intersected with the performance of some other activity. Below, we account for each of the seven identified activity intersections (see Figure 9.1).

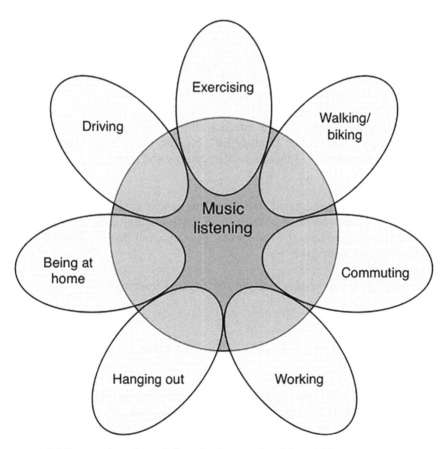

Figure 9.1 Intersection of music listening in everyday life activities

Exercising to music

The intersection between music listening and exercising is well known (e.g. Kerrigan et al., 2014), and was frequently mentioned in our interviews. While exercising to music has a long history, the respondents claimed digitalization had meant increased opportunities and comforts. Although most reported that they listened to digital music when exercising, the specific configuration varied, for example the kinds of devices used. Despite differences, three themes were prominent across the respondents.

First, exercising placed certain requirements on the equipment used for music listening. Body-fit was one issue, for instance problems with earphones falling out when running. This led to the use of particular earphones, or alternatively a headband to keep them in place. Another body-fit issue was related to the size of the music player:

> When I run, I use a small MP3 player. I think that the phone is too heavy and cumbersome, and it gives you sores, so I use that small MP3 instead.
>
> (IP3)

Second, and related, exercising was said to require uninterrupted music provision. Examples of interruptions included people sharing the same Spotify account or lack of connectivity, as in the following quote:

> I definitely do not change [music] when running. When I exercise, I always use the off-line [Spotify list], because the reception can be a bit bad in the forest [...] there are interruptions and such.
>
> (IP12)

Third, respondents suggested that exercising placed certain requirements on the kind of music you listen to. Nearly all had particular genres or songs they listened to when exercising. Unsurprisingly, tempo and rhythm were suggested to be of great importance:

> In the gym you need something that is more up-tempo.
>
> (IP4)

> [The choice of songs] depends on how fast I plan to run.
>
> (IP9)

As a result, some respondents prepared special playlists for exercising, often linking the name of the list to the intended use: "Running", "Exercising", "Workout", "Psyched-up", etc. The importance of tempo when exercising also meant that some respondents accepted listening to music that they otherwise did not like, for example music chosen by others. This was also linked to the perceived function of music when exercising. Many respondents specifically noted that for them, music was an exercising tool, which "is about keeping pace, boosting your energy, or psyching yourself up" (IP3). In addition to keeping a better pace, music made exercising more fun and/or provided a source of energy and motivation.

Thus, exercising influences what music to listen to and how, while music listening also influences the practice of exercising, making you go the extra mile, run faster, etc. The intensity of the intersection of music listening and exercising makes it qualitatively different from most other intersections. Music becomes an integral part of exercising to a much higher extent than it does with other intersecting activities.

Walking/cycling to work

Listening to music when walking or cycling from one place to another, for example to work or school,[1] was a very common type of intersection. Mobile devices for listening to radio or cassettes have long enabled pedestrians and cyclists to listen to music: "as long as I've been an active music consumer I've been able to bring music wherever I go" (IP4, born in 1990). Still, digital devices were recognized as having made this much easier. The respondents gave many examples: CD players, MiniDisc players, MP3 players, mobile phones with MP3 players, and smartphones with streaming services. Some also acknowledged that previous devices had not "really" been mobile (e.g. portable CD players). Besides the occasional exception, for example using an MP3 player despite access to streaming, most respondents currently streamed music on their smartphones, which they claimed they carried with them anyway:

> I mostly listen to music when I am walking somewhere … Then I always listen with the smartphone. I don't bring anything separate for it. On the smartphone I always listen through Spotify.
>
> (IP8)

When walking or cycling, the respondents used earphones for listening. However, one respondent emphasized using only a single earphone for safety reasons (being attentive to traffic and other pedestrians).

With a streaming service such as Spotify, Internet access was considered a key issue, and many used the possibility of offline listening to overcome this potential limitation. In addition to being online or offline, walking could also restrict music listening in other ways. For instance, one respondent pointed out that it was difficult to use YouTube when walking since that requires the phone to be open/active.

Walking or cycling to work typically has a fixed duration that frames music listening. The respondents gave examples of regularly listening during bike rides lasting 7 minutes up to 30 minutes. Similar examples were given for walks. In some cases, music even became integrated into the respondent's perception of time: "It takes about two songs to get to school, so then I try to pick the best songs ..." (IP5).

Compared to exercising, this activity intersection placed fewer constraints on the type of music our respondents listened to. Most claimed to listen to the same type of music when walking or cycling as they did during other activities. The type of music also varied over time: "When I walk to and from work now it is usually the summer list which is the latest, or it could be that I have heard a good song and listen to it a lot" (IP10). The choice of music could be related to the present mood and to what extent one could switch between different types of music. The mood could also be decisive in whether the respondent listened to music at all when walking. Finally, the choice of music could be made to induce a certain mood, like cheering you up in the morning on the way to school. Overall, mood comes across as an important aspect of the intersection of music listening and walking or cycling. The direction of influence runs both ways: the present mood can influence what music to listen to, and the particular music chosen can influence your mood.

Commuting by public modes of transport

This intersection refers to music consumption in connection with regular travelling through public modes of transport, such as bus, metro/subway, train, or car (if someone else is driving). Listening to music when commuting has many similarities to listening while using other forms of transport. Some respondents considered them identical: "[I listen] when I am on my way from one place to another either on the subway or when I am walking" (IP4). However, there are differences. Listening to music when commuting can also involve other activities, such as reading: "I commute so I sit with my earphones on the shuttle while reading" (IP2). Or it could be a substitute for those other activities: "On travels when I sit in a car or something I can't read because I get sick, so I listen to music instead" (IP5); "[I listen] instead of reading a book when I am tired or something" (IP8).

The respondents differed in terms of how they listened to music when commuting. Many streamed music on their smartphones: "On the bus specifically it is earphones and Spotify" (IP7). The equipment was often brought along for other purposes and not separately for music listening. Since commuting often involves limited or irregular access to the Internet and thus to streaming services, using an offline playlist was often preferred.

One form of listening when commuting was to combine randomness with some degree of control, e.g. using "shuffle play" with Spotify. This is random in terms of the particular song but controlled in terms of the set of songs on the playlist:

> I probably press shuffle play. On Spotify. And I have my earphones. I've compiled ... we have a number of different playlists on Spotify, so if I'm tired I pick the "sleep" list, and if I'm happy I may take the "psyched up"

list or the "goodies" list, or perhaps "Håkan" [first name of the Swedish artist Håkan Hellström]. Then you press shuffle play and hope something great comes on.

(IP11)

The degree of randomness could also depend on the time of day. One respondent chose more carefully in the mornings and used shuffle play in the afternoons.

A particularity of listening while commuting concerns the mixing of public and private spheres. Many respondents used earphones to shield off the surrounding environment, but also to protect that environment from their listening. Some respondents mentioned situations where others did not shield off the environment and how that frustrated them:

It happens that you hear, you know, young people who have their mobile phones, but on high volume, that is, without earphones, listening loudly on the bus. Then you almost get uncomfortable, like: "what's that ... damn ... shut it off ... put earphones on ... that's private!"

(IP6)

One important reason for listening to music when commuting was said to be to create a private sphere:

It has to do with the desire to enter your own bubble ... I think it becomes increasingly important because society is becoming more and more stressful. People need to escape somewhere to simply cope with everyday life, to enter into music is an incredibly useful tool.

(IP2)

Another reason was to make the commute more fun by adding music. Thus, music listening while commuting works as a form of micro-escapism. Similar to previous research on consumer escape (e.g. Molesworth and Denegri-Knott, 2009), which stresses the escape from routine in order to be or do something else, music dissociates from the environment, allowing focus on you, while contributing to make the activity more pleasant.

Working

Music listening when working was common among our respondents. For two respondents, music constituted a constant backdrop during work, while most others listened to music on and off. For our youngest respondents, the intersection concerned listening to music in the classroom. For our older respondents, it either meant playing music in the background, or listening to music to shut out other inputs at work. An important facet of this intersection concerned whether or not it was practically possible, or perceived as acceptable, to listen to music while working. This could depend on the particular task (e.g. having to express oneself in certain ways vs. answering emails), or situation (during opening hours). Whether or not it was allowed to listen to music in school was something that several respondents brought up. Here, there seems to have been a gradual liberalization. Respondents in their twenties indicated that it had not been accepted when they were at school (at least not before grade 10), while our youngest respondents said that unless the teacher was presenting or there were class discussions, this was a matter of personal responsibility.

One important difference among the respondents was whether music listening was private or a backdrop. Respondents who emphasized the creation of a private sphere tended to consume digitalized music, either using their smartphones or listening to music on the computer in parallel to working. The musical backdrop, on the other hand, was usually radio-based. The same person could use either form of listening, depending on situation:

> When ... we are open [retail store] then ... the radio is always on. Because then I need to hear when customers enter. When I'm [in the store] before or after hours then I always use headphones. I think the sound is best that way.
>
> (IP10)

For many respondents, listening to music when working was an active choice and a way of creating a private sphere that made working more fun (similar to commuting). However, it could also increase efficiency:

> I use headphones at work, because we sit in an office landscape and you kind of need to sit in your own little tunnel to get stuff done.
>
> (IP2)

> It feels like it makes things easier. You're doing something boring like maths, and then music turns it into a fun activity [...] I feel you can achieve a higher tempo if the song has a quick beat.
>
> (IP5)

> If you're working on something on your own, concentrating. Then you listen mostly to get inside yourself.
>
> (IP13)

In contrast to this, some respondents indicated that they did *not* consume music while working precisely because they found it difficult to concentrate on work when music was playing.

These responses suggest that music consumption and work practices can intersect in different ways. For some, listening to music was a tactical move to create an island of solitude that allowed them to concentrate on the work at hand. In some cases, adding music could even transform work from something boring to something fun. For others, music was simply something that went on in the background, and which did not interfere with work. For still others (or in certain situations), music consumption tended to take over, transforming the work/music consumption intersection to a pure music consumption practice.

Hanging out

Listening to music when hanging out involves many types of situations ranging from active forms of listening (e.g. going to concerts with friends) to more passive forms (e.g. having music in the background when playing board games). Digital devices differentially affected these situations. When going to concerts, digital devices made it easy to compile playlists before or after the concert. In other situations, music as such was more in the background and listened to more passively:

> Sometimes we sit and play [games] and listen to music. But it is not that we go and listen to music together. It is not the main thing.
>
> (IP13)

Parties were described as an example of hanging out where music listening was neither very active nor very passive but nevertheless significant. For parties, material devices such as speakers and docking stations and their quality were considered important. Listening to music in these situations often invoked conventions concerning what (and "whose") music to play:

> Usually when I am with friends I try to get my list played ... But if I have "music drought" ... then I can agree to play theirs. But if there is a song that is very soft or that I don't ... Well, then I ask them to switch song.
>
> (IP5)

> I never get the chance. I am the only one in my group of friends that likes to listen to Metallica, Iron Maiden, more rock and things like that. When we have pre-parties or so it is often House music. And then you just have to accept the fact that the majority likes it and just sit and listen.
>
> (IP7)

Here, the use of digital devices and services such as Spotify has clearly changed the conditions for music listening. One example is the procedure of *queuing*. One respondent explained that it was important to stick to the rules: "It is very important to queue songs, when you're at a party for example, so that it's fair." However, queuing can create problems when the rules are not followed, like if someone moves their song up the list: "No, that's the worst kind of people." One respondent described these situations:

[At parties] everyone should queue ... It becomes a war. You may think that the queuing system is okay, but then if someone breaks it and clicks on their song, then you get completely ... it becomes war. Because everyone wants to listen to their song ... And then the friendly atmosphere is spoiled.

(IP12)

Queuing can be prevented, for example, by locking the mobile phone:

[Y]ou can lock [the phone], but then people always approach you, "I want to queue a song". "Well, rather not ..." There is something called "Spotify Hitler". That's probably me.

(IP5)

There were also examples of a backlash for digital devices, partly due to the ease with which they allowed you to shift music:

A friend and her boyfriend have a vinyl player at home and two or three big boxes with records. They think that it's great to have at parties because then it's almost impossible for anyone at the party to just click for the next song in case they don't like it. So they can decide for themselves about the music and then you have to like invest 20 minutes in listening to one side of the record and then switch side. But this possibility to just jump between songs is not there and I think that this has contributed to the comeback of the vinyl.

(IP4)

There were several reasons given for listening to music when hanging out. At parties, music contributes to the mood and becomes more or less essential to the situation:

[At parties] it is nice [with music] and some party mood. [If it was quiet] it would be boring, there has to be some music at parties [laughter].

(IP1)

At other times music could have a more passive role, playing in the background. In some cases the situation offered an opportunity to discuss and discover new types of music and give recommendations to other people.

Being at home with music

This is probably the most heterogeneous intersection in our material. Still, since many respondents highlighted "being at home" as an important situation in which they consumed music, it warrants attention. Once again, very few (two) respondents described instances of exclusive music consumption in their homes. Instead, music accompanied other activities, like cleaning, cooking, working on the computer, watching TV (!), waking up, going to sleep, and indeed sleeping (!). Music listening at home was also among the most heterogeneous intersections in terms of material devices: radios, smartphones, tablets, computers, Internet radios, record players, CD players, docking stations, speakers, Wi-Fi streaming devices, and earphones were all used by more than one of our respondents. In many cases, respondents alternated between different devices. While ten respondents used Spotify at home, the music could also emanate from YouTube, their vinyl or CD collections, their MP3 library, an Internet radio channel, or the regular FM radio.

Given the heterogeneity of other activities with which music intersects at home, it is not surprising that its role varies. Two respondents clearly distinguished between two types of music listening: one involving active choice and a greater level of attention; and another, more passive type, where music provided background to other activities. Remaining respondents fit these categorizations quite well. Interestingly, active music consumption did not rule out intersecting activities. For instance, one respondent sometimes chose very specific records to listen to when cooking. Another example suggests that the relative weight of the intersecting activities can be important:

> At least once a week, I sit down in the evening and sort of: "Now I'm going to listen to music." And then I don't usually sit idly just staring into nothing listening to music, but usually I sit in front of the computer, surfing, kind of idle-surfing Web pages, so that you are still concentrated on the music. I don't do anything that takes over.
>
> (IP6)

So, the relative importance of music listening can vary quite considerably. At one end of the spectrum, there are intersections in which music is clearly subordinate, e.g. listening to music *while* sleeping. In other situations music listening is slightly more prominent, but still provides background to another activity, like cleaning or cooking. Then there are intermediate situations, where the relative weight is less clearly on one activity, like watching TV and listening to music at the same time. Here, we also find situations where music listening is integrated with other activities, similar to some work situations (e.g. doing homework). At the other end of the spectrum, there are situations in which music listening is the main activity, but where other activities can intersect as long as they do not interfere with that main activity.

Some respondents noted that music listening at home involves others (family members, friends, neighbours), and that this influences how and what you listen to. Finally, some highlighted more mundane aspects that influence the particular configuration of music consumption, including which entity was currently being charged, the difficulty of moving the docking station around when cleaning the house, or whether you would be able to hear when someone called for you.

The reasons given for consuming music at home varied and included breaking the silence, influencing your mood, providing a backdrop to other activities, shutting things out and providing comfort.

Driving to music

Listening to music when driving is a well-established intersection of activities. Since the introduction of the first in-car radio in the 1930s, cars have been equipped with ever more sophisticated devices for combining driving and listening (Berkowitz, 2010). The car also offers a relatively private space for enjoying music. Many respondents said they listen to music when driving and several of them regarded this as self-evident. "[Music in t]he car, yes, well that is a must, of course" (IP2).

For the consumption of digitalized music, however, driving to music is not necessarily the most important intersection. Many respondents claimed to listen to the radio when driving as an alternative to CDs, MP3 players or smartphones. There were several reasons for this. First, the existing infrastructure in the car placed restrictions on the consumption of digital music for some. This could lead to frustration:

> Unfortunately, I don't have that aux-input in the car, so I have to listen to the goddam radio. It's awful but then there is at least some music to listen to.
>
> (IP6)

Others took this in their stride:

> In the car it is mostly CDs, also because the sound is better. Because, I don't have anything with which to connect my iPhone to the speakers in my old Saab. So, then it's CDs.
>
> (IP8)

Second, the respondents suggested different motivations for listening and that this might influence their choice to consume digitalized music. Some suggested that music simply constituted a background to driving, thus implying that they did not care that much what was playing. To others, it could be very important to be in control. In one case, the respondent gave an example of what this could lead to:

> Sometimes in my car, when a certain song pops up in my head that I want to listen to, I've turned Spotify on and then you're sitting there like an idiot with your cell phone to your ear when driving just because you feel you have to listen to that song. But, of course, the sound is complete crap, but at least you get to listen to the song. Better than nothing.
>
> (IP6)

One respondent explained that the choice of listening to digitalized music or not depended on current preferences:

> If there is a particular song that I like, then I listen to it everywhere [...] but when I get tired of [a song] I might not listen to anything. Then, I just listen to the radio in the car.
>
> (IP1)

None of the respondents indicated that they felt driving placed any restriction on the kind of music they listened to. Consequently, they reported listening to a wide variety of music when driving. "When I drive, then it's all kinds of things [music]." Instead, the choice of songs or albums could depend on who else was in the car or indeed whose car it was. In particular, the presence of children introduces restrictions concerning what to listen to. Here, the proliferation of new digital devices also influences how music can be consumed:

> As long as the children enjoy it, the trip works well. However, during the last year there have been many iPads in the car. Then the adults can decide a little more [what to listen to], but at a lower volume then.
>
> (IP15)

There was also variation in terms of the unit of consumption when listening to music when driving. Some respondents clearly indicated that they consumed individual songs, while others consumed albums. This might be related to the kind of digital music technology they used: at least, respondents who consumed songs used streaming technology, while those who consumed albums used CDs. Also, respondents who used streaming in other situations expressed frustration over the fact that they could not stream in the car and thus control what they listened to:

> When I drive, I have to listen to the radio [due to a faulty aux cable]. But I *really* prefer to listen to my music rather than to the radio. Well, because they play a lot *over and over again*, and old songs, and such, so it's better to listen to your own.
>
> (IP5)

The music devices used by our respondents when driving included smartphones, MP3 players, car stereos (radio, CD, speakers, aux port, Bluetooth, etc.), aux cables, CDs (bought and ripped), playlists, and storage devices (for CDs). These were related to alternative configurations of their music consumption in the car: radio or CD, and streaming or radio. The example given above of holding the phone to your ear suggests that it is possible to break with available infrastructure and perform non-typical music consumption when driving (although it might not be recommendable!).

Some also highlighted that passengers can be important in the configuration of music listening in the car. The kind of music you listened to was adapted to the other persons present. This links to the varying meanings attributed to music when driving. We noted a few different types of listening above. For example, one of the respondents noted that going on longer trips could lead to specific preparations, like compiling a playlist. Others emphasized that in the car it was a matter of what was available at the time of driving, which could lead to frustration when choices were seen as too limited.

A typology of intersections of music listening in everyday life

The previous section outlined seven activity intersections involving music consumption. Combining this material with insights from previous work on consumption practices, notably Pantzar and Shove's (2010) ideas about the links between practices, we now ask: How does music listening relate to these other activities? Irrespective of whether music consumption is regarded as a practice performed in conjunction with another practice, or as an ancillary activity that is simply added to that other practice, we are interested in probing the different ways in which music consumption is combined with other activities as part of everyday life.

A first observation from our material is that the degree to which music consumption intersects with other practices varies. Two types of intersection can be identified in this dimension: separate and related. At one extreme there are situations where there is no actual intersection, so that the practices come across as separate. Some of the empirical examples border this extreme, suggesting that the intersection is coincidental or insignificant, for example music playing "in the background", or equating listening to the radio in the car to not listening to anything. At the other extreme there is complete intersection, in the sense that removing music from the situation would radically change its character. Here, then, music constitutes an essential part of the situation. Dancing would be one example, but there were also some cases of exercising where music consumption was suggested to be of critical importance. In these cases, it is appropriate to consider music listening and whatever other activity goes on simultaneously as constituting part of the *same* practice, even though they may exist as separate practices under other conditions (cf. Pantzar and Shove, 2010). Most intersections mentioned by the respondents fall somewhere in-between these extremes, i.e. music listening is neither completely separate from nor completely integrated with the other activities. Here we find various instances of what Pantzar and Shove (2010) call "cooperative", "competitive" and "prey–predator" relationships, depending on exactly how music listening relates to the other practice.

A second observation is that the way in which music consumption intersects with other practices also varies. Here, we have identified two basic logics: sequentiality and simultaneity. Sequential intersections are such that music consumption either precedes or follows some other practice, but is regarded as affecting or being affected by that other practice. On the other hand, intersections characterized by simultaneity are such that music consumption takes places while something else also is taking place. Most of the intersections in our material are of this kind, such as listening to music while driving, walking, commuting or working. By combining these two dimensions (the degree and kind of intersection), we can identify four types of intersections between music consumption and other everyday practices (see Figure 9.2).

The first type of intersection (or non-intersection) is the limiting case of *discrete practices*, i.e. practices that are separate and performed sequentially. In these cases, music consumption is a practice in and of itself; it is performed separately from and does not influence the next practice; it is delimited and independent. First you do X, then you do Y. The best examples of this type are the few indications of music consumption as a stand-alone activity that our respondents gave. However, as our material suggests, this is a relatively uncommon case. Indeed, none of our respondents listed this kind of exclusive consumption as one of the three most common situations in which they consumed music. Examples that fit the discrete type of (non-)intersection were commonly described as having occurred in the past, for example due to technological restrictions of mobile CD players:

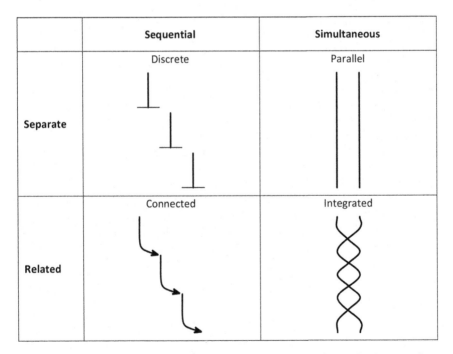

Figure 9.2 Typology of intersections between music consumption and other practices

It was so clumsy to bring along because it was so big. So I didn't bring it with me, only occasionally. It was rather that I used it in my room to sit and listen.

(IP12)

The second type of intersection involving music listening is *connected practices* (related and sequential). This type of intersection involves one practice having consequences for, gaining meaning from, or triggering the performance of another. Examples from our material include prospective connections where respondents listened to music in order to influence a future activity, e.g. listening to music to get psyched up for an athletic competition, or getting in the right mood for meeting friends at school, preparing a playlist for an upcoming party or trip, or listening to a band before attending a concert. There were also some examples of retrospective connections, e.g. listening to music to relive a particular situation, or some event during the day triggering a desire to listen to a certain song at a later point. As an example of a combination of prospective and retrospective connections, one of the respondents described how she listened to music before and after training and competition (the particular sport did not allow listening while playing):

I always listen to music before I practise and even before competing. When I compete it can make me calm down. And if I perform badly in a competition I always listen to music to calm down if I am sad.

(IP11)

In a few cases, music consumption was also noted to trigger other activities, for example when attending a concert triggered video recording. Needless to say, these examples in no way exhaust the possible ways in which music consumption can be sequentially related to other practices.

The third type of intersection is *parallel activities* (temporally co-existing but separate). As discussed above, this constitutes a limiting case. We find few instances where music listening in parallel does not somehow influence the other practice, although, for example, background music when working may come close. Many respondents also discussed listening to music while driving in this way, in no way indicating that they considered their music consumption to affect their driving. At the same time, some respondents implied that balancing music with a parallel activity could be tricky, for instance when listening to music while walking to school:

It is a little dangerous if people jump at me from behind because they know that I use both [earphones] so I have stopped doing that.

(IP5)

Sometimes, the difficulty of balancing two parallel activities made our respondents choose not to listen to music:

No I'm not usually able to [listen to music while working], because it is difficult for me to disregard it.

(IP4)

I'm the kind of person who sometimes can work to music and sometimes not. It depends on what I'm doing. When I am doing things that require me to express myself in a certain way, then I usually don't listen to music. It becomes too much in my head at the same time. But most of the time, when I'm editing, answering emails etc., then I can have music on without any problem ... It doesn't disturb.

(IP8)

Rather than viewing music as a potential disturbance, however, it was more common to recognize a positive influence on the parallel activity, making the experience more enjoyable:

It kind of makes it easier when you do something boring like ... sitting on a train and it becomes like an activity, a fun activity even though you are just sitting there and listening.

(IP5)

This takes us from parallel activities towards the fourth and final type of intersection, that of *integrated activities*. By changing the perception of the parallel activity (commuting in the quote above), music listening is no longer simply taking place alongside that activity. This is similar to parallel activities in the sense that music consumption is simultaneous to some other practice. It differs in the sense that music consumption is recognized as either influencing or being part of that other practice. As discussed above, there is considerable variation here from music affecting the perception of another practice (making your commute more enjoyable), via affecting the outcome of that practice (making you work better), to being an essential part of that other practice:

Whenever, you know, there's a problem with the link, or reception, because it's Spotify running [at the gym], then the whole gym stops and people immediately start screaming: "Put on the music!" People *have* to have music. It is so *unbelievably* important.

(IP6)

The two types of activity intersections that are sequential in character (discrete and connected) raise questions about "the here and now" versus the existence of prospective or retrospective links (cf. the distinction between because and in order to motives, Schutz, 1962). When music consumption is recognized as a sequentially related activity, it is part of some wider project, for instance, crafting your personal identity. As part of such projects, other activities may also become connected to music consumption, for example ways of dressing. In contrast, the two types of activity intersections that are simultaneous in character (parallel and integrated) raise questions about background and foreground, or in Piette's (2008) terms, about major and minor modes of being. If two activities truly go on in parallel, either one could supposedly stop without the other doing so. As a consequence, we can expect parallel activities to vary in prominence. Some of our respondents indicated that the ability to keep music in the background was important in certain situations, such as when working. Indeed, some chose not to listen to music when working out of concern that it would become too prominent. In other cases, the whole point of including music was for it to have an effect on the other practice, for example making a commute more enjoyable. In situations where music is highly integrated with another activity, on the other hand, there is a limit to how far into the background it can be pushed before the combined practice unravels (e.g. in the gym, or when dancing).

Concluding remarks: the consequences of digitalization for music listening

The purpose of this chapter was to identify activities with which music consumption intersects, delineate how music consumption is integrated with these activities, and explore how this integration affects music listening. We have identified and described seven intersections between music listening and other mundane activities. Based on these findings we have developed a typology of intersections along two dimensions resulting in the four types of intersections discussed above. In this concluding section one question remains: In what way can our typology of intersections between music listening and other mundane activities assist us in understanding the consequences of digitalization? As we have pointed out, digitalization is not a homogeneous phenomenon, but encompasses a range of different technological solutions. In the case of music, there are at least three co-existing digital regimes: CD, MP3 and streaming. This means that the consequences of digitalization may differ, depending on which regime one is studying. In particular, our study adds insights into the third generation of digital music – that of streaming.

However, we would argue that there are certain common consequences. More specifically, the increased availability and mobility of digital music tends to shift music consumption away from being a discrete activity to becoming an intersecting activity, either parallel to, connected to or integrated with a number of everyday practices. Our material suggests that the main effect of digitalization is to make music consumption a simultaneous activity, but by being readily available, there is also an increased possibility of enacting connected music consumption.

Kerrigan et al. (2014) argued that the integration of music listening and running led to a "musicalisation of running". Based on the accounts above we would suggest that influence also goes in the other direction, so that we get "runnification", "exercisification", "commutification" or "drivification" of music listening. Music listening becomes an activity that intersects with other activities to an increasing extent. This development shapes music listening both in terms of the ways we listen and the kinds of music we listen to, and in terms of the role music plays in our everyday lives.

While this certainly allows music to become ubiquitous, as Oakes et al. (2014) argue, we suggest that it also comes at the expense of dedicated consumption. Our material suggests that streaming contributes to a movement towards increasingly intersecting practices and away from exclusive listening. It seems that music is at the same time everywhere and nowhere. As one of our respondents self-critically put it, he felt that he "listened worse" (IP6) today than he used to.

Thus, a paradox with the digitalization of music listening seems to be that while it is easy to take music with you, share music, find out what others are listening to, etc., the integration of music listening with other activities makes it an increasingly private and asocial activity. In these cases music listening becomes a way of putting the world outside "in brackets" (Goffman, 1974) and entering your own private bubble.

Future work

This chapter is based on interviews with consumers. While this method is suitable for capturing information about contemporary music consumption and its development over time it has limitations in terms of how well it can capture everyday practices. Thus, we believe that the integration of music consumption with other practices needs to be further explored through other methods such as direct observation, diaries and other forms of self-observation. While one of the activity intersections that we identified has been more carefully explored, that of running (Kerrigan et al., 2014), the other intersections should be further studied to better appreciate variations and finer details. In particular, "being at home" and "hanging out" are highly heterogeneous categories that contain considerable variation and complexity requiring more careful and detailed analysis. Despite its shortcomings, the present chapter could offer a fruitful starting point for an extended analysis of how music consumption intersects with other activities, how its integration with other activities can be characterized, and how it affects music listening.

Note

1 There were various reasons for choosing to walk or cycle rather than go by bus or car (save money, increase health). In contrast to exercising, where health-related effects are in focus, the primary purpose here is to move from one place to another.

References

Akaka, M.A., H.J. Schau and S.L. Vargo (2013) "The co-creation of value-in-cultural-context consumer culture theory", in R.W. Belk, L. Price and L. Peñaloza (eds) *Consumer Culture Theory*. Bingley: Emerald, pp. 265–284.

Araujo, L. and H. Kjellberg (2009) "Shaping exchanges, performing markets: The study of market-ing practices", in P. Maclaran, M. Saren, B. Stern and M. Tadajewski (eds) *Handbook of Marketing Theory*. London: Sage Publications, pp. 195–218.

Arnould, E.J. and C.J. Thompson (2005) "Consumer culture theory (CCT): Twenty years of research." *Journal of Consumer Research* 31(4): 868–882.

Berkowitz, J. (2010) "The history of car radios. Car tunes: Life before satellite radio." *Car and Driver* (October).

Czarniawska, B. (2004) "On time, space and action nets." *Organization* 11(6): 773–791.

de Certeau, M. (1984) *The Practice of Everyday Life*. Berkeley: University of California Press.

Denegri-Knott, J. (2015) "MP3." *Consumption Markets & Culture* 18(5): 397–401.

Dholakia, N., I. Reyes and J. Bonoff (2015) "Mobile media: From legato to staccato, isochronal consumptionscapes." *Consumption Markets & Culture* 18(1): 10–24.

Fleischer, R. (2015) "Towards a postdigital sensibility: How to get moved by too much music." *Culture Unbound* 7: 255–269.

Fuentes, C. (2014) "Managing green complexities: Consumers' strategies and techniques for greener shopping." *International Journal of Consumer Studies* 38(5): 485–492.

Goffman, E. (1974) *Frame Analysis. An Essay on the Organization of Experience*. New York: Harper & Row.

Hagberg, J. (2016) "Agencing practices: A historical exploration of shopping bags." *Consumption Markets & Culture* 19(1): 111–132.

Halkier, B., T. Katz-Gerro and L. Martens (2011) "Applying practice theory to the study of consumption: Theoretical and methodological considerations." *Journal of Consumer Culture* 11(1): 3–13.

Hartmann, B. (2013) *Consumption and Practice: Unfolding Consumptive Moments and the Entanglement with Productive Aspects*. JIBS Dissertation Series No. 093. Jönköping: Jönköping International Business School.

Holt, D.B. (1995) "How consumers consume: A typology of consumption practices." *Journal of Consumer Research* 22(1): 1–16.

IFPI (2015) *IFPI Sverige Musikförsäljningsstatistik*. www.ifpi.se/dokument-och-statistik/musikforsaljningsstatistik.

Kerrigan, F., G. Larsen, S. Hanratty and K. Korta (2014) "'Gimme shelter': Experiencing pleasurable escape through the musicalisation of running." *Marketing Theory* 14(2): 147–166.

Kjellberg, H. and I. Stigzelius (2014) "Doing green: Environmental concerns and the realization of green values in everyday food practices", in S. Geiger, D. Harrison, H. Kjellberg and A. Mallard (eds) *Concerned Markets: Economic Ordering for Multiple Values*. Cheltenham: Edward Elgar Publishing, pp. 203–237.

Magaudda, P. (2011) "When materiality 'bites back': Digital music consumption practices in the age of dematerialization." *Journal of Consumer Culture* 11(1): 15–36.

Molesworth, M. and J. Denegri-Knott (2009) "Adults' consumption of videogames as imaginative escape from routine." *Advances in Consumer Research* 36(1): 378–383.

Oakes, S., D. Brownlie and N. Dennis (2014) "Ubiquitous music: A summary and future research agenda." *Marketing Theory* 14(2): 141–145.

Pantzar, M. and E. Shove (2010) "Temporal rhythms as outcomes of social practices: A speculative discussion." *Ethnologia Europaea* 40(1): 19–29.

Piette, A. (2008) "L'anthropologie existentiale: présence, coprésence et leurs details." *Antrocom* 4(2): 131–138.

Reckwitz, A. (2002) "Toward a theory of social practices: A development in culturalist theorizing." *European Journal of Social Theory* 5(2): 243–263.

Saren, M. (2015) "'Buy buy Miss American Pie': The day the consumer died." *Marketing Theory* 15(4): 565–569.

Schatzki, T. (2010) "Materiality and social life." *Nature and Culture* 5(2): 123–149.

Schatzki, T.R., K. Knorr Cetina and I. von Savigny (eds) (2001) *The Practice Turn in Contemporary Theory.* London: Routledge.

Schutz, A. (1962) *Collected Papers I: The Problem of Social Reality.* The Hague: Martinus Nijhoff.

Shove, E. and M. Pantzar (2005) "Consumers, producers and practices: Understanding the invention and reinvention of Nordic walking." *Journal of Consumer Culture* 5(1): 43–64.

Shove, E., M. Pantzar and M. Watson (2012) *The Dynamics of Social Practice: Everyday Life and How it Changes.* London: Sage Publications.

Shove, E., M. Watson, M. Hand and J. Ingram (2007) *The Design of Everyday Life.* Oxford: Berg.

Warde, A. (2005) "Consumption and theories of practice." *Journal of Consumer Culture* 5(2): 131–153.

Werner, A. (2015) "Moving forward: A feminist analysis of mobile music streaming." *Culture Unbound* 7: 197–212.

10 Marketing and cyberspace
William Gibson's view[1]

Barbara Czarniawska

Popular culture and marketing

Digital consumption is an expansive (and expanding) field, so I am limiting this text to its relationship to marketing, looking at the representation of both these issues in popular culture.

The claim that there is a circular relationship between culture and other fields of social endeavor is not new. This relationship is especially obvious in the case of popular culture, which transmits ideals and propagates identity models, reflects ongoing practices, but also teaches them to practitioners (Czarniawska and Rhodes, 2006). It also offers interpretative templates – patterns for sense making. It should not be surprising then if digital consumption and popular culture influenced one another. Yet what about such an allegedly rational organizational function as marketing?

The connection between popular culture and various management functions was noticed in accounting as early as the 1930s (Coleman, 1936), but it is only since the 1990s that this relationship has been studied systematically (see for example, Hassard and Holliday, 1998, on organizing in general; Beard, 1994, on accounting; Fitchett, 2002, on marketing; Czarniawska, 2012a, on finance).

It has also been suggested that fiction offers acute interpretations of actual developments and equally acute predictions of the future long before social sciences and humanities do (Kundera, 1988). This statement applies particularly well to science fiction, which prompted Martin Parker and colleagues in 1999 to edit a special issue of the journal *Organization*, dedicated to the connection between science fiction and organization studies. The message of this special issue was that organization theory could learn from science fiction how to report and reflect about actual and possible practices – a theme later developed by Rhodes and Brown (2005).

David Metz (2003) has suggested that science fiction offers identity models to the incumbents of new jobs and occupations – information technology freelancers and various temporary workers, for instance. Brian Bloomfield (2003) saw science fiction as a template for making sense of the relationships between human beings and advanced technologies. As Katherine N. Hayles had suggested, "visions of the future, especially in technologically advanced areas, can dramatically affect present developments" (Hayles, 2005, p. 131).

These observations have often been illustrated by the writings of William Gibson, whose works seem to be shaping the future as much as describing the present. He was, after all, the person who coined the word "cyberspace." As Douglas Kellner put it, it is "William Gibson and the cyberpunks who have carried out some of the most important mappings of our present moment and its future trends" (Kellner, 1994, p. 299). Gibson's interest in the contemporary economy is obvious in all his books (Czarniawska, 2012b), to the point that it is debatable if his genre is actually science fiction. As Hollinger (2006, p. 452) has noted, Gibson traded in "the tropes of sf [science fiction] for the strategies of mimetic realism." Some of his novels can be seen as ethnographies of what Hollinger called "future-present." Commenting on Gibson's writings, Fredrick Jameson (2005) suggested that a new genre – a "socioeconomic science fiction" – has recently emerged.[2] Its representatives, other than Gibson, were Neal Stephenson (e.g. *Reamde*, 2011, a political technothriller) and Gibson's previous co-author, Bruce Sterling (e.g. *The Zenith Angle*, 2004, which describes a world after 9/11).

Through its future-present setting, this new genre differentiates itself from another new trend in science fiction: a post-dystopian novel, best represented by Margaret Atwood's trilogy *Oryx and Crake*[3] and such recent films as *Elysium* (Neill Blomkamp, 2013) and *Interstellar* (Christopher and Jonathan Nolan, 2014). This type of fiction has its origins in earlier utopian and dystopian works, but it assumes an inevitability of a major catastrophe and explores possible new modes of life in the post-catastrophe world. It is always located in the future, unlike the "socioeconomic science fiction."

In several of his novels, but especially in *Pattern Recognition* (2003), Gibson analyzed the connections between cyberspace and global marketing, thereby also taking up the issue of digital consumption. This chapter summarizes his analysis and relates it to contemporary research trends.

Main characters and main issues in *Pattern Recognition*

The protagonist of *Pattern Recognition* (*PR*) is a young woman called Cayce Pollard. She is presented as a "dowser in the world of global marketing," and her talent consists of a "morbid and sometimes violent reactivity to the semiotics of the marketplace" (*PR*: 2). "Semiotics" is understood widely here, as Cayce is allergic not only to words, but to images as shapes as well. It is claimed that she is "sensing" pictures and objects. The intentions of the designers are of no interest to her; she serves "as a very specialized piece of human litmus paper" (*PR*: 13), as she is, quite literally, allergic to fashion – particularly to anything by Tommy Hilfiger, whose products are "simulacra of simulacra of simulacra" (*PR*: 17), "the null point [...] beyond which it is impossible to be more derivative, more removed from the source, more devoid of soul" (*PR*: 18). This is how Gibson explained it in an interview for *Wired*:

The Ralph Lauren brand is a simulacrum of something that was an American simulacrum of something that was originally British – it's sort of a receding hall of mirrors. But Ralph Lauren and Hackett both look astonishingly hyper real when viewed through Tommy Hilfiger ... There's a kind of infinite recession of simulacra going on. I don't know what I think about it, but it's there before me – and part of the way I deal with that is to write books like this. I hope I give the reader some perspective in which to frame the experience of that sort of simulacra, which is a huge part of daily life in this century. As soon as you step out the door you're confronted and informed by narratives, all of which have been very, very carefully crafted to attract you and their crafters would hope to convince you of the genuineness of the narrative – and the desirability of its applicability to self.

(Parsons, 2010)

You do not actually have to step out of the door anymore – the narratives await you on the screen of your computer, your tablet and your smartphone. It is a sign of passing time that in 2002 (when the action takes place), Cayce must actually go out onto the street to encounter fashion, instead of checking Instagram. At any rate, she is immune to such narratives, protected by her allergy. As she needs to be dressed, however, she only wears CPUs: "Cayce Pollard Units." They look like they were designed by Naomi Klein (*No Logo*; Klein, 2000):

CPUs are either black, white, or gray [...] What people take for relentless minimalism is a side effect of too much exposure to the reactor-cores of fashion. This has resulted in a remorseless paring-down of what she can and will wear [...] She can only tolerate things that could have been worn [...] during any year between 1945 and 2000 [...] [Her] very austerity periodically threatens to spawn its own cult.

(*PR*: 8)

As it is unlikely that Klein's book was already well known in February 2003, when *PR* was first published, it seems that Gibson foresaw even this development. Indeed, one result of *No Logo*'s popularity was that many a young person was wearing clothes from which the logo had been visibly removed, thus making it kind of a logo in itself (a no-logo). As Jon Elster (1983, p. 67) observed, "the anti-conformist is only a negative slave of fashion, who constantly has to monitor the choices of the majority so as to be out of phase with them" (supposedly unlike a nonconformist who simply does not notice fashion).

Cayce is a slave not so much to fashion as to her fashion allergy, but because she is allergic to the already fashionable, she is also capable of "hunting cool." She earns her living looking for new patterns in street fashion and pointing them out to the "commodifiers," who were going to "productize" and, hopefully, "monetize" them (*PR*: 86).

Is such cool hunting possible? Rinello and Golfetto (2006, p. 866), who studied a trade fair called Première Vision, concluded that it "promotes the idea that novel developments in society exist and that experts can somehow (by intuition or trained observation) spot them."

This idea is shared by another central character in *PR*, Hubertus Bigend, who employs Cayce:

> My passion is marketing, advertising, media strategy, and when I first discovered the footage [anonymous postings of short pieces of a video], that is what responded in me. I saw attention focused daily on a product that may not even exist [...] The most brilliant marketing ploy of this very young century.
>
> *(PR*: 65)

Cayce has been employed to discover the authors or producers of "the footage" – those short videos that are attracting the attention of crowds of fans. Obviously, Bigend's purpose is to commodify this digital product – an interesting aspect of digital consumption, as it means both digitalizing commodities and commodifying digital presences. Bigend is the owner of a company called Blue Ant. It:

> has a sub-unit called Trans, which is an abbreviation for either translation or transgression – nobody but Bigend knows. Trans contracts attractive freelancers, who go to clubs and restaurants and chat with unsuspecting people – usually of opposite sex. When certain products or services are mentioned in conversation, the Trans temps say they like it too. Thus positive reinforcement from an attractive person of the opposite sex is calculated to reward the opinion of the target person.
>
> *(PR*: 84–85)

How fictive is this? There is a Canadian company called "Blue Ant Media Inc.," and an Australian company BlueAnt Wireless, incorporated in 2003. Was it named after the company in Gibson's book? "Viral marketing" (*PR*: 84–86) exists:

> Viral marketing, viral advertising, or marketing buzz are buzzwords referring to marketing techniques that use pre-existing social networking services and other technologies to try to produce increases in brand awareness [...] through self-replicating viral processes, analogous to the spread of viruses or computer viruses [...] It can be delivered by word of mouth or enhanced by the network effects of the Internet and mobile networks [...] *Viral marketing may take the form of video clips*, interactive Flash games, advergames, ebooks, brandable software, images, text messages, email messages, or web pages.
>
> (en.wikipedia.org/wiki/Viral_marketing, accessed 21/12/2014, emphasis added)

Observe that even the idea of video clips, the main magical object in *PR*, already exists in marketing. Gibson did not invent "viral marketing" either; the authors of the Wikipedia article refer to earlier sources, such as Rushkoff (1996). Viral marketing described in *PR* is not digital at all; it most closely resembles buzz marketing, as described by Marie-Anne Dujarier:

> Specialists in what is called "buzz marketing" work to make the consumer the instrument of a subtle, discreet, and virtually painless type of advertising: word of mouth. They are asked to carry out unpaid work on promotional advertising in their own social and geographic environments.
> (Dujarier, 2016, p. 563)

In time, a certain compensation began to be used. The "buzzadors" (www. buzzador.com, accessed 24/06/2016) "pay using their opinions" when buying things from the site's Web shop. Apparently, there are as many as 400,000 buzzadors in the Nordic countries. Their opinions, it is claimed on the site, are more important to them than are those promoted by the marketers.

Is this a competition with traditional marketing or another step forward in marketing? In Bigend's opinion, "[f]ar more creativity, today, goes into the marketing of products than into the products themselves, athletic shoes or feature films" (*PR*: 67). Indeed, as one of the reviewers of *PR* observed: "Brand is the king: logos have become more important than the products they embellish" (Hitchings, 2003). In his review of *PR*, Konstantinou (2009) reminded readers that it was Naomi Klein who claimed in 2000 that "brand managers" were a new type of producer – not of goods or services, but of "meanings," reified into brands. Representational practices, as Kjellberg and Helgesson (2007) and many others after them have observed, are crucial in the making of markets. Yet the idea that merchants are selling symbols as well as products was suggested as early as 1959 by Sidney J. Levy. Still, what was a novelty to him has become normal practice by now.

The reason Bigend is so interested in those peculiar bits of video on the Web is that, like many other marketers, he believes in neuromarketing. This concept is based on "an image of the consumer as an entity that does not know why s/he buys certain products, whose purchasing decisions are largely motivated by subconscious forces" (Schneider and Woolgar, 2012, p. 178). This is how Bigend explains it to the uninitiated:

> You "know" in your limbic brain. The seat of instinct. The mammalian brain. Deeper, wider, beyond logic. That is where advertising works, not in the upstart cortex [...] The mammalian spreads continent-wise beneath it, mute and muscular, attending its ancient agenda. And makes us buy things.
> (*PR*: 69)

In other words, System 1, according to Plato and Daniel Kahneman (2011). Again, it was not Gibson who coined the term "neuromarketing," but Ale Smidts (2002) from Erasmus University in Rotterdam.

Does this mean that Gibson approved of neuromarketing? Hitchings formulated it well when he said at the end of his review of *PR* that:

> Its perspective is that of a tourist – we are constantly caressing the surfaces of things – but this is intentional [...] we are pressed up against what [Gibson] calls "the windshield of the present" – not searching for meaning, but, like Cayce, dowsing for it.
>
> (Hitchings, 2003, p. 3)

The story continues

Bigend and his Blue Ant advertising company are also present in two later Gibson books – *Spook Country* (2007) and *Zero History* (2010) – though the main topics of these books is different from *Pattern Recognition.*

Spook Country (*SC*) is a story about secret services and intelligence agents ("spooks" in slang), but Bigend is present because he sponsors what he calls "anomalous phenomena":

> I've learned to value anomalous phenomena. Very peculiar things that people do, often secretly, interest me in a certain way. I spend a lot of money, often, trying to understand those things. From them, sometimes, emerge Blue Ant's most successful efforts. Trope Slope, for instance, our viral pitchman platform, was based on pieces of anonymous Footage being posted on the Net.
>
> (*SC*: 105)

Trope Slope is a viral advertising campaign that inserted shoe ads into the footage from *PR*, "turning people's love for historic cinema into an opportunity to [...] 'sell shoes'" (Miller, 2014, p. 123). Gerard Alva Miller Jr. took a critical, Adorno-inspired view of Bigend's actions. To him, they illustrate:

> how corporations appropriate the desires of the multitude and transform them into moneymaking venues, and his commodification of Footage exemplifies how individuals cannot remain free from strictures of control – he is the representative of both capital and control in the novel.
>
> (Miller, 2014, p. 123)

However, Gibson's text opposes this simple interpretation. After all, Bigend is a son of a Situationist, a member of the movement known for its critique of commodity fetishism (Debord, 1967/1995).[4] As it seems that Bigend's relations with his mother are friendly, it is not the case of rebellion against parental ideology, either.[5] As he confides to Hollis Henry, a rock musician-turned-journalist, and one of *SC*'s many protagonists, he is fascinated by eversion. "Intelligence, Hollis, is advertising turned inside out" (*SC*: 106). "Secrets [...] are the very root of cool" (*SC*: 106). Rather, it seems that Bigend had read Franck Cochoy's (2016) book in which the author claims that curiosity is the key to understanding merchant seduction.

At any rate, it is clear that Blue Ant (or perhaps Bigend) has become more sophisticated than it was in *PR*. Bigend now favors "anti-buzz" ("Definition by absence," *SC*: 83):

> He doesn't want people to hear of Blue Ant [...] We're often described as the first viral agency. Hubertus doesn't like the term, and for good reasons. Foregrounding the agency, or its founder, is counterproductive. He says he wishes we could operate as a black hole, an absence, but there's no viable way to get there from here.
>
> (*SC*: 110)

No, indeed, not within the present legislation. Companies need to have a legal existence, that is, to become legal persons.

Zero History (*ZH*, 2010), continues with the same protagonists. Bigend continues to satisfy his curiosity. He is described as "[a]n overly wealthy, dangerously curious fiddler with the world's hidden architectures" (*ZH*: 18). In his view, his wealth is a by-product of his curiosity, and of his "fundamental disinterest in wealth" (*ZH*: 22). Yet it is his wealth that permits him to follow where his curiosity pushes him. As to the Blue Ant:

> We aren't just an advertising agency [...] We do brand vision transmission, trend forecasting, vendor management, youth market recon, strategic planning in general [...] Consumers don't buy products, so much as narratives.
>
> (*ZH*: 21)

However, this time, it seems, somebody beat Bigend to "a somewhat new way to transmit brand vision [...] A certain genuinely provocative use of negative space" (*ZH*: 23), through a secret brand of clothes, called Gabriel Hounds, which cannot be bought in shops and is not being sold on the Web, in spite of some Chinese attempts at selling fakes on eBay. The *cognoscenti* recognize them on the people wearing them. After having followed a chain of introductions, people queue in an open space to buy one item. "It is about atemporality. About opting out of the industrialization of novelty. It's about deeper code" (*ZH*: 116). It suggests that the digital consumers want to return to the real markets. But do they? It brings to mind a satirical program made by Turkish anthropologists about "contemporary Germans," who claimed that rich Germans need to hunt their meat, whereas the poor buy theirs in a supermarket. The paradoxical aspect of this desire to return to street markets is that, in order to get closer to Gabriel Hounds, people do a great deal of digital research: "I get an e-mail, if there's going to be a drop" (*ZH*: 162).

While people working for Bigend are tracing Gabriel Hounds, he has a yet bigger dream:

> I'd asked him what piece of information he'd most want to have, that he didn't have, if he could learn any secret. And he said that he'd want something nobody had ever been able to have [...] The next day's order flow. Or really the next hour's, or the next minute's [...] It's the aggregate of all the orders in the market. Everything anyone is about to buy or sell, all of it. Stocks, bonds, gold, anything. If I understand him, that information exists, at any given moment, but there's no aggregator. It exists, constantly, but is unknowable. If someone were able to aggregate that, the market would cease to be real [...] Because market *is* the inability to aggregate the order flow at any given moment.
>
> (*ZH*: 177)

Bigend, or Gibson, must have read Friedrich von Hayek:

> The peculiar character of the problem of a rational economic order is determined precisely by the fact that the knowledge of the circumstances of which we must make use never exists in concentrated or integrated form, but solely as the dispersed bits of incomplete and frequently contradictory knowledge which all the separate individuals possess.
>
> (Hayek, 1945, p. 519)

Thus the need for a market that can aggregate it. The market is out of the picture as soon as the order can be aggregated by one person, like Bobby Chombo, an expert in geospatial technologies and a consultant for the US military (at Bigend's request). Thanks to this aggregation, Bigend was able to buy the bankrupted Iceland.

Is that the possible future role of "big data"? It is, according to Jeremy Rifkin (2014), but not in Bigend's way. According to Rifkin, individuals will withdraw their bits of knowledge from capitalist markets and will create global collaborative commons. Time will tell who is right: Gibson or Rifkin.

As far as Gabriel Hounds is concerned, Bigend's plan is easy: he wants the US Army to buy the designer's product (with him as the intermediary, of course):

> If a great deal of men's clothing today is descended from U.S. military designs, and it is, and the U.S. military is having trouble living up to their heritage, and they are, someone whose genius lies in some recombinant grasp of the semiotics of mass-produced American clothing ...
>
> (*ZH*: 197)

To avoid spoilers, I will not reveal who that someone could be. Rather, I will emphasize another interesting observation from *ZH*. Bigend (or perhaps Gibson) thinks that "[t]he eBay sales [...] attract coolhunters, generate attention in the industry." If not, the ghost-branders may be interested. "They find brands, sometimes extinct ones with iconic optics or a viable narrative, buy them, then put out denatured product under the old label" (*ZH*: 216).

Do ghost-branders exist? Well, at least in "the trip hop/downtempo/ electronica track from Tabula Rasa's album 'Surfing the Sky'. The song is dedicated to the wondrous woman Naomi Klein," from 2012 (atomicdesign studios.com/projects/ghostbranders, accessed 28/12/2014). There also used to be a Romanian website, ghostbrander.com. The world seems to be going in circles.

A circuit of culture

All three novels illustrate the circularity of consumption, aided by digital means: material products become digitalized (or at least their representations, or their meanings, do), whereas digital products become commodified. Consumers are digitally buying, but also digitally selling, via eBay and other similar sites.[6] In fact, Gibson's trilogy contains many excellent examples of the phenomenon that Richard Johnson (1986–87) called "a circuit of culture." There is no border between inscribed cultures (texts, objects) and lived cultures, between science and fiction, between theory and practice. Texts are read; artifacts are consumed but also interpreted. Ideas shape practices, and practice gives rise to new ideas. Science feeds fiction, but fiction may guide scientific endeavors. It can be illustrated schematically, as shown in Figure 10.1.

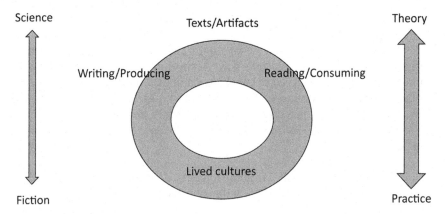

Figure 10.1 A circuit of culture
(Based on Johnson, 1986–87)

Science and fiction, theory and practice are extremes on the same dimension, rather than opposites. The acts of writing, and producing, have their origins in the lived culture, but transform it into texts and other artifacts. These, in turn, become read or consumed, and in this way re-enter the living culture. Dichotomies are the scientists' way of ordering knowledge, but are poor representations of the actual world.

This circle is perfectly illustrated by the works of William Gibson. He uses science (cybernetics, but also social science and literature); inspirations from Baudrillard, Debord, and Burroughs are obvious in these novels.[7] Science and engineering use his ideas – cyberspace, but also neuromarketing – the concept, if not the term. Neuromarketing is a notable phenomenon within digital consumption, and is being studied by both its critics and its enthusiasts. It may be humbug, but cyber-marketing certainly is not. There are a great many pictures of Cayce Pollard Units on the Web (e.g. dorotheacarney.com/picsnda/cayce-pollard-units, accessed 28/12/2014), and, of course, they can be purchased – for example, from www.polyvore.com/cpus_cayce_pollard_units/set?id=6147781, accessed 28/12/2014). Gibson himself appeared in an advertisement for a black Buzz Rickson MA-1 flying jacket (a CPU), which did not exist before the book was published (Konstantinou, 2009).

Does this mean that the phenomena described in *ZH* will turn out to be true, for example? Will exclusive brands become secret? Will markets return to the street? Will big data permit aggregation of the order flow, like Chombo did for Bigend? Is the very surname, Bigend, an allusion to big data? In other words, is Gibson predicting the future?

Not according to the "circuit of culture" theory. He is not even *speculating* about the future, as Margaret Atwood said of her work.[8] He is exercising his writer's imagination. Some of his ideas will catch on and some will not – as with any fashion product – in spite of all the efforts of trend setters and brand managers. As the scholars of fashion observed long ago,[9] nobody can control fashion, although many try. However, one of the points made obvious in all three books is that, as Palmer (2006, p. 479) pointed out, these "circles of production, distribution, reception, discussion" are constantly widening, thanks to cyberspace. The actual fashion may return to the streets, but cyberspace will remain its infrastructure.

Finally, one could ask what does Gibson, or at least his characters, think of digital consumption? Konstantinou called Cayce's stance "postironic," and concluded his essay on *PR* as follows:

> To be postironic in this sense is to be both producer and consumer of culture, something like a professional shopper. If this seems like a somewhat weak position from which to critique oppression and overturn class hierarchies, that is because it is.
>
> (Konstantinou, 2009, p. 97)

As to Gibson's stance, I believe that Neil Easterbrook might have diagnosed it correctly. He found in *PR*:

> Gibson's unmediated nostalgia for an unmediated real, a pure presence of the present, utterly authentic, outside all commodities: against the danger of "all experience having been reduced, by the spectral hand of marketing, to price-point variations of the same thing" (*PR* 341). Yet we know there are no aesthetics purely outside commodity aesthetics, no unmediated intuition of the real, no naïve experience untouched by language or irony or representation. "Cayce knows that she is, and has long been, complicit" (194).
> (Easterbrook, 2006, p. 498)

Aren't we all? Digital consumption only made it undeniable.

Notes

1   I would like to thank Hans Kjellberg and Magdalena McIntyre for their insightful comments.
2   In his latest book, *The Peripheral* (2014), however, Gibson "went back to the future."
3   *Oryx and Crake*, 2003; *The Year of the Flood*, 2009; *MaddAddam*, 2013. In an interview for *Wired* (2013), Atwood called her works "speculative fiction," as technology does not play much of a role in them.
4   Shukaitis (2014) pointed out the relevance of Debord and the Situationists for management and organization studies.
5   More on ambiguity of Bigend's persona in Easterbrook (2006).
6   On William Gibson's (the person) adventures at eBay, read Denegri-Knott and Molesworth (2010).
7   "Hollis thought he looked a little like William Burroughs, minus the bohemian substrate (or perhaps the methadone)" (*SC*: 294).
8   www.wired.com/2013/09/geeks-guide-margaret-atwood/ (accessed 28/12/2014).
9   For a review, see for example, Czarniawska (2005).

References

Atwood, M. (2003) *Oryx and Crake*. Toronto: McClelland & Stewart.

Atwood, M. (2009) *The Year of the Flood*. Toronto: McClelland & Stewart.

Atwood, M. (2013) *MaddAddam*. Toronto: McClelland & Stewart.

Beard, V. (1994) "Popular culture and professional identity: Accountants in the movies", *Accounting, Organizations and Society*, 19(3): 303–318.

Bloomfield, B. (2003) "Narrating the future of intelligent machines. The role of science fiction in technological anticipation", in Czarniawska, B. and Gagliardi, P. (eds) *Narratives We Organize By*. Amsterdam: John Benjamins, pp. 193–212.

Cochoy, Franck (2016) *On Curiosity. The Art of Market Seduction*. Manchester: Mattering Press.

Coleman, A.M. (1936) "The accountant in literature", *Notes & Queries*, 13 June, 428.

Czarniawska, Barbara (2005) "Fashion in organizing", in Czarniawska, Barbara and Sevón, Guje (eds) *Global Ideas. How Ideas, Objects and Practices Travel in Global Economy*. Malmö and Copenhagen: Liber and CBS Press, pp. 129–146.

Czarniawska, B. (2012a) "New plots are badly needed in finance", *Accounting, Auditing & Accountability Journal*, 25(5): 756–775.

Czarniawska, B. (2012b) "Business fiction: Global economy by William Gibson", in Quattrone, P., Puyou, F.-R., McLean, C. and Thrift, N. (eds) *Imagining Organizations.* New York: Routledge, pp. 31–52.

Czarniawska, B. and Rhodes, C. (2006) "Strong plots: Popular culture in management practice and theory", in Gagliardi, P. and Czarniawska, B. (eds) *Management Education and Humanities.* Cheltenham: Edward Elgar, pp. 195–218.

Debord, G. (1967/1995) *The Society of Spectacle.* New York: Zone Books.

Denegri-Knott, J. and Molesworth, M. (2010) ""Love it. Buy it. Sell it." Consumer desire and the social drama of eBay", *Journal of Consumer Culture*, 10(1): 56–79.

Dujarier, M.-A. (2016) "The three sociological types of consumer work", *Journal of Consumer Culture*, 16(2): 555–571

Easterbrook, N. (2006) "Alternate presents: The ambivalent historicism of Pattern Recognition", *Science Fiction Studies*, 33(1): 483–503.

Elster, J. (1983) *Sour Grapes: Studies in the Subversion of Rationality.* Cambridge: Cambridge University Press.

Fitchett, J. (2002) "Marketing sadism: Super-Cannes and consumer culture. *Marketing Theory*, 2(3): 309–322.

Gibson, W. (2003) *Pattern Recognition.* New York: G.P. Putnam's Sons.

Gibson, W. (2007) *Spook Country.* New York: G.P. Putnam's Sons.

Gibson, W. (2010) *Zero History.* New York: G.P. Putnam's Sons.

Gibson, W. (2014) *The Peripheral.* New York: G.P. Putnam's Sons.

Hassard, J. and Holliday, R. (eds) (1998) *Organization/Representation.* London: Sage.

Hayek, F. A. (1945) "The use of knowledge in society", *The American Economic Review*, 35(4): 519–530.

Hayles, K. (2005) "Computing the human", *Theory, Culture and Society*, 22(1): 131–151.

Hitchings, H. (2003) "Brand-savvy", *Times Literary Supplement*, 2 May.

Hollinger, Veronica (2006) "Stories about the future", *Science Fiction Studies*, 33(1): 452–472.

Jameson, F. (2005) *Archeologies of the Future. The Desire Called Utopia and Other Science Fictions.* New York: Verso.

Johnson, R. (1986–87) "What is cultural studies anyway? *Social Text*, 16: 38–80.

Kahneman, Daniel (2011) *Thinking, Fast and Slow.* New York: Farrar, Straus and Giroux.

Kellner, D. (1994) *Media Culture: Culture Studies, Identity and Politics between the Modern and Postmodern.* London: Routledge.

Kjellberg, H. and Helgesson, C.-F. (2007) "On the nature of markets and their practices", *Marketing Theory*, 7(2): 137–162.

Klein, N. (2000) *No Logo. Taking Aim at the Brand Bullies.* Toronto: Random House of Canada.

Konstantinou, L. (2009) "The brand as cognitive map in William Gibson's "Pattern Recognition." *Boundary 2*, 36(2): 67–97.

Kundera, M. (1988) *The Art of the Novel.* London: Faber and Faber.

Levy, S. J. (1959) "Symbols for sale", *Harvard Business Review*, 37 (July–August): 117–124.

Metz, D. (2003) "From naked emperor to Count Zero. Tracking knights, nerds, and cyberpunks in identity narratives of freelancers in the IT-field", in Czarniawska, B. and Gagliardi, P. (eds) *Narratives We Organize By.* Amsterdam: John Benjamins, pp. 173–192.

Miller, G. A. Jr. (2014) *Exploring the Limits of the Human through Science Fiction.* London: Palgrave Macmillan.

Palmer, C. (2006) "Pattern Recognition: "None of what we do here is ever really private." *Science Fiction Studies,* 33(1): 473–482.

Parker, M., Higgins, M., Lightfoot, G. and Smith, W. (1999) "Amazing tales: Organization studies as science fiction", *Organization,* 6(4): 579–590.

Parsons, M. (2010) "Interview: Wired meets William Gibson", 13 October, www.wired. co.uk/news/archive/2010-10/13/william-gibson-interview (accessed 10/11/2014).

Rhodes, C. and Brown, A. B. (2005) "Writing responsibly: Narrative fiction and organization studies", *Organization,* 12(4): 467–491.

Rifkin, J. (2014) *The Zero Marginal Cost Society: The Internet of Things, the Collaborative Commons, and the Eclipse of Capitalism.* New York: Palgrave Macmillan.

Rinello, D. and Golfetto, F. (2006) "Representing markets: The shaping of fashion trends by French and Italian fabric companies", *Industrial Marketing Management,* 35: 856–869.

Rushkoff, D. (1996) *Media Virus! Hidden Agendas in Popular Culture.* New York: Ballantine Books.

Schneider, T. and Woolgar, S. (2012) "Technologies of ironic revelation: Enacting consumers in neuromarkets", *Consumption, Markets & Culture,* 15(2): 1–12.

Shukaitis, S. (2014) ""Theories are made only to die in the war of time": Guy Debord and the Situationist International as strategic thinkers", *Culture and Organization,* 20(4): 251–268.

Smidts, A. (2002) *Kijken in het brein: Over de mogelijkheden van neuromarketing.* Rotterdam: Erasmus Research Institute of Management, Inaugural Lecture, 25 October.

Stephenson, N. (2011) *Reamde.* New York: William Morrow.

Sterling, B. (2004) *The Zenith Angle.* New York: Del Rey.

11 Digital advertising campaigns and the branded economy

Gustav Sjöblom, Oskar Broberg and Ann-Sofie Axelsson

On 14 February 2015, the Swedish football star Zlatan Ibrahimovic scored for his team, Paris Saint-Germain (PSG), in the home game against Caen. Ibrahimovic celebrated the goal by taking off his shirt, revealing no fewer than 50 new tattoos embellishing the upper part of his body. The event was filmed and posted shortly afterwards on YouTube. While not obvious at the beginning, the episode soon turned out to be part of an advertising campaign for the United Nations World Food Programme. The (fake) tattoos were 50 symbolic names representing the 805 million people who suffer from hunger today. This episode is our point of entry to show the central aim of this chapter: how marketing campaigns have evolved and today function as market devices.

A central aspect of the episode is the illustration of the way in which brands have, since the 1980s, become an important aspect of contemporary capitalism and "central components of the social fabric" (Arvidsson, 2006, p. 3).

Figure 11.1 Advertisement for the United Nations World Food Programme, 2015 (Image rights secured by Forsman & Bodenfors)

Brands function as a source from which consumers construct meaning, identity, social relations and shared experience. This consumer activity can in turn be mobilized by corporations that may appropriate (some of) the value created by consumer activity (Dujarier, 2016; Cova and Dalli, 2009; Arvidsson, 2006). Moreover, the World Food Programme campaign shows that Zlatan became a human brand that could be put to use in different settings and promote certain causes, but at the same time must be carefully managed (Thomson, 2006). Zlatan's brand-related actions had repercussions for him as a football player – the shirt removal during the Caen game resulted in Ibrahimovic receiving a yellow card, which banned him from the next PSG game.

Zlatan Ibrahimovic's brand attracts corporate sponsors who want to draw on his persona and performance in building their brands. Brands have become strategic to firms in that they enable a partial separation of production from the marketing and consumption, to the extent that today the latter constitutes the core value-creating activities of many firms (Willmott, 2010; Aaker, 1991). The structural implication of this process is that modern corporations, to some extent, re-orient their focus from the organization of production to the organization of consumption (Moor, 2007).

The organization of consumption is, however, no straightforward matter. Rather than presenting the product itself, the brand has become a context for how the product is used, a context that directs consumers towards certain actions. This opens up for processes of so-called collaborative, challenging the traditional borders between production and consumption (Dujarier, 2016). Successful marketing requires the inscription or entanglement of goods into the life-world of consumers in order to present the goods as objects that make sense. Marketing can be said to be a place of Foucauldian governmentality (Foucault, 2008), where one, rather than giving order or shaping actions, provides "an ambience in which freedom is likely to evolve in particular ways in order to posit the productivity of ordinary consumers so that it reproduces a given brand image" (Arvidsson, 2006, p. 74).

The need to position brands in ways that mobilize consumer action has increased brand owners' dependency on external actors who can mediate between production and consumption, including advertising agencies and expert consumers. The gradual digitalization of marketing since the 1990s has spurred this development further. Zlatan did not design the campaign by himself, nor did the brand owner; it was the advertising agency Forsman & Bodenfors (F&B).

This Swedish advertising agency has sustained the status of one of the world's most creative agencies for at least 20 years by winning international awards – a key to establishing and maintaining creative status within the advertising community. F&B has been particularly successful in combining traditional advertising channels and new digital formats (Veckans Affärer, 2007; Pratt, 2006; Resumé, 2004b). The World Food Programme campaign relied heavily on integrating digital channels into the campaign, bridging online and offline worlds, and mobilizing consumers using the power of digital communication. On the day preceding the PSG–Caen game, Zlatan posted an image of his new tattoo "Abdullah" on his Facebook, Twitter and Instagram accounts, accompanied by the text: "A very important name for me." The game was followed not only by a press conference, traditional paper posters and more than 4,600 articles in traditional media (including *The Guardian, The Independent*, and *USA Today*), but also by tweets and Facebook shares by celebrities such as David Beckham, Avicii and Enrique Iglesias, in addition to millions of ordinary individuals. Though the impact of advertising campaigns is notoriously hard to evaluate, it is evident that the campaign succeeded in its ambition to reach out on a global scale.[1]

In this chapter we particularly focus on digital advertising campaigns and the role of advertising agencies in contemporary branded capitalism. Through the lens of five award-winning advertising campaigns we trace the emergence of digital advertising campaigns as *market devices* (Callon et al., 2007) and of digital advertising agencies as *cultural intermediaries* (Nixon 2014, 2003; Cronin, 2004; Bourdieu, 1984). In this we follow the exhortation of Nixon to combine these two concepts to take into account, on the one hand, the subjectivity of key practitioners, and on the other hand, the socio-technical dynamics involved (Nixon, 2014).

Advertising as a market device

Market devices frame the encounter between supply and demand. For instance, Franck Cochoy has shown how retail spaces frame a set of consumer choices through the arrangement of retail space, shelving and the use of trolleys (Cochoy, 2007). At the heart of this process is the *qualification of goods*, the process whereby a good is disentangled from the world of the seller and re-entangled into the world of the buyer (Callon et al., 2002). Even though advertising campaigns are less tangible than the technologies studied by Cochoy, we argue that they play a similar role in qualifying goods. By mobilizing partly autonomous consumer action around brands, advertising campaigns offer new ways of building consumer relationships (Hagberg, 2008). Hence, advertising campaigns may be taken as an example of what Cova and Dalli call the "managed and dynamic platforms for consumer practice ... which, on the one hand, free the creativity and know-how of consumers, and on the other hand, channel these consumer activities in ways desired by the firm" (Cova and Dalli, 2009, pp. 232–3). In addition to the immediate impression on consumers and the advertising community, they furthermore introduce new and refined means of interacting around brands, involving certain technologies and cultural frames. As Nixon points out, the concept of market devices gives designers, advertisers, and other types of "professionals of qualification" a central role in the fixation of new sets of associations around products. The contribution of advertisers to the process of qualification is their ability to vary the media technologies and styles of representation in accordance with specific cultural contexts (Nixon, 2014;

Callon et al., 2002). We therefore argue that digital advertising campaigns are of special interest in this respect and that the practices related to innovative digital advertising play an important part in the emergence of new markets and the stabilization of already existing markets (Fliegstein, 2003).

The concept of *cultural intermediaries* draws attention to the role of actors, such as advertisers, in linking production with consumption in their capacity to help manufacturers and service providers manage their relationships with consumers. Bourdieu emphasized that advertisers as "new" cultural inter-mediaries display a proneness to combine high-brow and low-brow culture, distinguishing it from the established bourgeoisie. This openness to "newness" makes them more attuned to popular culture in terms of music, fashion, and style. The mixed cultural capital accumulated by these new cultural intermediaries has thereby given them the ability to forge economically valuable connec-tions between material objects and cultural value (Nixon, 2014; Bourdieu, 1984).

A focus on advertisers as intermediaries implies a clearer focus of the rules of the game that shape practices within the field of advertising (McLeod et al., 2011). Advertising agencies not only make profits and satisfy clients, but also build, by symbolic means, a cultural capital within the field of advertising (Alvesson, 2004; Bourdieu, 1984). Cultural capital is achieved by building peer regard and, especially, success at award shows. In the advertising indus-try, the most important institution for constructing the hierarchies of creativ-ity are international award shows, such as Cannes Lions, D&AD, Clio, and Eurobest.

While at first glance this esoteric institutional setup has little bearing on wider society, we argue that the rules that establish and maintain creative status are key to the role of advertisers as cultural intermediaries. Award-winning campaigns are, by definition, innovative. They constitute new ways of combining what is technologically feasible – including aspects such as con-sumer access and willingness to engage – with advertising craftsmanship, brand value, and cultural references. Once a particular campaign concept has been awarded, it is no longer a ground for winning further awards. On the other hand, it trickles out into daily consumer practices for how to engage with brands.

In this chapter we focus particularly on the emergence of digital advertising since the breakthrough of the Internet in the mid-1990s (Svenska Dagbladet, 2007a; Vision, 2000). The long-term trend towards increasingly reflexive and interactive branding has been taken a step further with the increasing ubi-quity and importance of the Internet (McStay, 2009; Arvidsson, 2006). Digi-tal advertising campaigns are built around platforms embodying core features of digital technology, such as interactivity, virtuality, and the malleability and mobility of content. On the Internet, brands can travel immaterially between places and across media platforms. The Internet can absorb the subject through visual experience, sociality, communication, and even tactility and muscular response. The Internet has the capacity to create "all-encompassing environments centred round a particular brand," where all actions are antici-pated by the program of the brand (Arvidsson, 2006, p. 96). This process, and by implication the practice of digital advertising, relies on consumer inter-activity and invites them "to participate in the elaboration of the brand, as well as the product or service that they purchase" (Arvidsson, 2006, p. 101). Consumers can be involved in several ways, such as rating, personalized design, or user-generated content. The challenge for digital advertising is to create social ties around brands that generate emotional and experiential ties that will affect the status of the brands in the minds of consumers, and thus its brand equity (Willmott, 2010).

Method

Currently, the close integration of online and offline channels and the mobi-lization of consumers online has become a necessity for a successful adver-tising campaign. This is, however, a relatively recent phenomenon. During the first years of the new millennium advertising on the Internet rose from negli-gible to substantial shares of advertising budgets, especially from 2005 onward with the development of participatory digital structures known as "Web 2.0" (O'Reilly, 2007). The use of digital technology in advertising during the first decade of the new millennium followed two trajectories. The lion's share of the digital advertising market is based on the Internet as a space for information seeking and the opening of new spaces for placing tra-ditional advertisements. The most salient case is Google, which, during the first decade of the 21st century, developed from an unknown search engine into the second most valuable brand in the world. (The international ranking of brands conducted by Interbrand valued Google at US$120 billion in 2015.) Google's rapid growth was part of a paradigmatic transformation in the advertising business, as search-engine optimization became a multi-billion-dollar industry. This part of the advertising business is closely connected to the development of the branded economy through the many new techniques and devices used to measure and control consumer attention through the use of big data (Broberg et al., 2016; see also Boullier's, and Pantzar and Lammi's chapters in this volume).

However, the process at the heart of this chapter is at the other end of the spectrum. Here we are concerned with the gradual development of sophisti-cated creative digital campaigns, which, over time, integrated campaign sites, viral YouTube clips, events, and mobile applications with more traditional advertising channels. In this chapter we analyze the connection between digi-talization and branding through the lens of five award-winning digital adver-tising campaigns, all – for reasons soon to be explained – produced by Swedish agencies.

The campaigns were chosen on the basis of two main criteria: that they made a mark within the field of advertising through winning awards; and that they represent important shifts in the nature of digital advertising. In the first decade of the new millennium, Sweden became a global leader in creative digital advertising, giving rise to the notion of a "digital wonder" in Swedish advertising. The campaigns studied in this chapter were created by two agencies: Farfar (including its forerunner Spiff), and Forsman & Bodenfors.

Farfar started as a small start-up launched in 2001 in the wake of the dotcom crash. The agency is representative of a number of internationally successful Swedish agencies, such as Great Works, Daddy, North Kingdom, and Kokokaka. Young entrepreneurs set up these agencies in the early years of the new millennium in reaction to entrepreneurs' negative experiences of the venture capital-driven hype of the 1990s. F&B, in contrast, is Sweden's most respected traditional advertising agency, which made a decisive move into digital advertising during the first years of the new millennium. By that time the Internet hype was gone but innovation developed. More widespread use of the Internet, increased bandwidth, and more sophisticated software made more elaborate digital advertising campaigns accessible to large audiences. Swedish firms and individual creatives were at the forefront of reshaping advertising practices and devising new means for creative consumer–brand interaction (Broberg et al., 2013; Sjöblom et al., 2011).

This study is situated in the interdisciplinary space between business history and the sociology of marketing. The legacy from business history is evident in the chronological structure and the ambition to emphasize the importance of treating this topic from a process and context-bound perspective, rather than as a constant. The methodological approach is based on business history, albeit grounded in an unorthodox combination of sources in the shape of oral history interviews, business press articles, and financial data. At the same time, the text is not a proper historical account of the development of digital advertising, but rather a way of using historically significant case studies to highlight two current themes in the sociology of marketing: market devices, and cultural intermediaries.

The main empirical sources consist of 19 oral history interviews conducted during 2010 and 2011 along the methodological premises suggested by the oral history tradition (Ritchie, 1994). We selected the interviewees on the basis of their roles as founders and/or creatives in Swedish digital advertising agencies that had received awards at the Cannes Lion Festival of Creativity – the most prestigious award show in the advertising field. The interviews varied in length between one and three hours, and focused on the entire life story of the interviewees, rather than just their involvement in digital advertising. The interviews were recorded, transcribed, edited and stored at Chalmers University of Technology. Business press articles were also an important source for this study, used in the tradition of business history (Hansen, 2004). First and foremost because seemingly simple details – number of awards, profits/losses, names of individuals – are not recorded or remembered in our other sources. Second, because press materials reveal circumstantial evidence about how corporate actions and strategies are transmitted to and perceived by the public. The easy availability, through the digitalization of press archives, makes it possible to scan large amounts of press material to find relevant data. We have used the Swedish database *Mediearkivet* to locate and download the articles referenced in the text (Retriever, 2016).

In the following we present a historical narrative – starting in 1994, ending in 2010 – of how digital advertising campaigns emerged as digital market devices, due to a combination of various competences and components. The advertising agencies were the cultural intermediaries that combined seemingly very different elements in order to find new ways of inviting consumers to interact with the brand in question. The focus of the analysis is on how the campaigns as assemblages qualify goods by enrolling consumers, evoking emotions, and building brand relations through new forms of interactivity and participatory actions.

Exploring the potential of the Web: the Posten webshop

The World Wide Web became widely available in Sweden in about 1994 and was immediately identified as a new site for marketing (Mattsson and Carr-wik, 1998). In the very first stage, being present on the Web was a marketing act *per se*, positioning the firm as part of the new technological wonder. By November 1996, 107 out of 127 firms on the Stockholm Stock Exchange A-list had their own websites (Affärsvärlden, 1996a). As more and more firms joined the ranks, mere presence on the Web no longer communicated novelty or generated consumer interest. Advertisers who wanted to use the Web for branding purposes had to resort to other means. Given the scarcity of bandwidth and software tools, the main outlets for early digital advertising campaigns were banners, advertising messages embedded in Web pages (Sjöblom et al., 2011).

The business and technology press assumed that Web advertising would be a domain for the incumbents in the market communication industry – the advertising agencies. With some exceptions, this did not become the case. Industry spokesmen and journalists often accused the advertising industry of conservatism and of once again failing to recognize a technological shift and business opportunity (Resumé, 1998; Affärsvärlden, 1996a, 1996b; Data-världen, 1996). The advertising agencies had a good business case for keeping a low profile. Digital advertising represented a negligible share of the total advertising market, the margins were low, and the agencies could afford to let others bear the development cost, and enter the market later as it matured.

Instead, the market for Web advertising in Sweden was dominated by a new breed of start-ups. Some of these start-ups, such as Spray, Icon Medialab, Framtidsfabriken, and Adera, subsequently broadened their scope into Internet consultancies as they were drawn into the venture capital-funded IT boom and bust – a journey that, without exception, ended in big losses, break-ups, and bankruptcies starting in 2000. Another type of start-up stayed far from the IT bubble and maintained their status as small Web agencies, working as subcontractors for the advertising agencies. In 1999, the main Swedish advertising award show Guldägget ("The Golden Egg") awarded the first ever "golden egg" in the Internet category to the webshop of the Swedish Post Office ("Posten").[2] The campaign used a conventional form of advertising, direct marketing, to send personal invitations to the webshop to a selection of Swedish celebrities and people in power, a typical recipient being Janne Carlzon, CEO of the airline SAS and a venture capitalist with interests in information technology. Once at the webshop, the invited celebrity was offered instantaneous free delivery of a select number of products. As it turned out, most of the participants chose a live lobster, which subsequently arrived on their doorsteps (Interview Matias Palm-Jensen, 2010).

The campaign's display of the usefulness of the Web as a channel for marketing and sales created an echo in Sweden, directly through the persons involved in the campaign and indirectly through media buzz and the Guldägget award. The Guldägget jury labeled the campaign "an ingenious collaboration between two worlds: the Real-Reality world and the Virtual-Reality world" (Resumé, 1999). The jury also praised the design of the website for being innovative and entertaining without standing in the way of the message. For the creatives behind the campaign, the key idea was to make use of the low cost of Internet advertising to buy a lot of banner ad space and to combine new and old advertising channels targeting high-profile people to spread the gospel of the usefulness of the Internet (Interview Nicke Bergström, 2010).

Posten had a high profile in the early Swedish Internet. Swedish policymakers deregulated the postal market in 1993 and turned the Post Office into a state-owned joint stock company in 1994. Posten management was well aware of their vulnerability to market exposure and technological change and made heavy investments in the Internet. The main venture was Torget ("the market square"), an online community and e-commerce site launched in May 1996. Posten had a well-defined business model. Torget would enable Posten to make money through advertising spending on Torget, delivery services to customers, and payment through its Postgirot payment service (Göteborgs-Posten, 1996).

Given the prominence of Posten in the early Swedish Web ecosystem, it was hardly a coincidence that they became the first winner of a Guldägget Internet award. At the same time, it appears that Posten's role was limited to that of procurement competence. The creative success of the campaign owed more to the advertising agency, Romson, and particularly to the small Web agency, Spiff, that produced the campaign. The core element of the campaign – mixing digital with other channels and innovative design with elements of humor – was soon to be the hallmark of Spiff's founders (Interview Nicke Bergström, 2010).

The campaign did not create success for Posten Torget. On the contrary, the number of daily visitors to the site declined from 200,000 in March 1999 to 167,000 in July of the same year (Svenska Dagbladet, 1999). E-commerce was not yet mature and Internet users increasingly preferred other points of entry to the Web. Posten sold Torget in 2000 and 2001. According to an estimate from 2003, the venture cost Posten SEK 900 million (Dagens Nyheter, 2003). The advertising agency Romson was sold in 2002, despite a number of high-profile digital campaigns. The main beneficiary of the campaign – besides consumers – was Spiff, or rather the individuals behind Spiff. While Spiff was drawn into the destructive debt-driven maelstrom of the IT bubble and disappeared from existence, the award-winning campaign established the firm's creatives as leading authorities on advertising campaigns that linked digital and traditional channels through strong messages and a sense of humor. In 2001 they found a new outlet for their skills and ambitions at a new agency: Farfar (Broberg et al., 2013).

The user-generated viral video: the Milko Music Machine

The dramatic end of the IT boom in 2000–01 made the Internet unfashionable, but did not prevent Internet advertising from maturing. In 2000, the small Swedish dairy producer Milko launched a new online campaign site to boost sales of their sour milk product Milko Fjällfil. The site was designed as a "Milko Music Machine," where the visitor could manipulate a dancing and singing cow and record music videos. The visitor first selected a genre and then sequences of dance moves and mooing, which together made up a complete music video. The site gave each video a unique ID so visitors could share their videos with friends (Stenius, 2013).

The website became one of the very first viral success stories in advertising. It was one of the first interactive sites that allowed the visitor to combine graphics and music. Noting the immediate success of the Swedish website, its creators added an English-language site a month later. According to the agency's own figures, the campaign attracted more than 5 million visitors in the first year. The campaign broke new ground in market communication over the Web and won the most prestigious award in advertising, a Cannes Lions Grand Prix, in 2001 (Dagens Reklamnyheter, 2001; Vision, 2001a).

The Milko Music Machine was at the same time low-tech and high-tech. The video was composed of (low-tech) stop-motion animation using a plastic cow doll and revamped clothes from Barbie dolls. The programming, in contrast, was done in Macromedia Shockwave, at a time when most Web campaigns were more or less static HTML sites with GIF animations in banners. The stop-motion technique looked modern in relation to the pixelated computer game graphics that dominated Web visuals at the time. The quality of the video was improved by matching the beats per minute of the music with the frame rates of the graphics to synchronize the dance. Its creators labeled the campaign a low-tech production for a high-tech format (Interview Matias Palm-Jensen, 2010). Its success rested on a form of technical knowledge that centered more on knowing what is feasible in terms of limitations in programming and the narrow bandwidth of users mostly relying on dial-up connections.

The Milko Music Machine was produced by Farfar, a small Swedish Web agency set up only a year earlier by the same people who had been responsible for Spiff. The success of the campaign can be interpreted as the result of a conscious plan by Farfar to use entertainment value to build brands. The Milko Music Machine was a low-budget production. In fact, the entire agency spent two months of work for a puny revenue of SEK 100,000. The campaign was mainly created by Farfar working for free for the customer. Or, from another and perhaps more accurate perspective, the campaign was a conscious investment in Farfar's own brand. Building on the success of the Milko Music Machine, Farfar became one of the world's leading digital advertising agencies – if not in terms of revenue then at least in terms of status within the community and the number of prizes awarded (Vision, 2001b).

After Cannes, Farfar signed a prestigious contract with one of the most highly valued brands at the time, Nokia. Farfar's leading creatives were invited to serve on the juries of the Cannes and Clio award shows, thereby gaining further impact in the international advertising market. In 2006 the owners of Farfar capitalized on this brand investment when the company was sold to the global media conglomerate Aegis (Broberg et al., 2013; Resumé, 2004c). Farfar's success relied on a combination of skilled people, a superb sensibility for trends in popular culture and pushing the limits of available technical platforms, and, last but not least, an ability to utilize their successful campaign for status building. As stated by one of the founders (Interview Matias Palm-Jensen, 2010): "Suddenly, the whole world knew who Farfar was. Of course this was a good campaign for us as an agency. The Grand Prix itself did not matter as much as the fact that everybody suddenly knew about us."

The Web as the platform – Volvo XC90 launch

In December 2002 a seemingly mysterious advertising campaign appeared in Sweden. With national coverage, a large number of outdoor commercial spaces were filled with large photos of beautiful scenes of Swedish nature. Similar landscape photos were seen in prime-time television commercials. The landscape images showed an aesthetic craftsmanship of high quality. The pictorial language was also distinctive and repeated in several campaigns that followed, drawing the contours of the special "universe" with which the brand wanted to be associated. None of the photos revealed the marketed product, but instead only listed the campaign website address and the brand name (Resumé, 2003a).

The purpose of the TV and outdoor advertisements was simply to draw traffic to the website. At the time, making a website the focal point of the campaign was a unique and daring move. The site was constructed like a long photo, a panorama of animated stills, of which only a small part was visible at first. Scrolling to the right would take the viewer through the different scenery, an imaginary journey through Sweden – from the remote wilderness all the way to the city. There the viewer would end up in an urban

Figure 11.2 Advertisement for the launch of the Volvo XC90, 2002
(Image rights secured by Forsman & Bodenfors)

environment and, finally, find the product of the campaign – the XC90 Volvo SUV (Resumé, 2003a, 2004a).

The campaign launched Volvo's first SUV. The launch was crucial since the XC90 was a late arrival in the SUV segment, with many competitors already on the market. Volvo needed something different and exclusive to position the new car. Volvo had a longstanding relationship with F&B, already the leading traditional advertising agency in Sweden. With the XC90 launch, F&B took an important step in fully incorporating the Web into its toolbox (Interview Martin Cedergren, 2010; Resumé, 2003b). Basing an important product launch on a website was a bold step in 2002 and had not previously been done by national or international agencies. The decision to base the campaign on a Web platform was made quite late in the creative process, when a more traditional format had already been worked out and launched to a pilot audience. The original campaign was well received, but it was clear that it did not substantially stand out from other car advertisements. The creative team therefore decided that something totally new was needed and so made the Web the focal point of the campaign (Interview Filip Nilsson, 2010; Resumé, 2003b).

Up until the XC90 launch, Web-based advertising was mainly based on low-tech solutions and humorous content, and had a low status in the advertising community. On this occasion, F&B contracted an internationally acclaimed photographer, Peter Gerke, to shoot over 2,000 nature pictures which were put together to form the illusion of one large photo. Rather than introducing the car, they wanted to make people dream. The success of the XC90 campaign was not, as one may think, due to the introduction of interactive elements. Rather, the opposite is the case. When Mathias Appelblad and Martin Cedergren, the creators of the campaign, later described the process, they mentioned websites of other car companies as negative examples (Interviews Mathias Appelblad, 2010; Martin Cedergren, 2010). Around 2000, websites for cars were often produced with limited resources. Interactivity was restricted to opening and closing the door of the car. To Mathias and Martin, that was something you would do at the auto dealer. In their minds that was not premium. Based more on storytelling and film production, they wanted to convey a feeling (Interview Mathias Appelblad, 2010): "Internally, we said that if the XC70 – launched a couple of years earlier and not a proper SUV – was for those out camping, the XC90 is for those who have or rather dream of a lounge in Aspen."

Technically, the site combined cutting-edge art Flash programming with adaptation to the viewer's bandwidth and computer platform. The challenge, in a time when most Web users had limited bandwidth, was to convey high-resolution pictures to as many viewers as possible. The production combined the traditional advertising skills of F&B, the creativity of the company's recently hired "Web expert," and technically skilled sub-contractors (Paregos, Itiden, and Kokokaka). The fact that F&B and Volvo had cooperated for almost a decade also guaranteed a substantial amount of trust in the creative ideas of the advertising agency. This trust was clearly tested when the whole campaign was remade late in the production process and focused on the Internet (Interview Mathias Appelblad, 2010).

In 2002 a URL with its "www" was just mystical enough to spur interest. During the first month the campaign site attracted 170,000 visitors (Resumé, 2003b). However, again, the campaign's success did not only boost the brand (this time Volvo), but was also an international success for F&B. In 2003 the agency was awarded no fewer than seven prestigious prizes in international advertising competitions, in the Cyber and Integrated categories.[3]

The social Web – the Heidies' 15 MB of fame

As we saw in the examples of Milko and Volvo, up until the middle of the first decade of the new millennium, the degree of interactivity in digital advertising campaigns was limited by the available technological platforms and existing consumer culture. This changed dramatically with the rapid spread of what became known as Web 2.0. Once again, the creatives at Farfar led the way in devising new ways of connecting brands and consumers (Svenska Dagbladet, 2007b).

On 24 January 2007, two young women calling themselves "the Heidies" kidnapped a Diesel sales executive and laid their hands on the new and unreleased Diesel underwear collection he was carrying. The Heidies locked themselves in a hotel room with the Diesel executive for five days with the purpose of getting their "15 MB of fame" as Diesel supermodels. The women also hijacked Diesel's website and used six video cameras to show the world what they were up to on www.diesel.com, non-stop live for five days. The growing audience could watch the Heidies upload pictures and videos to the Diesel website. Crucially, they could also interact with the Heidies and their hostage using a wide range of digital platforms. Chat messages from visitors on the website were displayed on a large TV screen in the room. The Heidies and their followers were active not only on the Diesel website but also on MySpace, YouTube, Flickr, and blogs (Interview Nicke Bergström, 2010; Macleod, 2007).

Moreover, the campaign allowed visitors to influence and participate in the action through votes, text messages, emails and music videos, where participants expressed their wishes for how the Heidies should dress themselves and the sales executive, the colors of the hotel room walls, or what music the three should listen and dance to. The campaign was also packed with references to the world of celebrities and popular Internet phenomena. One online vote chose the ultimate celebrity animal, a vote won by actress Paris Hilton's dog. On one occasion participants in the campaign guided the Heidies to try Mentos in champagne. The scenes often took a messy, sexy, and even violent turn. The campaign mobilized thousands of young consumers on the live chat. The YouTube clips from the event appeared on the top ten list of the most watched video clips on day two. The number of Google searches increased from 74 to 13,000 in only five days (Internetworld, 2007).

The interactive elements of live streaming in social networks definitely strengthen the experience of being a part of what is going on and give the consumer a stronger sense that what is desired is also within reach. The possibility to connect and communicate in real time, with the advertisement and, indirectly, the product, is something with which newspaper or TV ads cannot compete. However, a digital format creates a buzz not only when the campaign is active; still today, eight years later, traces of "The Heidies" are easily found on the Internet – not least because the award shows leave many traces in the form of articles, comments, and discussions (Heidies, 2007; Macleod, 2007). Not many newspaper or TV campaigns can so easily be found or watched. Furthermore, "the Heidies" was more like a reality show than a conventional product ad; it even had product placement. Showing young, beautiful, and happy people doing fun and crazy things together – instead of models showing the latest underwear collection – was probably a large part of the success.

The creative team for the campaign wanted not so much to *tell* the audience what values were important – or "buzzwords," as Matias Palm Jensen called them – but to *show* them in the campaign. One way to develop this storytelling was to bridge the gap between online and offline, but also to dare to do the unexpected. Farfar argued for what is referred to as pinball effects of innovative campaigns, where effects cannot be planned to happen in a certain place or moment, but instead suddenly occur. To some extent the whole campaign rested on this premise, as it was basically designed without Diesel knowing what would come of it. However, when Farfar wanted to keep some of the campaign budget for follow-up events and tried to persuade Diesel to continue to build on the campaign by, for example, using the two "Heidies" as models on the catwalk in the next fashion show, the customer was not interested (Interview Matias Palm-Jensen, 2010; Internetworld, 2007).

Giving up control over the brand and handing it over to consumers can seem like a wild and daring idea. However, the fields of advertising and branding have further developed these ideas over the past few years. For example, Coca-Cola is today increasingly directing their marketing budget towards "conversations and story-telling." By labeling this strategy *liquid marketing*, Coca-Cola highlights content development outside the control of the advertising company (Fisk, 2014).

The success of the Diesel campaign must also, to a large extent, be understood in terms of timing. In early 2007 new forms of social media were spreading rapidly and Web 2.0 was just becoming acknowledged as the next big step in Internet development. What the advertising agency Farfar did was combine the technological frontier with a punky format that could appeal to European teenagers (Richardson, 2009): "We brought together different elements that were hyped at the moment. We said that this would be pop-culture 2.0. It is not something I am particularly proud of, but it is interesting to see how we managed to elevate the feeling to a new level."

The use of sexual references and that two young women were running around in (Diesel) underwear throughout the campaign was crucial to the attention-seeking strategy. The creative team described the campaign as a comment on current phenomena, such as docu-soaps and celebrity hype, but without too much lecturing (Internetworld, 2007). The campaign may, however, also be interpreted the other way round – as capitalizing on and potentially reinforcing these trends. The creative leader Matias Palm-Jensen reflected on this critique and argued that had the Italians or Spaniards produced the campaign there would have been far more nudity; he also pointed to the fact that they turned traditional gender roles around when they let the two women, rather than the sales executive, take charge of the situation.[4] By assembling this popular culture into a form that perfectly matched technological availability and a nascent consumer readiness for social media, Farfar and its creatives further established their status as superstars in digital advertising. At the Cannes Lions festival they were awarded another Grand Prix Cyber Lion for the campaign (Resumé, 2007a, 2007b).

The mobile Web – the World's Biggest Signpost

With the number of people online steadily growing and the technology used gradually integrating more social elements, one thing was yet to come: mobility. Even at the end of the first decade of the new millennium, Internet users still tended to rely on computers and access Web content from home, work, or in libraries. However, by 2010 the convergence of the Internet and mobile telephony was just around the corner, virtually putting the Internet in people's pockets. With the new smartphone technology, people became, for the first time, *mobile* Internet users, able to access websites on the go (Phillips, 2014).

Farfar had gained Nokia's confidence in 2003 following the success of the Milko Music Machine, and retained the contract throughout the decade. In the new world of mobile Internet, Nokia asked the agency to raise people's awareness regarding the company's online and mobile navigation services. The task was demanding. Services are more difficult to visualize that tangible products and navigation in particular is difficult to talk about, and may therefore need to be experienced. Farfar's solution was to inspire consumers to experience Nokia's navigation using "the World's Biggest Signpost." Farfar visualized navigation by materializing it into a giant (60-ton and 50 meter-high) interactive signpost set up in central London in June 2010. Passers-by could submit their favorite location – "share the good things," in the wording of the campaign – by sending the Nokia service a text message with their mobile phone. Alternatively, people could drop a pin on a map online whereby the signpost – in fact a building crane – would turn to point its arrow in the direction of the location and display the name and distance of the location. The arrow was as big as two double-decker buses. Due to the massive response to the invitation, a two-queue system was implemented where SMS submissions were given priority. During the two-week period all available display slots were filled (Guldägget, 2010; Helloyoucreatives, 2010).

Just like Farfar's previous campaigns, the novelty of the World's Biggest Signpost rested on a combination of relatively simple existing elements that linked the online and offline worlds: the physical installation (the signpost and the people texting on their mobile phones), an online map (the Nokia service displaying submitted locations on a map), and the campaign site (where the installation was on live display through webcams; people could submit their locations and find out more about the navigation services). The campaign was well received not only by its users and viewers, but perhaps most of all by the advertising community. In 2011 the campaign was recognized by the Gunn Report as the most award-winning piece, with eight Cannes Lion awards in five different categories. For Farfar, it was yet another success thanks to the simple but strong visualization of how navigation services work, the smartness of connected online and offline activities, and, once again, the trust in the crowd to provide content (Broberg et al., 2013; Dagens Industri, 2010; Resumé, 2010).

The campaign may have added to the Nokia brand and sales in the short term, but in the long term the campaign could do little to prevent Nokia's demise in a market where content and design was becoming increasingly important. Services (like navigation) are typically not associated with a particular brand and are therefore difficult to market in strong competition with others offering hardware and software in a stylishly designed bundle. This is neatly summed up by Farfar's case video of the campaign, which starts with a message stating, "When people think about navigation, they don't think about Nokia" (Helloyoucreatives, 2010). That was probably true before the campaign, and probably still true after the campaign. It is more likely that the people remembering the campaign are advertisers (thinking of Farfar).

Digital devices and cultural intermediaries

With this chapter our goal has been to shed new light on advertising agencies and the central role of digital advertising campaigns in the branded economy. Based on five award-winning campaigns, we have argued that the campaigns can be seen as digital market devices, and their creators – the advertising agencies – as cultural intermediaries. By combining technology and popular culture in a way that aligns with the maturity of the technology and the readiness of the consumers at particular points in time, the campaigns suggest new ways for consumers to interact with brands and with each other in the context of brands. These campaigns were part of bringing digital media culture into existence, guiding the way into the digitally branded universe. The chapter focuses on the content and production of five successful campaigns. We cannot make any claim to provide evidence of their eventual impact on consumer behavior, attitudes, and actions. Nevertheless, we believe that it is reasonable to assume that in a counterfactual world without these digital advertising campaigns, the ensuing forms of social interaction around brands would have been different.

Each of the five campaigns presented a new way for consumers to socialize around brands. By bridging the online and offline worlds, the campaigns contributed to making the new technology more accessible and palatable while simultaneously situating action in relation to particular brands and to brands in general. The Posten webshop made use of the low price of the yet immature digital advertising channel to display the Web's superiority when it comes to the speedy satisfaction of consumer desires, thus manifesting the business model of the advertiser, Posten. Moreover, the campaign positioned online actions for offline desires as belonging to the domain of the elite associated with the new economy. The Milko Music Machine was the first to invite Internet users to create content that combined music and graphics and to share the results virally. In this case, the brand in question functioned rather as a backdrop, perhaps with little bearing on the campaign. The XC90 launch marked the maturity of the Internet as a site for an important product launch – the choice of a website as the hub of the campaign signaling novelty itself. While not inviting consumers to generate content, the campaign required them to work by following the traces and waiting out the animation that led them to the car, all the time under the aegis of the Volvo car brand. By hiring a respected photographer and making the most of the technical limitations, the campaign helped make the Internet respectable as a site for mainstream consumer–brand interaction. The Heidies' 15 MB of fame took digital advertising into the world of Web 2.0, drawing on the popular docu-soap format and basing the campaign on user-generated content on a wide range of social media platforms. Here the Internet user interventions had consequences in the strange branded ambience between online and offline that the campaign represented. Finally, the World's Biggest Signpost made use of a very tangible real-world physical installation to unveil to consumers the potential inherent in Nokia's navigation services.

However, the process by which digital advertising campaigns function as market devices cannot be understood without attention to the advertising agencies and the context in which they operate. The advertising agencies act as intermediaries between the producer/advertiser/brand and the consumer, possessing the capability to assemble seemingly disparate entities into a whole that combines technology and popular culture in a way which mobilizes consumers for a particular brand. The campaigns studied in this chapter reveal that the most prominent aspect of brand building related to award-winning campaigns is that of building the brands of the agency and its creatives. For Forsman & Bodenfors, as well as for Farfar, the prospect of strengthening the brands of the agencies themselves was a key tenet for the choice of partners, the design of the campaign, and the agencies' investment of time, money, and effort on participation in award shows.

One key to a successful campaign is to put consumers to work for the brand through collaborative (Dujarier, 2016). The campaigns introduced new assemblages of technology and popular culture where consumers choose to take part actively in the generation and distribution of content under the umbrella of the brand. Consumers use brands to construct social relations and share emotions and personal identity. The Heidies and Milko campaigns put sociality at the forefront, engaging consumers and thereby making them part of the brand-building process, knowingly or unknowingly. The Posten webshop and the Heidies campaigns also reveal how the branding process is partly outsourced to expert consumers in the form of celebrities and pop culture artifacts, which gives further credibility to the campaign and leads the way for other consumers.

By putting consumers to unpaid work for branding and brands, digital advertising campaigns pave the way for a new form of appropriation of surplus, where consumer labor is subsumed under capitalism (Willmott, 2010; Arvidsson, 2006). At the same time, the campaigns do not reveal the extent to which these new marketing strategies represent an exploitation of consumers and the extent to which they represent the empowerment and enrichment of daily life. The campaigns do not point to a coherent performativity. Moreover, they tend to combine adherence to established norms with a degree of resistance.

As the introduction and chapters of this book suggest, digital sources are often instrumental in providing consumers with new calculative capacities, such as tracing product information and comparing prices (Cochoy, 2012; Licoppe, 2008; see also Hansson, this volume). However, while most of the other chapters on digital devices as assemblages focus on a tangible physical technology, we broaden the scope. The campaigns certainly have a material base in the form of code, the medium on which the code is stored, by-products such as images, user-generated content, and walk-through presentations. However, the point of the campaigns is the way in which material and non-material components are assembled to integrate technology and cultural content in order to generate emotions and non-calculative capacities – all done in order to build brand equity (Willmott, 2010). Digital advertising campaigns are transmitted via computers and/or mobile devices, and are normally at the technical forefront. By exploring the technology's potential connections to specific services, the campaigns not only usher users in a new direction of technology use, like the Posten webshop, the XC90 launch, or Nokia's signpost, but they also try to capitalize on this frontline in order to strengthen the brand in question. These campaigns all deliberately explored the limits of people's imaginations on what the new technology could do/be.

Zlatan Ibrahimovic covering his torso with fake tattoos in order to bring attention to the fight against poverty was a typical example of the role of advertising in a new media landscape where global exposure is reached through a combination of online and offline strategies. The campaign was orchestrated by the agency Forsman & Bodenfors, with its creators acting like cultural intermediaries in the process of assembling seemingly different entities (football, celebrities, the UN, poverty, viral advertising) into an effective message that reached millions of people worldwide. This qualification of goods connects production and consumption in new ways, challenging traditional ways of thinking around value creation (Broberg et al., 2016). Thereby the advertising agencies become pivotal in their role of building/maintaining brands, but also in how their campaigns act as digital market devices.

Notes

1 According to Forsman & Bodenfors' figures – which should admittedly be treated with caution – the campaign reached 1.2 billion people and led to 4.4 million actions by consumers (FB, 2015).
2 Guldägget introduced an Internet category in 1997, but did not find any submissions of sufficient quality in the first two years.
3 Cannes (Grand Prix, Gold), New York festivals (Grand Award, Gold, Gold), Epica (Bronze), Clio (Gold).
4 In our interview with Matias Palm-Jensen (2010), he stated that: "So we turned around the concepts a bit. But I agree, it is still shabby popular culture."

References

Literature and press material

Aaker, D. (1991) *Building Strong Brands.* New York: The Free Press.
Affärsvärlden (1996a). "Vinnarna på internet," 20 November 1996.
Affärsvärlden (1996b). "Reklambranschen 1996: Sega reklambyråer," 8 May 1996.
Alvesson, M. (2004) *Knowledge Work and Knowledge-intensive Firms.* Oxford: Oxford University Press.
Arvidsson, A. (2006) *Brands. Meanings and Value in Media Culture.* London: Routledge.
Bourdieu, P. (1984) *Distinction: A Social Critique of the Judgement of Taste.* London: Routledge.
Broberg, O., Axelsson, A.-S. and Sjöblom, G. (2013) "Entrepreneurial exploitation of creative destruction and the ambiguity of knowledge in the emerging field of digital advertising", In McKelvey, M. and Lassen, A. (eds) *How Entrepreneurs Do What They Do. Case Studies in Knowledge Intensive Entrepreneurship.* Cheltenham: Edward Elgar, pp. 105–118.
Broberg, O., Gianneschi, M. and Jonsson, S. (2016) *Svensk reklam. Annonser, varumärken och marknadskommunikation 1975–2012.* Stockholm: Dialogos.
Callon, M., Méadel, C. and Rabeharisoa, V. (2002) "The economy of qualities," *Economy and Society,* 31(2): 194–217.
Callon, M., Millo, Y. and Muniesa, F. (eds) (2007) *Market Devices.* Oxford: Blackwell.
Cochoy, F. (2007) "A sociology of market-things: On tending the garden of choices in mass retailing," *The Sociological Review,* 55: 109–129.
Cochoy, F. (2012) "The pencil, the trolley and the smartphone: Understanding the future of self-service retailing through its sociotechnical history", In Hagberg, J., Holmberg, U., Sundström, M. and Walter, L. (eds) *Nordic Retail Research: Emerging Diversity.* Gothenburg: BAS, pp. 215–233.

222   *Gustav Sjöblom et al.*

Cochoy, F. (2015) "Consumers at work, or curiosity at play? Revisiting the presumption/value cocreation debate with smartphones and two-dimensional bar codes," *Marketing Theory*, 15(2): 133–153.

Cova, B. and Dalli, D. (2009) "Working consumers: The next step in marketing theory," *Marketing Theory*, 9(3): 315–339.

Cronin, A.M. (2004) "Regimes of mediation: Advertising practitioners as cultural intermediaries?," *Consumption Markets & Culture*, 7(4), pp. 349–369.

Dagens Industri (2010) "Dags för VM i reklam," 16 June 2010.

Dagens Nyheter (2003) "Torget kostade Posten nära 1 miljard," 3 March 2003.

Dagens Reklamnyheter (2001) "Milkos kossa gör nya konster," 22 March 2001.

Datavärlden (1996) "Reklambyråerna missar tåget," 11 November 1996.

Dujarier, M.-A. (2016) "The three sociological types of consumer work," *Journal of Consumer Culture*, 16(2): 555–571.

F&B (2015) "805 million names," available at: www.fb.se/work/world-food-programme/805-million-names [accessed: 20 May 2016].

Fisk, P. (2014) *Gamechangers: Creating Innovative Strategies for Business and Brands*. Chichester: John Wiley & Sons.

Fliegstein, N. (2003) *The Architecture of Markets: An Economic Sociology of Twenty-first Century Capitalist Societies*. Princeton, NJ: Princeton University Press.

Foucault, M. (2008) *The Birth of Biopolitics. Lectures at the College de France 1978–79*. Basingstoke: Palgrave Macmillan.

Gothenburgs-Posten (1996) "Internet det nya varuhuset," 25 February 1996.

Guldägget (2010) "The World's Biggest Signpost," available at: guldagget.se/vinnare/the-worlds-biggest-signpost-2/ [accessed: 16 May 2016].

Hagberg, J. (2008) *Flytande identitet NetOnNet och e-handelns återkomst*. Borås: Responstryck.

Hansen, P. (2004) "Writing business history without an archive", In Gadd, C.-J., Granér, S. and Jonsson, S. (eds) *Markets and Embeddedness: Essays in Honour of Ulf Olsson*. Gothenburg: Department of Economic History, School of Economics and Commercial Law, Gothenburg University.

Heidies (2007) "Heidies 15 MB of fame," available at: www.youtube.com/watch?v=pSc-Z7lLB14 [accessed: 16 May 2016].

Helloyoucreatives (2010) "Nokia's the World's Biggest Signpost," available at: www.youtube.com/watch?v=a7rrpwAQVLs [accessed: 16 May 2016].

Hörnfelt, E. and Hansson, M. (1999) *www.torget.se. Den fantastiska historien om ett av världens mest framgångsrika internetprojekt*. Stockholm: Bonnier Icon Publishing.

Internetworld (2007) "Tonårstjejer kapade sajten," 21 June 2007.

Lazzarato, M. (1996) "Immaterial labour", In Virno, P. and Hardt, M. (eds) *Radical Thought in Italy: A Potential Politics*. Minneapolis, MN: University of Minnesota Press.

Licoppe, C. (2008) "Understanding and reframing the electronic consumption experience: The interactional ambiguities of mediated coordination", In Pinch, T. and Swedberg, R. (eds) *Living in a Material World*. Cambridge, MA: MIT Press, pp. 317–340.

Macleod, D. (2007) "Heidies 15 MB of fame with Diesel," available at: theinspirationroom.com/daily/2007/heidies-15-mb-of-fame-with-diesel/ [accessed: 16 May 2016].

Mattsson, N. and Carrwik, C. (1998) *Internetrevolutionen: 1000 dagar som förändrade Sverige*. Stockholm: Bonnier Icon.

McLeod, C., O'Donohoe, S. and Townley, B. (2011) "Pot Noodles, placements and peer regard: Creative career trajectories and communities of practice in the British advertising industry," *British Journal of Management*, 22: 114–131.

McStay, A. (2009) *Digital Advertising*. Basingstoke: Palgrave Macmillan.

Moor, L. (2007) *The Rise of Brands*. Oxford: Berg Publish.

Morris, M. and Ogan, C. (1996) "The Internet as mass medium," *Journal of Communication*, 46(1): 36–50.

Nixon, S. (2003) *Advertising Cultures: Gender, Commerce, Creativity*. London: SAGE.

Nixon, S. (2014) "Cultural intermediaries or market device? The case of advertising", In Smith Maguire, J. and Matthews, J. (eds) *The Cultural Intermediaries Reader*. Los Angeles, CA: SAGE, pp. 34–41.

O'Reilly, T. (2007) "What is Web 2.0: Design patterns and business models for the next generation of software," *Communications & Strategies*, 1(17): 17–37.

Phillips, C. (2014) "How smartphones revolutionized a society in less than a decade," *Chattanooga Times*, 20 November.

Pratt, A.C. (2006) "Advertising and creativity, a governance approach: A case study of creative agencies in London," *Environment and Planning A*, 38(10): 1883–1899.

Resumé (1998) "Brindfors tar strid med webbyråerna," 29 January 1998.

Resumé (1999) "Romson får Guldägg för Postens Webshop," 22 April 1999.

Resumé (2003a). "Volvos jeep säker segrare," 16 January 2003.

Resumé (2003b). "En skön revansch för F&B," 19 June 2003.

Resumé (2004a). "Hantverk i världsklass," 15 January 2004.

Resumé (2004b). "Svensk design och webb i främsta led," 2 December 2004.

Resumé (2004c). "Nokia väljer Farfar för global satsning," 2 September 2004.

Resumé (2007a). "Svenska triumfer i cyber," 21 June 2007.

Resumé (2007b). "Palm-Jensen: Vi står upp för Sverige," 9 November 2007.

Resumé (2010) "DDB vann Cannes-kampen. 46 lejon totalt bästa svenska insatsen någonsin," 1 July 2010.

Retriever (2016) "Mediearkivet," available at: www.retriever-info.com/sv/ (accessed: 16 May 2016).

Richardson, W. (2009) *Blogs, Wikis, Podcasts, and Other Powerful Web Tools for Classrooms*. Thousand Oaks, CA: Corwin Press.

Ritchie, D.A. (1994) *Doing Oral History*. New York: Twayne Publishers.

Sjöblom, G., Axelsson, A.-S. and Broberg, O. (eds) (2011) *Internet, IT-boomen och reklambranschen under andra hälften av nittiotalet: transkript av ett vittnesseminarium på ABF-huset i Stockholm den 17 februari 2010*. Gothenburg: Department of Economic History, School of Business, Economics and Law, Gothenburg University.

Stenius, P. (2013) "Milko Music Machine," available at: perstenius.com/projects/m ilkomusicmachine/ [accessed: 16 May 2016].

Svenska Dagbladet (1999) "Posten Torget tappar ännu mer," 20 August 1999.

Svenska Dagbladet (2007a). "Byråer i brytningstid," 5 September 2007.

Svenska Dagbladet (2007b). "Farfars lejon ryter högst," 21 June 2007.

Thomson, M. (2006) "Human brands: Investigating antecedents to consumers' strong attachments to celebrities," *Journal of Marketing*, 70(3): 104–119.

Veckans Affärer (2007) "Reklamindustrin – Jakten på guldägget," 19 April 2007.

Vision (2000) "Varumärke och kommunikation är det nya i den nya ekonomin," 21 December 2000.

Vision (2001a). "Storslam för Sverige," 21 June 2001.

Vision (2001b). "Vinnarna: Snart finns det bara tio webbyråer kvar," 21 June 2001.

Willmott, H. (2010) "Creating 'value' beyond the point of production: Branding, financialization and market capitalization," *Organization*, 17(5): 517–542.

Interviews

Mathias Appelblad, former employee of Forsman & Bodenfors, 29 September 2010, New York.

Nicke Bergström, founder of Farfar, 28 September 2010, New York.

Martin Cedergren, former employee of Forsman & Bodenfors, 18 February 2010, Stockholm.

Filip Nilsson, Executive Creative Director at Forsman & Bodenfors, 30 November 2010, Gothenburg.

Matias Palm-Jensen, founder of Farfar, 25 May 2010, Stockholm.

12 From the logs of QR code readers

A socio-log-y of digital consumption

Franck Cochoy and Jan Smolinski [1]

In 1991, Morris Holbrook, the well-known consumer researcher, published a paper entitled, "From the Log of a Consumer Researcher: Reflections on the Odyssey." Holbrook reported his personal experiences as a participant in the Consumer Behavior Odyssey, a famous research trip undertaken in 1986 by a group of deviant marketing scholars with the hope of renewing consumer research. More precisely, the Odyssey consisted of team members physically traveling throughout the United States on a bus and visiting various market-places. The aim was to move away from laboratory experiments and quantitative research which dominated marketing research at that time. Through this spectacular and well "advertised" adventure, they wanted to promote qualitative, interpretive, naturalistic and field-based consumer research. Indeed, they argued that the former type of research had lost all connection to real, situated and full-flesh consumer behavior. They believed that this new method provided the means to overcome this deadlock and reconnect consumer research with the down-to-earth experiences of consumption (Cochoy, 1998). Along these lines, or rather along these routes – the report's title is *Highways and Buyways*! – Morris Holbrook's "log" was a paper notebook where the researcher recorded, in a literary style, handwritten field notes about his direct observations and thoughts, following the classic tradition of ethnographic accounts in anthropology.

Since then, the meaning of words has dramatically changed. At a period when consumption has largely entered the age of the Internet, the digital world and the so-called "big data" and "cloud computing," "logs" no longer refer to the qualitative, interpretive, analog-type notebooks of anthropologist-like consumer researchers. Rather, they encompass the massive array of "digital traces" left in opaque yet powerful databases by any single, individual and local consumer action. As a consequence, the irony may well be that the reconnection between marketing and real marketplaces targeted by the Odyssey faces the danger of disconnecting us from more recent consumer practices, starting with situated shopping activities and going beyond them through the Web. Hence, the need exists for a new "reconnection" between market science and market matters (Araujo et al., 2010). Indeed, if consumer research and the sociology of consumption are about following the phenomena that (re)shape consumer behavior, we may well have to shift logs, abandon paper field notes, and renew (one more time!) the procedures of consumer research in order to take emerging consumer practices and data into account.

In 1986, the move was from etic, positivist, hypothesis-testing quantitative-based consumer research to emic, constructivist, interpretive, naturalistic and qualitative field-based consumer research. Does following consumers' digital traces stocked as "big data" mean that we need to step back to previous quantitative, statistical, number-crunching approaches? Yes and no. Yes, in the sense that what was impossible before, i.e. tracing the real moves of each consumer in the market, is now workable, provided we use data-processing software and statistical techniques. No, in the sense that the approach is now completely different: consumer "logs" are not data designed and produced for controlled research programs and experiments, but rather emerging traces of ordinary consumer practices. As such, these data blur the distinction between qualitative and quantitative, emic and etic, inductive and deductive, descriptive and explanatory research and call for new research procedures. Fortunately, the latter are increasingly addressed and described in the literature (Boullier, this volume; Rogers, 2013), but they still need to be discussed and enriched.

In this chapter, we propose to contribute to such discussions and enrich-ments by considering what kind of insights we may gain when conducting the research "from the logs of consumers," that is, through an exploratory, empirical analysis of the traces left by the reading of QR codes, i.e. the bi-dimensional barcodes that provide access to the Internet when read with a smartphone. The use of such cryptic pictograms in European markets, although very recent, is now widespread and well known (Cochoy, 2015). One interesting contribution of such codes is the shift from massive one-way advertising to the advent of what we call "self-marketing" (Cochoy, 2012). Instead of blindly pushing the same single unsolicited message to a large audience, at the risk of annoying a large crowd to seduce just a few, QR codes reverse the communication relationship. They offer consumers the optional opportunity to obtain, on a voluntary basis, additional commercial information (hence the idea of "self marketing," in the sense of "help yourself" by selecting addi-tional market data). On consumer markets, a QR code works as an extension of the packaging by providing a variety of additional services and information on company Web apps or websites.

How are such codes managed? Although free code generators abound on the Internet, some companies have developed a business aimed at providing more sophisticated services to QR code users. It is thanks to a partnership with such a company, Unitag, that the conduct of our study was possible.

Unitag is a French start-up company that offers QR code services through a Web interface on a global scale (www.unitag.io/qrcode). Unitag's clients include a wide range of companies, ranging from very small unknown busi-nesses to large global corporations like Spotify, T-Mobile, Volvo, and so on. The services offered, organized along a now classic "freemium" scheme, include the free generation of advanced QR codes free of charge, with the

Figure 12.1 Advanced QR code

possibility of customizing bits of information, colors, "eyes," including a logo, etc. (see Figure 12.1 for an example). They also propose paying features, such as the possibility of redirecting the codes toward other or new addresses, obtaining statistics and maps about how and where the codes are used, etc. Our study is based on a secondary, extended analysis of the logs of three Unitag-assisted QR code campaigns for three "fast moving consumer goods": a table box of salt (salt box), a sweet snacking good (chocolate bar), and a bottle of water (water bottle).

The remainder of the chapter is organized into three sections. First, we present the data, the research purposes and the ways we approach them. Second, we provide results. The concluding section reflects on what can be learned from such results in terms of digital consumption and digital methods; this section also traces some possible routes for further analysis of the same type of data.

Elements of socio-log-y

Reversed thunder

As stated above, QR codes help consumers entering the age of self-marketing where commercial information is not (only) imposed on them, but often requested by them. This provides an unprecedented situation which allows companies immediately to test the performativity of their advertising promises. Previously, advertisers could not know whether or not their campaigns were read, except through costly surveys or through the fragile clue of sales, which often depends on reasons other than advertising, despite appearances. QR codes provide an intermediary access to consumers' attitudes, because they measure consumers' attention, their curiosity, their desire for information and their willingness to learn more (Kessous, 2015; Cochoy, 2016). The idea is that of a literal (half-)revolution (180° angle). Whereas advertising was previously like a storm, where lightning came from the sky and hit some rare consumers, while the majority escaped its fire at the cost of its "noise" (both in the acoustic and figurative senses), QR codes invent a reversed kind of storm, as if the lighting were coming from the ground and going into the sky, or rather into the cloud(s), i.e. the digital places where companies store their marketing data (hence its silence, accuracy and effectiveness).

A few years ago, when QR codes were a complete novelty, methods like quantitative surveys and case studies through experiments with focus groups were appropriate research strategies. Indeed, these methods helped researchers grasp not only the expectations but also the practical difficulties attached to this new device: a representative survey of 500 French people showed that consumers who were inclined to read QR codes were young, male, technophiles and interested in the product at stake; focus groups, however, showed that such goodwill was strongly challenged by technical obstacles like the time needed to activate the QR code reader, the difficulty of focusing on the codes in difficult lighting conditions, and so on (Cochoy, 2015). Today, however, QR code reading is no longer a situated experiment but a pervasive market practice. Consequently, we have to address a much larger field than a case study can offer. Even a survey or a series of interviews would be limited. These methods may, of course, help collect information about social practices over a vast population and territory, but given their reliance on questions addressed to human informants, they have two main flaws. First, they tend to exaggerate people's reflexivity about their practices; they sometimes even lead them to answer questions they would not have raised themselves (Bourdieu, 1979). Second and more importantly, surveys and interviews would accurately reflect people's behavior, but in so doing, they undermine the contribution of technical devices to this behavior, or rather they overlook the hybridity of contemporary behavior, which combines human and non-human agency: a shopper does not shop the same with or without her shopping bag (Hansson, 2014; Hagberg, 2016); a citizen experiences the city differently with or without her car (Normark, 2012); a teenager develops contrasted abilities with or without her phone (Serres, 2012); and of course, a consumer does not consume the same with or without her smartphone (Hansson, this volume; Hagberg and Kjellberg, this volume). One way to overcome this latter difficulty would be to observe QR code reading behavior "in the wild," for instance by placing a camera over a billboard or a shop window and observing how people use QR codes, used in combination with the quantitative video ethnography with which we experimented elsewhere (Calvignac and Cochoy, 2016). However, despite their growing spread, the reading operations of the same physical codes are still so rare that implementing such a method would probably be too costly given the time needed to collect sufficient observations for a relevant study.

From locks to logs

In order to understand QR code use, why should we waste time in constructing costly and questionable observation tools when the field at stake does the job itself and does it in a way that overcomes all the difficulties just raised? The peculiarity of QR codes is their "self-observational" character: they collect traces of their own use, and they do so in a systematic manner. Each time a code is read, a log file is produced that records some aspects of the operation. The logs also account for the user's action: the user reads the code according to his or her personal mood, local environment and social properties (age, gender, and so on); the logs also express the phone's characteristics that are involved in the reading operation (Web provider, Web browser, operating system ...). If we want to understand QR codes, a relevant approach is to follow the logs attached to them. In a previous study, we presented the QR code as a keyhole through which curious consumers (and/or customers made curious by the device itself) may look to discover what hides behind the product door. According to the curiosity metaphor (Cochoy, 2016), following the logs consists of shifting places to look at the same issue from the other side of the lock. In other words, the socio-log-ical approach is about inverting the curiosity device. Whereas curiosity is often about peeping at a forbidden scene through a keyhole, with a QR code one looks through the keyhole to see who looks at it.

The collection of logs gathers the traces of successful QR code reading operations. In this sense, our new empirical material is the opposite of our previous data. In 2009, when testing bi-dimensional codes, consumers experienced many frustrating attempts, mistakes or failures (Cochoy, 2015). In contrast, what we see through the logs are rather details about successful scanning gestures. Indeed, a recorded log exists only when the code has been successfully read and the Internet connection established (at least for the activation of the first URL, with no guarantee and/or information about the accomplishment or failure of what follows). We observe no more local experiments, but rather massive and widespread practices. Furthermore, what we discover when studying such codes, at least indirectly, is the behavior of the user but also the intentions and expectations of the professionals who design the lock.

Comprehensive socio-log-y

QR code reading also helps us revisit the classic opposition between business actors and researchers. Business actors are concerned with the pragmatic urges of managerial operations, which combine or alternate between sophisticated, heavily equipped methods, and lighter and softer "rule of thumb" processes. This contrasts with the slow, reflexive, methodologically equipped inquiries dear to researchers. Beyond these differences, the researchers who study computer logs share the same data, point of view and questions as the professionals. Even if the theoretical views, the techniques used and the objectives of both types of actor often diverge. IT professionals have become market analysts to the point that they tend to challenge the position of classic marketers as market experts and intermediaries, and may also challenge the knowledge of economic sociologists (Cochoy et al., 2015). Looking at QR code logs is an interpretive work, not only in the original Weberian sense of intellectual sharing and understanding of others' meaningful representations, but also in an extended sense, in which the sharing and understanding of professionals encompass the material aspects of their practical activities. In our previous study, the focus was on understanding how consumers handle the code-reading operation and why they encounter difficulties and even failures when doing so. When browsing the logs, professionals and researchers are more likely to misunderstand the data than users are. Both may fail to make sense of the collected data or to interpret them correctly.

Comprehensive socio-log-y is all about experiencing such difficulties and grasping the ambivalent potential of digital traces. On the one hand, such traces offer an amazing opportunity to gather and analyze systematic information about all QR code reading behavior, as if an instant, complete census had replaced limited case studies or surveys. Having access to such data gives to the researcher the impression of benefiting from an informational treasure; the promises of the possible treatments and findings are a source of great excitement. This echoes the current view and discourse about big data. These huge digital archives are repeatedly presented as a source of power and control. The media denounce big companies working as "big browsers" who know everything about us through the digital traces we leave and who use this knowledge to infringe upon our privacy and manipulate us without our consent or knowledge. On the other hand, having the opportunity really to look at such data may paradoxically invert such impressions. In our case at least, the information collected is surprisingly poor, lacunar and asymmetric. As a consequence, its possible meaning is obscured by large uncertainties. Looking at the logs means experiencing the marketers' puzzlement and worry when facing market data (Schwarzkopf, 2015) and feeling their will to overcome this uncertainty by making sense of any bit of information, even if limited, contradictory, and obscure.

For each log, the recorded information includes the identifier of the QR code being read, an anonymous identifier for the user, the name of the product and company, the exact time of the reading operation, the name of the city where it occurred, the brand and model of the phone, the name and version of the Internet browser, and … that's all![2] On the one hand, we have a very large number of entries – nearly 70,000 logs for the three campaigns at which we will look. These logs, apart from a few omissions, and thanks to the well-known precision and control of automatic digital reading and writing procedures, are incredibly "clean" and faithful to the situation to which they refer, as if all the respondents to a classic survey had systematically answered (almost) all the questions, without committing any mistakes and without being dishonest. On the other hand, these logs reflect only some discrete and rare aspects of the rich experiences to which they relate. What is worse, they are strongly asymmetrical, given that the information they record, apart from time and place circumstances, is restricted to technical aspects attached to the phone (a brand, an operating system, a browser ...), rather than personal data attached to the consumer. Apart from a hermetic user code automatically created for each visitor (for instance, "879681dcb1a037c1"), which tells us if the same person has read the same QR code more than once, we cannot know anything about this person's identity from QR code logs; we are deprived of information about the user's gender, age, education, revenue, occupation, and other "social characteristics" dear to sociologists and market analysts.

The archaeology of digital data

In the following sections, we nevertheless would like to explore our asymmetrical, biased data, and examine their possible connection to these human aspects they are supposed not to include. The idea is to test the robustness of the unequal division between human and non-human data constructed by the law. Since technical characteristics are the only data we have,[3] we will try to study the smartphone identities, trace their behavior, pursue different objectives from the ones chosen at the moment of data collection, and so on, and, it is hoped, reveal what they may convey about their users. At this stage, we do not pretend that we will be successful. As we said, our data are poor, asymmetrical, and selective. We will experience the limitation of market knowledge based on such data, as well as travel some routes that may reveal that closed paths may sometimes lead further than we might think. Our objective is thus to reveal the ambivalence of the intelligence of digital market data. Such knowledge is less powerful than people usually think, but the idea that one cannot know anything about people's behavior without any personal data may also be incorrect.

There are two different ways to conduct this archaeology of digital traces. A first way consists in taking the data as they are, with their limitations, and following the stream along the routes traced by the actors (i.e. the variables as defined by the actors themselves) and stopping where it stops. This is the approach implicitly proposed by Dominique Boullier (this volume), who relevantly notes that digital data lead us away from society or public opinion and the underlying individuals, but move us toward a world of circulating entities. These entities travel inside large electronic networks: see tweets on Twitter, profiles and "likes" on Facebook, and (of course) logs in company databases. They experience their own lives, have their own special characteristics, and deserve to be observed and described as such and on their own, without necessarily looking at the outer "real world" or "individual human users" they are supposed to have come from (or lead to). Accounting for the digital life of traces and the kind of pictures it produces is a reasonable and innovative option that clearly deserves to be enacted.

A second approach that we privilege here adopts a different rationale based on the assumption that traces, by definition, come from somewhere, and that they have no meaning or existence until they lead somewhere else, until they may be observed, seen and used "from the outside" for a given purpose. This is particularly true in a marketing context, where the production of traces is just a means, a market mediation aimed at bridging real consumers with real goods and services. Classic sociologists of organizations, while describing in great detail the internal games played by actors within an organizational context, have often overlooked that such games exist only if the organization where they occur has an external purpose that is recognized as such. Without voters, a political party is nothing; without believers, a church disappears; without clients, a company cannot survive (Crozier and Friedberg, 1980). In keeping with this reasoning, it would be mistaken to think that logs have any meaning independent of their uses by consumers and by companies. Without the market they come from and lead to, digital traces are nothing. As a consequence, we should not stop where the traces end in the database, but also try – like the market professionals, along a fully interpretive logic – to "trace the traces" beyond them, to explore their forgotten, broken or possible connections, to see what they could mean or where they may lead.

In the second part of this chapter, we will implement but also hybridize these two approaches: we will follow the traces as a population of their own. We will do so in order to understand their rhythm, geography, and ecology, but we will also follow them farther. Like any detective or archaeologist, we will try to find the means to reveal deleted connections, go beyond the Web, and trace correspondences between digital logs and analog behaviors.

Following the population of logs: time and space

Let us first take the easiest road by monitoring, as suggested by Boullier (this volume), the aggregate life of the logs in their integrity and despite their sub-characteristics inside the database. It should be noted that even this first lazy quest needs some further work, since the logs present themselves as a long list that does not reveal anything except maybe their aggregated count. They only become meaningful when we find the means to organize the flow, for instance by looking at the duration of a given campaign, and then calculate, in chronological order, how many logs were recorded per day, so that we may trace the evolution of the campaigns and compare their profiles.

As stated previously, we will focus on three QR code campaigns for different products at different scales: a box of salt (salt box), a bottle of water (water bottle) and a worldwide brand of chocolate bar (chocolate bar). In each case, the code is printed on the package. The code printed on the salt box celebrates the 80th birthday of the company by leading to its Facebook page where it organizes contests, animates its mascot, circulates information, and so on. The code printed on the bottle of water leads to a website where the bottling company promotes its actions in favor of the environment. The code printed on the chocolate bar complements the information already present elsewhere on its packaging by indicating how the product fits into a balanced diet, providing portion advice, and suggesting recipe ideas. It also leads to information about the product's environmental impact, like how much water and energy were used over its entire life cycle.

Please note, however, that our study is strictly focused on the use of the QR codes, and does not include the information to which they lead. We also restricted our analysis to campaigns and visits observable in the territory of metropolitan France in order to homogenize distances and also exclude geographical areas (like overseas territories) where visits are too few to establish meaningful analyses. For each product, we have taken into account QR code visits from the moment there were fewer than two consecutive days without visits. This eliminates the early tests conducted by the companies that implemented the QR codes: these tests are of no interest for the study of consumer practices. Given these restrictions, the campaigns gathered 28,712 visits from 20 November 2012 to 8 March 2015 for the chocolate bar, 14,794 visits from 24 March 2014 to 6 March 2015 for the salt box, and 22,041 visits from 22 October 2013 to 5 March 2015 for the bottle of water. From these data, we excluded all the visits for which the location information was missing. Ultimately, we kept 11,880 visits for the chocolate bar, 10,006 visits for the salt box and 13,441 visits for the bottle of water. On this basis, we extracted a random sample of 30,000 visits (10,000 per product) in order to give an equal weight to each campaign.

Each reading operation of a QR code results in a two-way information flow: the user receives the information available on the website through the QR code; in exchange, the company that manages the flow receives a certain amount of information about the user, or rather his or her phone. Since the collection of information is processed without the knowledge of the user, the law forbids the collection of personal data. The data collected are thus purely technical. As mentioned above, these data include the moment (the date and exact time), the location of the visit (the accuracy of which is limited by authorities to the level of municipality) and a series of characteristics such as the make and model of the phone, the name and version of the operating system, the name of the operator, and the name and version of the Internet browser.

Is there a way to "re-socialize" the data that describes the phone without saying anything about the social characteristics of its users? Yes, by using the location data. When we know the city, the region or the department of an event,[4] we can check to see if there is a link between the collected traces about this event and the social characteristics of the involved geographical area. Certainly, doing so moves the observation from the individual level to large population groups, at the risk of significant uncertainties about the validity of the possible results. For example, observing a certain type of social practice that occurs in an area where the population is older does not guarantee that the observed practitioners are themselves older. This criticism has been well known since the famous article by William S. Robinson (1950) that labeled such hazardous association between the practices of a given group and the characteristics of the larger population to which it belongs as "ecological fallacy." However, since in our case the geographic "re-socialization" of our data is the only possible strategy, it is worth trying as an exploratory approach and with all the caveats attached to such a procedure.

We will limit the comparisons to regional and urban scales, because the data available at the departmental level are often too scarce to establish reliable analyses. For reasons of population size (and also for reasons of clarity), we will restrict the observations at the urban scale to the five largest French cities. The aggregation of individual data at the regional level was not automatic because the system provided the name but not the GPS coordinates of municipalities. Therefore, we had to connect our data with other databases providing the GPS coordinates of French municipalities, the names of the regions, and the characteristics of the population for such geographic areas. This proved to be extremely problematic and time consuming to operate, due to some technical problems such as small variations in city naming conventions across databases. We set up a procedure to ensure correct coordinates for all the cities and to point out the problems and then correct them ... by hand. In our sample of 30,000 visits, we corrected the mistakes by hand until the number of errors fell to less than 1% of the total visits. Other operations were also necessary, such as re-coding certain data into simplified categories (see, for instance, the operating systems, which were reduced to Android, iOS and "others"). Accounting for this complexity and time-consuming manual work is important because these difficulties show that "big data" not only cannot talk automatically, but must almost always be cleaned up and reformatted (Denis, 2015) to "have them talk."

With the help of Excel, SPSS and QGIS softwares, we conducted a statistical and geographical analysis of our reformatted data. We will first focus on the spatial and temporal variations in QR code reading operations. We will push this analysis further by monitoring the variations of the same operations at the regional and city scales. Finally, we will study the particular case of the iterative reading of the same QR code by the same phone/visitor.

Let us first examine the distribution of the number of QR code visits in each city (Figure 12.2, top map) and then observe, for cities with more than 10,000 inhabitants, the number of visits per 10,000 inhabitants (Figure 12.2, bottom map). The first map, which displays the absolute number of visits for each visited city, is very predictable, and thus rather disappointing. Indeed, the observed variations faithfully reflect the urban population: the greater the population levels, the more the QR codes are visited.

However, the picture changes if we neutralize the size of population. In this sense, the map that displays the number of visits per 10,000 inhabitants (for the cities that are sufficiently populated for this calculation to be meaningful) helps introduce some interesting corrections, if not inversions: the most "active" cities are not necessarily the most populous ones. Among the 30 most "scanning" cities, i.e. cities where we observe between 23.6 visits (Lieusaint) and 12.3 visits (Olivet) per 10,000 inhabitants, unsurprisingly we find four of the 30 most populous cities: Paris, Lyon, Dijon and Clermont-Ferrand. However,

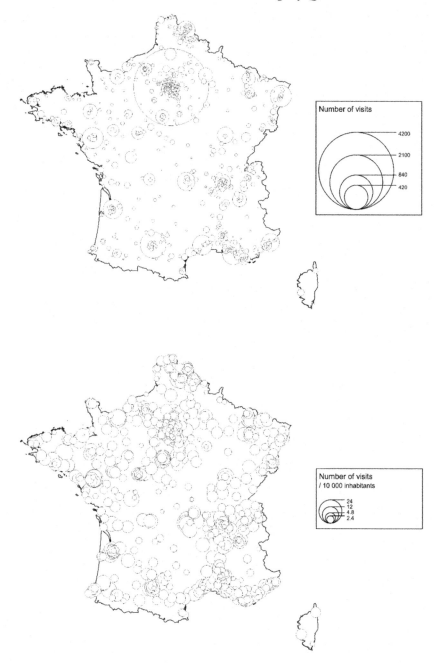

Figure 12.2 Visits of QR codes for cities with more than 10,000 inhabitants (top); number of visits per 10,000 inhabitants (bottom)

some major cities like Toulouse, Nice and Nantes do not belong to this list of most scanning cities, and several large cities were often outperformed by smaller communities, such as Gerzat, Lieusaint and Saint-Orens de Gameville. Among these cities, the case of Nice deserves particular attention. Indeed, despite its position as the fifth most populous city in France, Nice counts only 7.3 QR code visits per 10,000 inhabitants, placing it 231st of all French cities of more than 10,000 inhabitants. Ironically, since May 2010, Nice has been presented as a pilot city for digital practices, and has had ambitions to be the laboratory of future "contactless cities."[5] These first results show the existence of significant regional variations that deserve to be explored further, notably along a temporal dimension.

For each campaign, QR code visits occurred in a non-linear and product-specific way, as illustrated by the graph in Figure 12.3, which displays the average number of daily recorded visits (on the basis of seven days' moving averages)[6] over a period of almost a year for the three campaigns. Examination of the three curves produces some interesting findings. The curves show that the reading of QR codes strongly differs from the reception of conventional advertising because the unique and one-shot temporality imposed by promotional campaigns is replaced by the "consumption" of commercial information that extends over a much longer period of time. The observable pattern is a

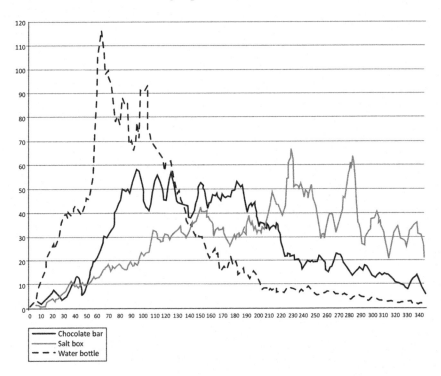

Figure 12.3 Number of daily visits for the three QR code campaigns over a year

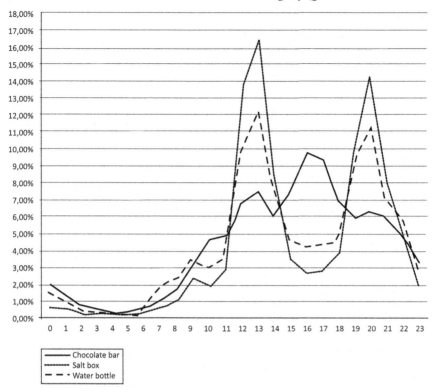

Figure 12.4 Distribution of visits over the day for three QR code campaigns

response to consumers' appetites for product communication rather than the marketing strategies of companies. More specifically, we discovered that the profile of reading operations differed from one campaign to another. While the QR codes printed on the packaging of the bottles of water were read quickly and massively soon after their distribution,[7] those on the chocolate bars and salt boxes were read on a more delayed and persistent basis, especially the salt box. Everything seems to indicate that the reading rhythm varies according to consumption practices: mineral water is bulky to store and frequently restocked; it therefore entices a highly reactive consumption of the bottles' contents as well as of the codes printed on the bottles. On the contrary, the chocolate bar and the salt box are more favorably read over time, especially the salt, which does not expire for years. Thus, we begin to understand that QR codes allow informational exchanges that are situated and adjusted to local practices of consumption and opposite to the blind nature of classic advertising communication.

The variation of reading operations over time is also observable on a smaller scale over the course of a day. Indeed, if one aggregates all the visits for each campaign by hourly slots, it is possible to examine their daily "consumption," giving a particular illustration of the rhythm of digital traces (see Pantzar and Lammi, this volume). The underlying logic behind the different curves is easy to grasp. The number of reading operations is unsurprisingly near zero at night and grows as the day moves forward. However, we also see considerable variations that are clearly linked to the nature of the products: the frequency of salt and water QR code visits peaks at lunch (1:00 pm) and dinner time (8:00 pm), with higher numbers for the salt, the consumption of which is more related to other food intakes. The chocolate bar experiences a visit profile that contrasts with the other products, with a continuous growth until midday, marked by two peaks corresponding to the sluggish feeling before noon and snack time in the afternoon, whereas its presence is much lower at mealtimes. These observations suggest that the reading of some QR codes (here focused more on brand loyalty rather than product information, see above), far from occurring in store and before buying as a complement to labeling and packaging information when selecting products, is performed after buying the product and at home.[8] This shows that packages are subject to many reading operations that are more frequent as they approach the moment of use, as if the consumption of products and of given information go hand in hand.

This is confirmed when we observe how the temporal variations vary according to space, again probably related to the physical characteristics of the products as well as to the social characteristics of the population. The six graphs in Figure 12.5 show, for each product, the evolution of the number of visits per 1,000 inhabitants for the different regions and the five largest French cities halfway through the period of observation (174 days: left column), and at the end of the same period (348 days: right column). The comparison of these maps confirms some general trends, including the fastest pace of the visits paid to the QR codes printed on the bottle of water compared to the other two products. However, the same comparison also reveals some curious variations that depend on the city or the region where the visits occur.

We notice some interesting differences between the large cities, where the performance of Paris, Lyon and Toulouse are in contrast with the modesty of Nice and Marseille in terms of QR code reading, regardless of the product, without it being possible to interpret these differences. It seems easier, however, to seize and analyze the observations at the regional level. Specifically, we notice that the activation of QR codes expresses a double "adhesion": reading the codes adheres not only to the message, which is decoded voluntarily, but also to the territories where they are read. For example, the highest level of bottled water QR code consumption occurs in the region where this water is produced (the center of France), but also in Brittany, an area where bottled water consumption is very high because of ground and surface water contamination problems caused by pesticides and nitrates.[9]

By combining the QR code data for each region with some social characteristics of the populations established by INSEE, the French statistical agency, we get a series of significant correlations, some of which are

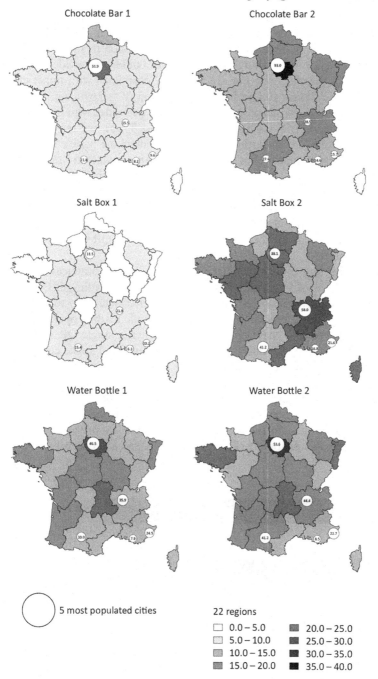

Figure 12.5 Number of visits per 1,000 inhabitants, by product after 174 days (left) and 348 days (right), for the regions and the five largest French cities

remarkable. For instance, the number of visits to the QR code on the salt box is negatively correlated with the number of visits to the QR code on the chocolate bar, as if craving for salt resulted in an aversion to sugar, and vice versa (r = −0,681; sig. = 0). Many other examples could be provided: visits to the QR code on the chocolate bar are positively correlated with upper-class categories (r = 627; sig = 0) and income per region (r = 0.670, sig. = 0); visits to the QR code on the bottle of water are positively correlated with the rate of retired people per region (r = 0.428, sig. = 0.047), etc. These two results reflect more or less predictable consumption patterns like snacking habits of urban professionals or health concerns of aging people. Other results are more enigmatic, like the strong link between iOS users (measured with an iOS/[Android and other operating system] ratio) and salt box readers (r = 0.653; sig. = 0). Last but not least, some anticipated relationships were not observed: see the lack of significant correlation (positive for salt and chocolate; negative for water) between the prevalence of obesity and the visits to QR codes printed on the three products.

Examining the observable variations of individual practices confirms and clarifies this very strong adhesion logic between the reading of QR codes and the local circumstances of product use. In order conclusively to strengthen the link between consumption situations and QR code reading operations, we propose to observe how these operations vary when a single QR code is subject to multiple visits by the same visitor, both in time and space contexts.

Figure 12.6 measures the more or less sedentary or nomadic characteristic of multiple visits, by giving the proportion of different categories of maximum distances observed during all the visits made by the same person for each product. Distances were calculated based on the GPS coordinates of the visited cities according to the requirements imposed by privacy protection regulations (see above, note 2). The maximum distance between the visited cities

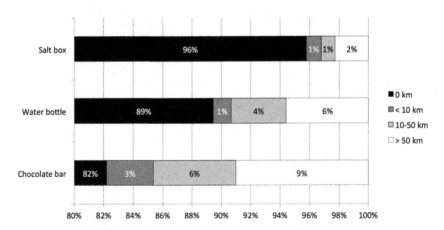

Figure 12.6 Distribution of the maximum distances observed during several visits to the same QR code by the same visitor

is estimated by calculating the length of the diagonal that connects the couple formed by the minimum observed latitudes and longitudes for all visits to the QR code by the same user, and conversely, the coordinates of the maximum latitudes and longitudes observed for the same visits. As we will see, calculating these distances informs us about the propensity of goods more or less to follow consumers' physical movements and practices. As a matter of readability, we present the results with a broken scale (starting beyond the 80% level).

Figure 12.7 shows the results of a comparable and complementary calculation aimed at tracking the distribution of the maximum time elapsed between the first and last visits to the same QR code by the same visitor, for each of the three products. The calculation provides insights about the extent to which the codes are interesting for the consumers, or (conversely) about technical difficulties they may encounter.

Once again, the observed practices seem closely associated with the physical properties of the goods. The most sedentary readings are unsurprisingly related to the salt box, the bulky characteristic and low "continuity" (in terms of physiological needs) of which suggest a sedentary lifestyle. Conversely, the chocolate bar, designed to fit in the pocket and accompany people's movements in order to satisfy or arouse sudden cravings, is one that is the most favorable to remote and nomadic reading operations. The bottle of water, more cumbersome than the chocolate bar but more frequently desired than salt, occupies an intermediate position, less sedentary than salt, less mobile than the chocolate bar. The spatial mobility of visits leads to some temporal extensions. The more sedentary the product, the more often the "replay" readings occur within a short time interval, and vice versa; the more mobile the product, the more widely the replays are spaced in time.

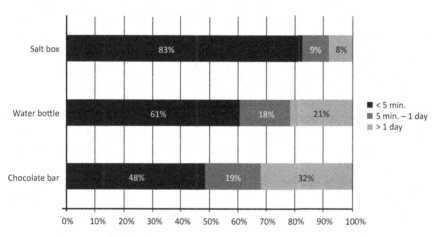

Figure 12.7 Distribution of maximum periods observed between several visits to the same QR code by the same visitor

Conclusions

The study of QR codes and their use via the digital traces left by their reading presents a triple challenge. The first challenge is methodological: we have to find a way to make sense of traces, the collection of which is massive and systematic, but that does not speak alone. In other words, one has to overcome the tension between the supposed omnipotence of big data and their relative lack of meaning in their raw state. Trying to meet that challenge captures, beyond the results themselves, the effort in which big data professionals are engaged. This study reveals the necessary strengths and weaknesses of this kind of approach when one is forced to assume that the characteristics of the general population can be used to approximate the users' social characteristics. In this respect, our study is a first exploratory attempt to conduct the socio-log-y of the varied traces that pave the way of digital consumers, and thus move beyond classic ethnographies formerly introduced in consumer research by the Consumer Behavior Odyssey from which we started.

The second challenge is theoretical: we have to wonder about the different ways to account for digital traces and their implications. We can explore these traces themselves and for themselves, and in this case we rely on the third generation of social science as shown by Boullier (this volume), who promotes a view that postulates the existence of an endogenous ecology of traces, independent of their origin and destination. Or we may study new digital data and the ordinary empirical world on an equal basis in order to trace the relationships between the two, and we may hybridize rather than substitute the different generations of social sciences. The decision between these two approaches may refer to a particular conception of society, or depend on very prosaic empirical constraints, i.e. the choice to favor the inner life of digital traces at the expense of their origin and destination is, largely related to the (not insurmountable) unavailability of exogenous data. It is also dependent on the objectives that are assigned to the research and on the nature of the objects under scrutiny. If one is interested in political expressions and the emergence and circulation of opinions and the intricacies of social networks, the hypothesis of a "life of traces" is obviously as appropriate as it is stimulating. If one is interested in market phenomena, where seizing traces is not an end in itself but rather a means to strengthen a business relationship or warn the public against the danger of such control, it becomes clear that tracing the links between people, the activation of traces and economic performance, is highly difficult.

This is the third challenge, which urges us to think about the performativity of the promise of technical devices. On the one hand, QR codes are now well-rooted and common in the commercial landscape. They facilitate the advent of a "self-marketing" regime in which business information is deliberately sought by consumers, in sharp contrast to the situation where advertising appears as pollution made up of unsolicited messages. QR codes also offer companies a way to trace this new relationship between consumers and products. On the other hand, the significance of this mediation is extremely fragile because it is based on a propensity for curiosity that is very weak (Cochoy, 2016) and because the data are incomplete, rarely able to say anything by themselves, except limited and sometimes risky clues once they have been properly reframed. Finally, the QR code technology is fragile because it may be ephemeral. It faces possible replacement by other solutions, like the direct recognition of images. Nevertheless, the advent of the QR code technology, beyond its modest extension, limitations and uncertainty, contributes to paving the way for a new business relationship scheme centered on the development of an interactive and local exchange between consumers and products that is not a matter of political consumerism but of commercial citizenship in the simple sense of participation.

Notes

1 The research this chapter rests upon was financed by the Digcon project (Digitalizing Consumer Culture) funded by the Swedish Research Council (grant number: 2012-5736), and the Omniscan project funded by the Région Midi-Pyrénées (France, Agile-IT program).
2 We also had the latitude and longitude of the phone antenna used for the connection, but the French agency regulating the use of personal digital data denied us the possibility of using it. We thus limited geographic information at the city level, by using the latitude and longitude of the city.
3 Our data are biased in the opposite direction: classic surveys miss technical agency; logs know everything about the technique but lack personal information.
4 A department is an administrative division of the French territory; France contains 96 departments.
5 Certainly, the Nice experiment involved payment via near-field communication (NFC) devices, so we expected that the use of smartphones for contactless operations also extended to the reading of QR codes ... but it did not (www.investincotedazur.com/fr/info/news/fr-nice-ville-du-sans-contact-mobile-lancement-le-21-mai-2010/).
6 The calculation of moving averages helps to smooth the large daily variations and thus makes the graph more readable.
7 Our records start from the first reading operation of each QR code. The QR codes were printed for at least a year, see our period of observation in Figure 12.2.
8 In France, the average time allocated to provisioning is 23 minutes a day. However, this activity is less and less done on a daily basis: the three thirds of the provisioning activity are performed in large supermarkets located in the suburbs and during the weekend (www.insee.fr/fr/themes/document.asp?ref_id=ip1533#figure3).
9 See eaumineralenaturelle.fr/chambre-syndicale/leau-minerale-en-chiffres.

References

Araujo, L., Finch, J. and Kjellberg, H. (eds) (2010) *Reconnecting Marketing to Markets: Practice-based Approaches*, Oxford: Oxford University Press.
Bourdieu, Pierre (1979) "Public opinion does not exist", In Mattelart, A. and Siegelaub, S. (eds) *Communication and Class Struggle*, New York: International General, pp. 124–130.

Caliandro, A., Beraldo, D. and Barina, S. (2013) "Etnografia digitale di #boicottabarilla: Il boicottaggio all'epoca di Twitter," *Centro Studi Etnografia Digitale*, 7 October, www.etnografiadigitale.it/2013/10/etnografia-digitale-di-boicottabarilla-il-boicottaggio-allep oca-di-twitter/.

Calvignac, C. and Cochoy, F. (2016) "On vehicular agencies: Lessons from the quantitative observation of consumer logistics," *Consumption, Markets and Culture*, 19(1): 133–147.

Cochoy, F. (1998) "Another discipline for the market economy: Marketing as a performative knowledge and know-how for capitalism", in Callon, M. (ed.), *The Laws of the Markets*, Sociological Review Monographs Series, Oxford: Blackwell, pp. 194–221.

Cochoy, F. (2012) "The pencil, the trolley and the smartphone: Understanding the future of self-service retailing through its sociotechnical history", in Hagberg, J., Holmberg, U., Sundström, M. and Walter, L. (eds) *Nordic Retail Research, Emerging Diversity*, Gothenburg: BAS, pp. 215–233.

Cochoy, F. (2015) "Consumers at work, or curiosity at play? Revisiting the prosumption/value co-creation debate with smartphones and 2D barcodes," *Marketing Theory*, 15(2): 133–153.

Cochoy, F. (2016) *On Curiosity, The Art of Market Seduction*, London: Mattering Press.

Cochoy, F., Smolinski, J. and Vayre, J.-S. (2015) "From marketing to 'market-things' and 'market-ITing': Accounting for technicized and digitalized consumption", in Czarniawska, B. (ed.) *A Research Agenda for Management and Organization Studies*, Cheltenham: Edward Elgar.

Crozier, M. and Friedberg, E. (1980 [1977]), *Actors and Systems. The Politics of Collective Action*, Chicago, IL: The University of Chicago Press.

Denis, J. (2015) *Le travail invisible de l'écrit, Enquêtes dans les coulisses de la société de l'information, mémoire pour l'Habilitation à Diriger des Recherches*, Université Toulouse Jean Jaurès, 26 June.

Hagberg, J. (2016) "Agencing practices: A historical exploration of shopping bags," *Consumption, Markets & Culture*, 19(1): 111–132.

Hansson, N. (2014) "'Mobility-things' and consumption: Conceptualizing differently mobile families on the move with recent purchases in urban space," *Consumption, Markets & Culture*, 18(1): 72–91.

Holbrook, M. B. (1991) "From the log of a consumer researcher: Reflections on the Odyssey", in Belk, R.W. (ed.) *Highways and Buyways: Naturalistic Research from the Consumer Behavior Odyssey*, Provo, UT: Association for Consumer Research, pp. 14–33.

Kessous, E. (2015) "The attention economy between market capturing and commitment in the polity," *Œconomia*, 5(1): 77–101.

Normark, D. (2012) "Sutured and sundered: The order-productive cohort of carsons, mophonkers and other consumer-assemblages visiting a petrol station", in Hagberg, J., Holmberg, U., Sundström, M. and Walter, L. (eds) *Nordic Retail Research, Emerging Diversity*, Gothenburg: BAS, pp. 269–285.

Robinson, W.S. (1950) "Ecological correlations and the behavior of individuals," *American Sociological Review*, 15(3): 351–357.

Rogers, R. (2013) *Digital Methods*, Cambridge, MA: MIT Press.

Schwarzkopf, S. (2015) "Data overflow and sacred ignorance: An agnotological account of organizing in the market and consumer research industry," Copenhagen Business School, working paper.

Serres, M. (2012) *Petite poucette*, Paris: Le Pommier.
Simakova, E. and Neyland, D. (2008) "Marketing mobile futures: Assembling constituencies and creating compelling stories for an emerging technology," *Marketing Theory*, 8(1): 91–116.
Tedlow, R.S. (1990) *New and Improved: The Story of Mass Marketing in America*, New York: Basic Books.

Index

Printed in the United States
by Baker & Taylor Publisher Services